A
More Perfect
Union

How I Survived the
Happiest Day of My Life

HANA SCHANK

ATRIA BOOKS
New York   London   Toronto   Sydney

ATRIA BOOKS
1230 Avenue of the Americas
New York, NY 10020

Copyright © 2006 by Hana Schank

Library of Congress Card Number: 2005053659

ISBN 978-0-7432-7737-2

First Atria Books trade paperback edition February 2007

10 9 8 7 6 5 4 3 2

ATRIA BOOKS is a trademark of Simon & Schuster, Inc.

Designed by Kyoko Watanabe

Manufactured in the United States of America

For information about special discounts for bulk purchases,
please contact Simon & Schuster Special Sales at
1-800-456-6798 or business@simonandschuster.com.

For Steven,
the best person I know

A MORE PERFECT UNION is a true story, although some names and details have been changed.

Contents

1

Welcome to Wedding Land

Marry your son when you will and
your daughter when you can.
—*French proverb*

HERE IS THE DIFFERENCE BETWEEN A TWENTY-eight-year-old man telling his parents he has just become engaged and a thirty-year-old woman doing the same: When Steven called his parents, they said something along the lines of "Really? Well, okay. Whatever makes you happy." When I called my father, he said, "Well what do you know. It's about fucking time."

"Yes, thank God I'm off your hands," I said. Daughter successfully married off. Check.

He then told me that I sounded like one of those girls I'd been making fun of for the past few months, giddy and excited that someone would actually want to marry her.

"I do not," I insisted. "It's just cool that I'm, like, getting married and stuff. It's weird."

"You do," he said. "Maybe you don't want to admit it, but you do."

From my mother, a woman whose general level of seriousness would make a two-year-old depressed, I got squeals of delight. So I did the only thing that seemed reasonable. I squealed back.

I'd never really pictured myself married. My childhood fantasies

1

had always involved either sharing a funky SoHo loft with my fabulous (undiscovered) artist boyfriend, or heroically struggling to raise my kids on my own while pursuing a high-powered career that required owning lots of designer suits. Wearing a big white dress and twirling across the floor to "A Groovy Kind of Love" had never entered into my imagination. So it had been a long and involved process to get to this point, to go from being someone who wore two worthless rings on her right hand (one bought at a flea market to commemorate a long-overdue breakup with an ex-boyfriend, the other purchased on a business trip in a moment of boredom) to one of those women I always saw on the subway lugging around glaciers on their fingers. There had been two years of friendship, two years of dating, and one year of living together before either Steven or I even uttered the word "marriage." But once spoken aloud, it was soon followed by other related words like "engagement ring," "proposal," and finally, "wedding."

And then before I knew it, I was flashing my own little chunk of ice at my friends. With the ring on, my hand no longer looked like mine. It looked like it belonged to someone older, someone who lived in a sprawling Upper East Side apartment, someone who referred to herself as Mrs. So-and-so and had a nanny and a closet full of Manolo Blahniks organized by color. I found that I couldn't stop staring at this foreign entity that had taken up residence on my hand. I snuck peeks at it as I walked down the street, watching it flash in the sun, wondering how it looked in the rain, when it was overcast, when there was wind. My friends seemed a little obsessed too.

"How do you feel?" asked my friend Jami, the resident rocker chick in my life, over sushi in the East Village a few days after I had officially become engaged.

"Ridiculous," I told her.

She grabbed my ring finger and pulled it towards her. "Let me see it one more time. I may never get this close to one of these things again."

I stared at her. Jami is a woman who maintains a website detailing her sexual exploits. We used to stay out at clubs till all hours, spend Sundays lazing around Tompkins Square Park, eating bagels and peanut butter frozen yogurt, and complaining about work and men. My understanding had been that we didn't care about getting married or owning diamond engagement rings. When people we knew got married, we rolled our eyes.

"You'll find the right guy," I said, suddenly the authority on how to properly trap a man into marriage.

She picked up a spicy tuna roll with her chopsticks and inspected it. "You know, when I turned thirty it was fine. Thirty and single is cute, you're part of a trend, single thirty-year-olds loose in Manhattan, blah, blah, blah."

I nodded.

"But thirty-one and single," said Jami, "that's not so cute."

The engagement ring, it seemed, shone as bright and loud as the lights of Las Vegas, and everyone noticed it. It wasn't a huge ring, but to me it felt like I was carrying around the Rosetta stone on my finger. I was getting my hair cut when the hairdresser asked me if I was planning on wearing my hair up or down at the wedding. I was getting my eyebrows waxed when the waxing lady asked to see my ring. ("Oh," she said, hot wax in hand. "Your fiancé is so . . . thoughtful." I took this to mean she thought the diamonds were small.) I was at an interview in a large midtown office building when the twenty-something guy conducting the interview asked when the wedding was.

"What wedding?" I said.

"I saw your ring."

"Oh," I laughed. "*My* wedding. Um, we're thinking next fall. Labor Day weekend. Probably something small."

I was surprised at how easily these facts rolled off my tongue. In just a few weeks they had become my new vital statistics. What I did for a living, what neighborhood I lived in, what I hoped to accomplish in life—all these facts had now become secondary to the single, all-encompassing fact that soon I would be someone's wife.

When I stopped by my friend Ellen's store I got the feeling she was staring at my ring, so I put my hands in my pockets. Ellen and I used to work together years ago in the Internet division of a fancy ad agency. Back then she had bleached blond hair and wore patent leather stiletto boots because that was what one wore in advertising. But these days she owns a home furnishings store just east of SoHo, has grown her hair back to its natural brown, and is usually in some flavor of trendy sneakers and jeans.

"I'm thinking," said Ellen, "that you're not letting yourself be happy about this."

"What do you mean?" I asked. "I'm happy."

"But you should be really happy. It's okay. You're getting married."

I shrugged. "I'm happy. I cried when he asked me—I don't know why."

"Because you were happy," she said.

The door opened and two Japanese tourists walked into the store.

"Let me know if you have any questions!" Ellen called out to them.

"How's the store?" I asked, lowering my voice.

Ellen sighed. "Oh, it's fine."

"That one's nice," I said, nodding towards a curvy green glass vase. "You just get it in?"

"Yeah." Ellen reached out and moved it two centimeters to the left. "I just need to find a husband, is what it comes down to. I'm sick of worrying about money."

I stared at her blankly, not sure if she was serious or not.

"Thank you! Come again!" Ellen called out to the two tourists, who were silently making their way out the door. "Anyway," she continued. "Be happy."

"I am happy," I said. "I just don't want to get divorced."

Ellen rolled her eyes. "Oh Lord. You're not going to get divorced."

"Over half of marriages end in divorce."

"I'm not having this conversation. Be happy. You're getting married."

I shrugged, and looked down at the cement floor.

"Plus," she said. "We've got wedding planning to do."

Yes, there was wedding planning to be done. Now that I had a ring and a fiancé, it seemed that the only reasonable thing to do was to figure out what kind of wedding Steven and I were going to have, which sounded simple enough. It wasn't until I wandered over to the wedding planning section of my local bookstore that it began to dawn on me that I had done more than simply decide to commit myself to the man I loved: I had entered Wedding Land.

"You've died and gone to heaven" read the introduction to *Planning a Wedding to Remember.* "He, you know—the one—finally popped the question and you said (no surprise here) YES! Your feet haven't touched the ground since."

I stood in the bookstore, frilly pink book in hand, not knowing whether to laugh, cry, or throw up. Thinking that perhaps I had selected a particularly obnoxious wedding planner, I put the book back and picked up a second one.

"Congratulations on your engagement!" cried the *Easy Wedding Planner, Organizer and Keepsake.* "You must be looking forward to what will be the happiest day of your life—your wedding!"

I didn't realize, of course, that this was the sort of language and the kind of mentality that would engulf my life for the next year, that from the moment Steven placed a ring on my finger until the last wedding guest left I would inhabit a world filled with ribbons and menu choices and useless facts, like the difference between engraving and thermography. I figured that over time people would stop noticing my ring (it would get duller, right?), stop asking me wedding questions, move on with their lives. But this was foolish, and I believed it because I had not yet opened a wedding magazine.

The engagement up until that point had been an oddity, a funny little thing that I'd gone and done. A slice of American kitsch that Steven and I had enacted in our living room. But one day, killing time at the airport before a flight, I crossed into flagrant wedding planning mode: I bought *Martha Stewart Weddings.* All my life I had passed by racks of wedding magazines, and now, finally, I had undergone the rite of passage required for me to actually open one. I had to find out what secrets of womanhood were revealed in those pages. What was it that made the white-clad women on the pastel magazine covers look so serene and pleased with themselves? Did they say if the ring got duller? Did they explain why no one mentioned divorce?

It turns out that the world of wedding magazines is one in which every bride has waited her whole life for her wedding day, where women have favorite flowers and signature mixed drinks, and every marriage ends in happily ever after. Advertisements for vacuum cleaners and silverware abound, sandwiched between articles instructing the bride on how to carve her own chocolate bride and groom figurines, or extolling the virtues of ruffles. The magazines are like an alternate universe in which the years between 1953 and now never happened. One article in my issue of *Martha Stewart Weddings* entitled "Figuring Out Your Taxes" showed a black-and-white photo of a 1940s-looking couple, the woman sitting on her husband's lap, smiling as he writes a check, because, of course, he is so wise and in charge of all their finances, and she is in charge of looking cute and sitting on his lap. This, despite the fact that most wedding magazines come with a wedding budget planner. Apparently women are capable of managing a wedding budget that involves signing potentially dozens of vendor contracts, but paying the cable bill is beyond them.

It seems hard to believe that anyone can take this stuff seriously. And yet women buy more bridal magazines every year. I had noticed the ever-expanding rack of wedding magazines on the newsstand, and wondering if it was just my imagination or if there really were more of them than I'd ever seen before, I did some investigating. I discovered that bridal magazines took a hit in the sixties, when the idea of a perfect wedding for most brides involved exchanging Native American vows while standing naked under a waterfall rather than walking down a church aisle to "Here Comes the Bride." The then-editor of *BRIDE'S* magazine has said that back in the sixties, "people would laugh at me at parties."

No one would be laughing today. In recent years, while ad pages for the magazine industry have been falling, bridal magazines have seen their ad pages rise. In 1999, *BRIDE'S* broke the Guinness World Record for magazine size, weighing in at 4 pounds 9 ounces, a total of 1,242 pages—and you can bet it wasn't because they'd added so many more articles. And in the past five years, a bevy of new magazines have begun to line the magazine racks: *InStyle Weddings, The Knot, Elegant Bride, Wedding Bells,* just to name a few. Which is not surprising, when you consider that the wedding industry on the whole is expanding—at last count it raked in approximately $70 billion annually, making it the same size as the entire U.S. food processing industry. But then, of course the industry brings in that much money, given that the average wedding today costs $22,000. Let me repeat: that is the *average.* To put that number in perspective, consider that the average household income in the U.S. in 2002 was $42,000. But how can you put a price tag on the Happiest Day of Your Life?

As I read through the magazines and books, and as I talked to my friends, I began to wonder if I was the one who was out of step with the rest of the planet; perhaps I was the one living in an alternate universe. They were all so obviously in agreement, and they all shared the same mantra: your wedding is the happiest day of your life. It is your day to shine, your shot at the spotlight, says everyone. Don't fuck it up.

"This is your moment," said one Estée Lauder ad I flipped past.

"It's your day," cooed an ad for the bridal salon at Saks Fifth Avenue.

Leafing through these magazines, engulfed in a world of women who vacuumed and men who went to work and paid the bills, I was utterly lost. Since when was my wedding supposed to be the happiest day of my life? What about the day I graduated from college? Landed a great promotion? What if I won the Nobel Peace Prize? Would that day still come second to my wedding? And how did all my friends seem to know this already, this Happiest Day thing, and how had I missed it? All this time I'd thought that we were focused on our careers, on our lives as fulfilled single women. If a man came along, great; if not, that would be okay too. Had it all been a charade? Had I just been puttering along while everyone around me waited to be swept off their feet by Prince Charming?

The Happiest Day mythology is so deeply imprinted on people's brains that it crops up in the strangest of places. Recently I was watching a reality TV show where a bunch of wannabe fashion designers were challenged with the task of designing wedding gowns for a group of fashion models, none of whom were actually getting married. The designers all immediately freaked out at the prospect of creating garments for what they endlessly referred to as "the most important day" in the lives of their fashion models, despite the fact that the day was hypothetical. Some of the models were all of sixteen years old, and yet they too promptly began acting as though they were really about to be married, referring to their "big day" as though it were just around the corner.

The notion of the wedding as the most important thing that could ever possibly happen in a woman's life has been around since the days when it actually used to be true, and it goes hand in hand with the concept of the princess bride, who is allowed to throw temper tantrums because her bridesmaids' nail polish is the wrong shade. After all, if this were guaranteed to be the most important day in your life, wouldn't you want everything to be perfect? I wondered if I could find out when the bride-as-princess concept first originated, and turned up a reference in *The New York Times* from 1905.

"On her wedding day," the article explains, "if never before or afterward, she [the bride] is permitted to do as she pleases, so long as she does not upset the established conventionalities."

My friend Cameron had gotten engaged a few weeks before I did, and I called her to discuss.

"I'm thinking about taking a year off to plan my wedding," she said before I could ask about the Happiest Day.

"Seriously?" I asked. Cameron was a senior-level brand strategist at an advertising agency and was, until that moment, one of the most career-oriented people I knew.

"Totally," she said. "It'll be fun. I'm already designing my save-the-date cards, and I love it. It's so creative."

"What about your job?" I asked.

"My job sucks," she said. "I want to make save-the-date cards."

"I loved planning my wedding," my friend Kimberly told me on the phone. "Of course, I took off a year to do it. Not everyone has to do that."

"Hmm," I said.

Kimberly was one of my oldest friends, and that she felt this way should have come as no surprise. Within moments of our meeting in college, Kimberly had informed me that all she really wanted to do in life was what her mother did: play bridge and get manicures. This was not the kind of goal one owned up to at our fairly competitive university, so she said it with a laugh, and at the time I thought she was joking. We had been discussing her major, and I pointed out that she probably couldn't major in bridge, so instead she picked political science, the default major for people who didn't know what else to study. (This was a process I was intimately familiar with since I, too, was a political science major.) Kimberly, it turned out, was great at political science, went on to win prestigious Capitol Hill internships and ultimately landed a spot at a top law school. I pretty much forgot about her homemaker dream until a few years later when, after a short stint as a lawyer, Kimberly got engaged and promptly quit her job. Now she lives in Connecticut and is married to a dermatologist.

"Actually," she said, drawing me back to our conversation. I've been thinking lately that I might become a wedding planner." The economy was in a slump and since she was through with law, Kimberly was always coming up with new career plans for herself. One day she was going to go to cooking school, the next she was deciding between starting a gift basket business or studying medicine.

I guess it should have come as no surprise that lots of women love weddings because as a nation we love weddings. The film *Four Weddings and a Funeral* was an unexpected success in 1994, and almost every year since, Hollywood has turned out a blockbuster in which a wedding is central to the plot. In four of those years, a wedding film ranked in the top ten at the box office. And two of the most recent wedding movies, *My Big Fat Greek Wedding* and *Meet the Fockers*, rank among the top fifty of all time highest-grossing U.S. films.

Based on the nation's movie-watching habits, it seems that people like fantasy weddings as much as real weddings, which helps explain the existence of fantasy wedding planners—women who have started selecting locations, dresses, and flowers, even though there is no one in their life at the moment that they plan on marrying.

"Editors of wedding magazines and websites say many of the letters and e-mails they receive are from single women who are not currently engaged but enjoy planning their future weddings as a form of entertainment," reported one article I came across.

"Men aren't a part of planning the real wedding," said a woman quoted in the article, "so why should they be a part of the virtual one?"

And then there are the women of the wedding website The Knot who inhabit a world so consumed by the wedding life that they even have their own language: FI for "fiancé," FMIL for "future mother-in-law"; and after the wedding (for these women continue to participate in wedding discussions long after the bouquet has been tossed), there is DH for "dear husband." I'd known about this site for a long time because I had a friend who worked for them during the dot-com boom. But had I not already known about The Knot, I'm sure somehow it would have entered my consciousness one way or another, because it is the epicenter of Wedding Land. So, soon after my engagement was official, I logged on to check it out.

The women who post messages on The Knot call themselves Knotties, and each creates an online bio for herself detailing the basic information about her wedding. Or at least, that is the ostensible purpose of the bio. In practice, many of the women turn these bios into virtual scrapbooks of obsession, pasting in images of their engagement rings, shoes, flower arrangements, flower girls, endless bouquet options, hair-style choices, invitations, and, of course, wedding gowns. And then, when they are done, they invite other Knotties to "critique" their bios.

No topic on The Knot is too small to obsess over, no detail too stupid or mundane.

"I'm planning on having Victorian Lilac dresses for my bridesmaids," wrote one Knottie. "I've been looking for ribbon and other accessories to match, but cannot find the right shade! Help!!!"

Ribbon for what? I wondered. Was there some reason I needed to be amassing a collection of Victorian Lilac ribbon?

"I just ordered a fabric aisle runner," wrote another. "Anyone else worried about tripping? Would paper or vinyl be better? I thought fabric would be nicer now I'm second-guessing as it is softer and might be harder to walk on. Any opinions?"

Some women posted their wedding nightmares: one dreamed she missed her entire reception looking for her lipstick, another that her maid of honor stopped on her way down the aisle to sell raffle tickets. There were dreams of blizzards in May, ruined pictures, ruined hair, smeared invitations. The stress level of these women oozed right out of the computer screen, and I found myself stressing for them. And yet, the amount of effort they were spending on their weddings—some seemed to be planning three years in advance of the date—left me in awe. How could it possibly be that these women were so utterly focused on wedding planning? Did they really buy into the Happiest Day mythology? Did they think it was 1950? Did they wish it was?

Perhaps women have so little control over their lives that we feel this, our wedding, our "big day," is at last something we can control down to the last insanely small detail. Perhaps we are so rarely the center of attention in the real world that we find ourselves enthralled with the one event at which we will be, for a brief moment, the star. Whatever the answers, I knew that my wedding would be different, and I smiled with the knowledge that I would not become an obsessive-compulsive bride. I would have some sort of wedding, I would be married, and that would be that.

"So where do you want to have this shindig?" I asked Steven one night as we were cooking dinner. Or rather, he was cooking and I was standing in the hall observing because at the time we had a one-person kitchen. Our division of labor in the kitchen usually went like this: I was in charge of all oven-related dishes, like roast meats and baked potatoes, and Steven was in charge of all stove-top cooking, which meant mostly pasta sauces and stir-fry. Since we both liked to cook, it was a division that worked out pretty well, although we'd discovered that none of our parents believed us. ("So you cooked?"

Steven's father was always asking him. "Or really Hana cooked and you're taking credit?")

"I don't know," Steven said. "What do you think?"

"Well, the magazines say that a good way to start planning a wedding is to pick a theme, and everything else follows."

"Oh man," he said, chopping up an onion. "What kind of theme?"

"They suggest things like 'Hearts and Flowers,' or, you know, 'The Wild West,' that kind of thing."

"Like, 'Romance Under the Sea'?"

"Yeah," I said. "I'm thinking maybe we should go with 'Man's Inhumanity to Man.' "

"What about, 'Anti-Semitism Through the Ages'?" asked Steven. "I mean, it is going to be a Jewish wedding."

"Ooh, good one. We could do a Czarist Russia table, a Spanish Inquisition table, a Nazi Germany table."

"The possibilities are endless, really. That's what makes it a good theme."

Steven tossed the chopped onion into a frying pan and adjusted the burner heat.

"Seriously," I said, leaning against the wall. "What do you think of when you think about our wedding?"

"When I think of our wedding," he said, "I think: casual."

"Casual, like twenty people in a restaurant, or casual, like, in a field?"

"I don't think we can do twenty people in a restaurant. I'm sure my parents want to invite more than twenty people."

"Yeah."

"What do you think of when you think of our wedding?" Steven asked.

I sighed. "I think, oh my God, my parents are going to be in the same room."

"Oh, babe," he said. "They'll behave."

My parents really wanted me to elope. Or more accurately, my father really wanted me to elope. Even though they had been divorced for six years by that point and he was now remarried, he was horrified by the thought of being in the same state as my mother, let alone the same room. The best thing you could say about their divorce was that it was speedy. One day I was out for a weekend drive in the country with my parents, a week later my mother had moved across town. A few months after that my father sold their apartment and moved out of the state. Silly little scraps of my childhood that had been carefully tucked away for years suddenly vanished. Poems I'd written, papers with gold stars on them, the one or two awards I'd managed to win over the course of fifteen years of schooling, and my birth certificate all disappeared in the tornado of lawyers, mediators, and divorce papers. So when my father recommended elopement, I understood what he meant. My mother, on the other hand, said she had no opinions. But my guess was that, secretly, she was rooting for an elopement too.

Steven's parents, on the opposite end of the spectrum, subscribed to the "whatever makes you happy, honey" school of parenting. We'd had them over for dinner once when they were in town, and when Steven asked them what they wanted us to cook, they both said, "Oh, whatever, it doesn't matter." "Fine," Steven replied. "We'll make you a pork roast." "Oh no, don't make pork," they said in unison. "Then what do you want?" he asked. "You know," they said. "Whatever you want to make."

This was the policy they employed when it came to the wedding too. Whatever we wanted. Whatever made us happy. But not at City Hall. Not too small, either. They had a lot of friends with whom they wanted to share their joy. But whatever we wanted was just fine.

To be fair, if we'd insisted on getting married at City Hall, they would have gone along with it, and my parents would have probably breathed huge sighs of relief. I thought a lot about City Hall, about what it would be like to get on the subway in a little white dress, or maybe we could spring for a taxi. We'd get down there, we'd wait on line, we'd sign something, and we'd be married and that would be it. I talked to an acquaintance who'd done just that, who described the waiting area as looking like a subway car had just emptied out into it—all the people you see on the subway, she said, they're all in there with you, waiting to get married. As much as I didn't want to move to Happiest Day Land, I also wanted something more special than signing a piece of paper at City Hall. Something that at least paid a tiny homage to the fact that what Steven and I were doing was Big and Important.

Because, even though I had not been dreaming about my wedding since I could walk, it had been there, in the back of my mind—how could it have not? At my bat mitzvah, when I complained to my parents that there was no band, just a stupid string quartet, and how come I didn't get to pick out stuff—I didn't know what stuff, but surely there was stuff to be picked out—my father said, "This isn't your party. This is for your mother and me. Your wedding will be your party." And back when my parents were married, my mother used to like to pick out pretend locations for my nuptials. She would call me and say, "Today we saw the most beautiful garden, it would be perfect for your wedding." Even though I had not been thinking about flower arrangements and wedding colors and ribbons, I had imagined the general feeling of my wedding. My family would be there, everyone would be happy, and I would be happy.

And I wonder if this is what the whole 1950s-era Happiest Day of My Life thing is about. The generation of women getting married today grew up in the era of divorce. We were children in the seventies and eighties, when the divorce rate reached its peak, and even though we know there is no such thing as happily ever after, we want it stubbornly, irrationally. We believe that our marriages will be different, and we start by proving it with our weddings, which harken back to a Disneyfied view of the 1950s, when the men went to work and the women took Valium and people got married and stayed married and everyone was happy.

No matter that the world was not the way people like to imagine it, that divorce is as much a part of American life as getting drunk and blowing things up with fireworks on the Fourth of July. No matter that American divorce actually predates America, with the first recorded divorce issued in 1639 in Massachusetts. American culture is rife with rose-colored views of the past. Politicians like to talk about getting back to family values, as though we had only recently left Eden and with the enforcement of a few little laws could quickly find our way back. Fashions repeat endlessly on themselves—when

I was a teenager the little white socks of the fifties were in; in college it was sixties-era tie-dyes and ratty jeans, giving way to a brief attempt circa my early twenties to reintroduce the bellbottoms of the seventies; and just the other day on the street I saw two women wearing leg warmers, the fashion statement of the eighties. Each generation tries to recapture the feeling of the previous generation, of the eras we lived through but barely remember or never lived through at all, but surely they were better than they are today, because today sucks. Generations X and Y are seemingly obsessed with their childhoods: the other day on the subway I heard two people my age discussing the collection of Star Wars figurines they owned twenty years ago ("Dude, you had the Millennium Falcon? Can you imagine what that would be worth on eBay?"). So why should weddings be any different? Why not take a nostalgic trip back to the era when we pretended that everything was okay?

The first location we looked at was the Boathouse in Central Park. We wandered in one sunny afternoon in T-shirts and cargo pants, looked at all the well-dressed ladies lunching, picking at their salads as they admired the lush landscape of the park. It was a quiet, elegant little corner of Manhattan, and we felt completely out of place.

"Don't you think it's a little weird that we're looking at booking a place for our wedding that we can't afford to eat in?" I whispered to Steven.

"I was just thinking the same thing," he whispered back.

Someone came by and brought us fresh iced tea, and we sat for a while in two enormous high-backed leather chairs, our feet dangling above the floor as though we were children. When the wedding coordinator arrived, we went through the motions of looking at the space and reviewing the menu options, both of us knowing that never in a million years would we get married here. It was a lovely spot, but it was everything I didn't want in a wedding: a large hall, those big round tables where everyone has to yell to be heard, a band leader forcing everyone to get up and Hava Nagila themselves around the room (and there was always that moment, at those weddings, where some uncle or other would squat down on the floor and try to do some sort of Russian kicking thing while everyone else worried that he might have a coronary and eventually his wife or daughter would plead with him to get back to the table). I had no idea what I wanted from a wedding, but it wasn't that.

The wedding magazines clearly thought they were full of all different kinds of weddings—weddings for every taste and budget, some claimed—but to me they all looked like the same general idea. There was a bride in a white dress, a groom with a silly boutonniere, a marriage ceremony, and then everyone ate. Usually there was dancing. The weddings I'd been to tended to blend together in my head. There were nice hotels and ugly hotels, there were weddings with sushi and weddings with jalapeño poppers, but in the end they were all just a bunch of pomp and circumstance, a scene meant to duplicate every TV or movie wedding because no one knew what else to do.

But, truth be told, there had always been a voice in my head at these weddings that said, "Well, at *my* wedding . . ." At my wedding there won't be a band, at my wedding we'll rent out Shea Stadium and there will be a big softball game and I'll get married at home plate, at my wedding the toasts will be witty and articulate, at my wedding it won't rain. Because that was the fun in going to other people's weddings, right? Finding things to criticize, determining the overall cost of the wedding, and placing bets on how long the marriage would last—these were, as far as I could tell, the main activities people indulged in at weddings.

None of this would help us pick a location, so I went out and bought *Locations* magazine, which listed hundreds of places in New York where one could get married. There were a vast assortment of hotels and catering halls, echoing industrial spaces in SoHo, something billed as a "photographer's studio," Park Avenue mansions where you could pretend to be Edith Wharton, churches and synagogues, private clubs, and endless restaurants. None of them spoke to me. Or rather, they did speak. They said: this isn't for you.

Part of the problem was that neither Steven nor I are really from anywhere. Had things been different, I would have been perfectly happy to get married in the house where I grew up. Unfortunately, I was no longer related to anyone who lived in it. I grew up in Connecticut, but my mother now lived in Chicago in an apartment I'd never seen, and my father lived in a house in Florida that had been slowly transformed into a still-life menagerie by his new wife's passion for decorating with ceramic animals. Steven's parents had only recently moved to Atlanta; and while they generously offered up their home for the wedding, given that we didn't know a single person in Atlanta, it would have been an odd choice.

So that's how we ended up with Vermont. We spent a few nights flipping through *Locations*, making gagging noises. I called a few Manhattan caterers and, upon hearing their price ranges, promptly hung up. And then, one rainy evening, I took *Locations* and threw it across the living room.

"There is nowhere in here to get married," I said, "So, I guess the wedding is off."

Steven was sitting across the room in our blue overstuffed chair-and-a-half, reading *War and Peace*, which he had recently begun in preparation for his impending entry into a graduate program in Russian Literature. Steven and I had met at work, back when we were both writing for a news website. Since then I'd stayed on in the Internet world, becoming a freelance web designer, but Steven had ventured on a long and occasionally treacherous career path that had found him at various points making bagels at midnight in Seattle, writing reviews of Tex-Mex restaurants or Carpathian Mountain ski resorts in Ukraine, and most recently, editing the most boring academic journals ever published. Ever since I'd met Steven he had been fighting the impulse to go to graduate school and study something arcane and inconsequential to humanity. He maintained that he wanted to be *in* the world, not just locked in an office reading about it. "I would give anything," he sometimes said, "to be interested in something practical." But, after two months of editing *Human Factors and Ergonomics in Manufacturing*, he decided arcane and inconsequential sounded pretty darn good, and applied to graduate school. He would begin school three days after our wedding.

Steven book-marked *War and Peace* and looked over at me.

"Don't say things like that," he said.

I glared at the carpet. "I'm sorry," I said. "I didn't mean that. I just . . . I just don't know what the hell we're going to do and I'm sick of looking at all these pictures of stupid industrial spaces. And I thought we were going to do this together."

"We are doing it together. We looked at the Boathouse. We looked at that magazine. What do you want me to be doing?"

"I want you to pick a location."

"Fine."

Pause.

"Have we figured out how many people we're inviting?" Steven asked.

"I dunno. Well, your parents probably want to invite some people, and then there are our friends, and I guess some of my family. Do you think we could do, like forty people?"

"That sounds nice. Forty people sounds good."

"Okay."

"Okay."

Steven looked up at the ceiling, as though our location might be up there somewhere. I walked across the room and picked up the *Locations* magazine, which had landed on the floor with its pages splayed out.

"What about that place in Vermont?" Steven said.

"Which place?"

"You know, that inn we went to a few summers ago."

I smiled at the memory, thinking of the tangy local cheese we'd stuffed ourselves on, the spider-filled shuffleboard court where we'd whiled away the better part of an afternoon, the charmingly freezing swimming hole. We'd been together for about a year at that point, and it was our first real vacation as a couple. When you've been dating for a while and you go on vacation, it's a little like experimenting with living together. All your stuff is in the same room for the first time, and you learn things like who takes up more space on the bathroom counter. It's the first time you don't have the option of saying, "Well, I guess I'll go home now." And that trip was, I think, the first time I knew that this could really be it. This could be my life.

"That place was nice," I said.

"And that way we could keep it small."

"Right, because who would want to drive all the way up to Vermont?"

"Yeah, it's hard to get to."

"Omigod," I said. "It's perfect. We'll have a little country wedding and no one will come and it'll be great."

"See," said Steven. "That wasn't so hard. Anything else you want me to do?"

"Yeah," I said. "Call Vermont and tell them we're coming."

And with that, I imagined that the hard part was done. I would plan a lovely Vermont wedding. It would be small. There would be a wedding coordinator at the inn who would take care of most of whatever needed taking care of. I would not have a theme, no one would play "Hava Nagila," and I would not become obsessive about Victorian Lilac aisle runners. And then we would be married and that would be all there was to it.

2

The Princess Diaries

Girl, do not exult in the wedding dress;
see how much trouble lurks behind it.
—Syrian proverb

THE TIME THAT ELAPSED BETWEEN THE END OF Steven's marriage proposal and the beginning of the wedding dress discussions felt like about twelve seconds. It was almost as though my friends and family, sensing engagement in the air, had all run out and purchased six back issues of *BRIDE'S*. There was no discussion about how I felt about getting married, whether I was sure I had picked the right guy. Everyone just wanted to make sure I got the right dress.

"Are we going to Kleinfeld?" asked Ellen. "We have to go to Kleinfeld."

Kleinfeld Bridal is a New York institution—women have been buying gowns there since the 1940s—that claims to carry the largest selection of wedding gowns in the city.

Jami beeped in on my call waiting.

"Vera Wang, right?" said Jami. "You're taking me to Vera Wang with you."

"You want to go to Vera Wang?" I asked. Jami owned an entire wardrobe of ironic, hipster clothing; Vera Wang was for celebrities, wanna-be-society girls, *the* name brand in wedding gowns. Jami was not a Vera Wang girl. "I can't believe you've even heard of Vera Wang."

"Are you kidding?" she said. "You *have* to take me."

As soon as I hung up with Jami the phone rang again.

"So what kind of dress are you thinking about? A-line? Mermaid? Princess? Basque Waist?" said a voice that sounded like my mother, though the words couldn't be hers. My mother, who skipped down the aisle in a white velvet micro-minidress to "Feelin' Groovy"; my mother, who when asked what her wedding reception was like replied, "I was so stoned, I have no idea."

"Who is this?" I asked.

"I've been reading *Modern Bride*," she said. "They say you should know what kind of dress you want before you go to a bridal boutique."

Whoa, Mama.

There is probably nothing else in wedding culture that makes people think "wedding" as much as the bride's dress. Most of us only need to see a picture of a woman in a wedding gown to have a whole range of emotions conjured up, from pleasure to nausea. Which is probably why the wedding industry assumes that, if you are female, you have been fantasizing about your wedding dress for years now, and therefore the majority of your wedding planning efforts will be directed towards locating and purchasing your dream gown. In my brief foray onto The Knot I'd noticed an entire board devoted to The Dress. The bridal magazines I'd been flipping through seemed to consist almost entirely of wedding gown ads; and the remaining ads, which were for things like tuxedos, Slim-Fast, or furniture, all had pictures of wedding gowns thrown in for good measure.

The planning books I'd looked at assumed even worse.

"Ever since a Victorian bride wore the first white wedding dress, women have devoted weeks, months, even entire childhoods to the contemplation of this utterly romantic garment," asserted the *Bride's Book of Etiquette*. "Your wedding gown is the dress of a lifetime."

Unfortunately, I spent my childhood in other ways, and so I had no idea what to ask for when I walked into Kleinfeld a short three weeks after becoming engaged. My mother had flown in from Chicago just for the occasion. Kleinfeld is in the Bay Ridge section of Brooklyn, a neighborhood famous the world over for being home to the disco-with-the-flashing-floor of *Saturday Night Fever*. No flashing floor for Kleinfeld, though; decorated in standard-issue bridal salon pinks and beiges, it has classical music piped into the lobby and an incongruous coin-operated coffee machine occupying one wall.

Gloria, the bridal sales associate who had been assigned to me, showed my mother and me into a fitting room.

"What do you want to look like on your wedding day?" she asked. "A lot of brides want to look like a princess. Or maybe you want something more rustic—you said the wedding was in Vermont?"

The question caught me completely by surprise, although if I'd thought about it for a minute before entering the store, this was just the type of topic for which I should have had a prepared answer. I want to look like me, I thought. I had no Cinderella fantasies, no desire to be transformed into a virginal bride about to be carried off on a white horse by her shining prince.

I looked at Gloria, who was waiting impatiently for some answer that would enable her to start bringing out gowns for me to try on.

"I'm looking for something, um, not so bride-y," I said.

Gloria eyed me as if to say, are you sure you walked into the right store?

"If you have anything that's, maybe, not white, that would be good too," I added.

Gloria smiled. "Oh, brides almost never wear white these days."

"Really?" I asked hopefully.

"Absolutely not. Almost every dress we have comes in ivory."

"Oh."

I bit my lip and tried to think how to counter the idea that ivory and white were two wildly different colors. "I meant, like an actual color. Maybe something purple? I don't know how likely that is."

"Some dresses also come in champagne and blush," she said helpfully.

The first dress she brought me was a traditional-looking white organza confection with a fitted bodice and a huge, billowing skirt.

I stared at it, thinking, *Did you not hear what I just said?* Getting into the dress was a three-person affair. Gloria held the bottom of the dress over my head and reached through the neck for my arms while my mother tugged the skirt down over me. For a minute I was drowning in tulle, looking through the neckline of the dress helplessly for someone to pull me through to the other side. Gloria grabbed my arms and yanked me out of the tulle eddy, zipped up the back, smoothed the fabric of the bodice, and then spun me around to face the mirror.

"Let's see it with the veil," she said, pinning a long white veil into my hair.

I stared into the mirror, transfixed by the stranger staring back at me. The person in the mirror was young and innocent and eager to share her meatloaf recipe with you. She had never owned a pair of black leather pants, had not for one second doubted the institution of marriage, had never lied to her parents or stolen lipstick from CVS. She had spent her entire life dreaming of the one glorious moment when she would become a bride.

"I love it," said my mother.

"I think I'm going to hurl," I said.

"What's that?" asked Gloria.

"It's a bit much," I told her. And yet I didn't want to take it off. I wanted to spend the rest of my days here in this little white box in Brooklyn, staring at the strange and splendid creature in the mirror. I stepped up onto a little circular platform in the center of the dressing room and fluffed the skirt of the dress over it, watching the folds of the fabric fall noiselessly down. I pirouetted on the platform and the skirt flared out like a dancer's costume. I heard the soft rustle of the tulle crinoline against the silk lining of the dress. I found myself to be simultaneously enchanting and horrifying.

"Please," I said. "Get me out of this dress."

For two hours we played dress up. I was a living Barbie doll, and Gloria and my mother zipped me into crinolines, attached hooks to eyes, snapped buttons closed, lived out entire imaginary lives in the Kleinfeld dressing room. We were girls at play, dreaming how fabulous our lives would be once we were married off to stable, loving husbands. And for every imagined life there was a dress. I was the princess and Gloria and my mother were my handmaidens, readying me for the ball. I was Nicole Kidman, Gloria and my mother my celebrity handlers, dressing me for my red carpet walk to the Academy Awards. Whatever the fantasy, it was in that room in Kleinfeld, just waiting to be enacted.

I tried on dresses with bows, lace, ruffles. I left my thirty-year-old woman-with-a-401(k) persona at the door and became a little girl who needed help putting on her clothes. There were pink dresses that reminded me of Little Bo Peep (I couldn't resist crying out, "I've lost my sheep!" once Gloria finished zipping me into it. She ignored me.), dresses meant to evoke Jackie O, dresses with cathedral trains and lace so heavy it was an effort just to breathe. Every single one made me look like I'd just walked off the top of a cake. And in every single one I felt ridiculous. Because as enticing as it was to become the women that these dresses demanded of me—pampered, innocent, absurdly feminine, consumed with my own beauty—standing in them I felt like a fraud. I had not been waiting my entire life for my wedding day, but these dresses said that I had.

As I pushed my way out of the dressing room two hours later, depleted, I wove my way through scores of other brides who had been promoted to the large mirrors in the main room, such was their dress-trying-on prowess. They all stood on their little round platforms, their dresses billowing out to the walls, their veils floating in the air like a tulle electric storm. They stood there and they smiled at their reflections, at their adoring mothers, their jealous best friends, at the Kleinfeld associate who months later would be receiving a photo of the bride on her wedding day, wearing that same smile. They smiled because they were satisfied. They had won the race to the altar.

I walked out of Kleinfeld and struggled to catch my breath. I was relieved to be back outside in a world where women wore regular clothes and colors other than white. I didn't know much about what I wanted from a wedding dress, but I did know this: I didn't want to look like a bride. I didn't want to be a white-swathed child, virginal, pleased as punch that I had gotten my man. I didn't want to be Cinderella at the ball, or Princess Diana or Princess Grace or any stupid goddamn princess. I wanted to be me. But there was no wedding gown that would let me do that.

It is not without reason that the vast majority of wedding dresses are about making the bride feel and look like a fairy-tale princess. This is probably the most frequent request dress designers and bridal salons get. At the majority of the bridal salons I visited (and I made it to the bulk of the ones in the New York area), the sales associates always began by saying, "So, you want to look like a princess, right?" I did a little poking around to find out when women started craving royal sensations from their gowns, and found a book published in 1972, the year I was born, which reported that 90 percent of brides who responded to an essay contest on the subject "Why I Chose My Gown," wrote something like, "It made me look like a fairy princess."

Other women take the Cinderella fantasy literally, shelling out thousands of dollars to top designers for Disney-inspired Cinderella gowns. Or they get married at Cinderella's castle in Disney World, in a ceremony complete with horse-drawn glass pumpkin coach, footmen dressed to look exactly like the footmen in Disney's cartoon *Cinderella* (although one assumes these footmen will not turn back into mice at midnight), and Disney characters at the reception.

"Discover a place where little girls' dreams come true. Where magic and matrimony join together to create the perfect day," gushed a bridal magazine ad for Disney's Fairy Tale Weddings division.

Even women who aren't terrifyingly obsessed with Cinderella generally harbor some kind of princess fantasy. Several of my otherwise well-adjusted married friends admitted to me that they bought their wedding dress because it made them feel like a princess. Advertisers in the wedding magazines I looked at promised honeymoons "where fairy tale romances come true"; the ads for wedding dresses designed by Romona Keveza boasted dresses "inspired by the world's most celebrated women," a list that included Princess Diana, Grace Kelly, and Audrey Hepburn. Note that Marie Curie, Eleanor Roosevelt, and Amelia Earhart did not inspire wedding gowns. If wedding gowns are all about enacting dream lives, then why is it that the only dream catered to is the one involving being royalty? And why is it always princess? Why does no one fantasize about being the queen, which might actually be an interesting job (depending on the era one is fantasizing about— more interesting to be a queen who actually governs and chops off people's heads than one who just stands on a balcony and waves). But of course the fantasy is about being young and in love and, I suppose, lacking any sort of decision-making abilities, whereas queens are old, already bored by their marriages, and might actually have to make a decision or two.

The implication of the Cinderella fantasy, of course, is that you want to look like Cinderella because you are marrying your prince, the man who will take care of you, install you in a castle, and buy you glass slippers while you sit around looking pretty and doing volunteer work. No one in the wedding industry has accounted for women who might want to fantasize about having any other profession. Where are the wedding gowns that make you look like an astronaut, a Nobel Prize-winning physicist, or the head of the United Nations? My personal childhood fantasy involved being President of the United States, flying around the world making speeches and signing peace treaties. But no one asked me if on my wedding day I wanted to look like the President.

I decided that if I was going to be forced into looking like a princess, I at least wanted to know why, so I read up on a little wedding gown history. It turns out that part of the reason wedding dresses today are all about royalty is due to Queen Victoria, who popularized the white wedding gown. Prior to the 1840s, women wore colored dresses, or simply their best dress, to their wedding. Around the world women married in a range of hues: American Revolution brides wore red as a symbol of rebellion, Norwegian brides married in green, Puritan women wed in gray gowns, Spanish women in black. But after Queen Victoria's wedding, it became standard for women to not only wear white but oddly, dress like someone from the 1840s. Because when today's women say they want to look like a princess, what they are really saying is they want to look like some version of Queen Victoria. It is as though our wedding fashion sense has gotten stuck 160 years in the past. We are told that this is what a wedding dress should be, and we all listen and obey, as though it is not possible that women have ever gotten married in any other costume. In an era when women have more freedom and greater opportunities than ever before, the most popular fantasy we can enact is one from a time famous for valuing repression and depriving women of opportunity.

Some of the blame for the Queen Victoria trend must fall to the wedding industry, which has so successfully enforced the idea of what a wedding should be that even in Japan, where the tradition for thousands of years was for brides to be wed in an embroidered kimono, women are now overwhelmingly opting for flouncy white gowns. But perhaps the bulk of the Victorian fetish can be explained by our collective nostalgia for things past, and especially in an era where nearly half of the women buying these wedding gowns will eventually get divorced, perhaps it is an expression of wishful thinking, of a longing for a nonexistent time when, as in fairy tales, all marriages ended in happily-ever-after.

Even though I didn't spend much time as a kid thinking about what I would be wed in, I did have a few ideas from time to time. I knew I wanted to wear lilac. For many years I was madly in love with the wedding dress from the "November Rain" video (yes, that would be Guns N' Roses), which was miniskirt length in front but swooped out into a huge train in back. I knew I would wear comfortable, sensible shoes. I knew that I would look beautiful. But one by one, even the few things that I knew for sure began to erode.

"You have to wear white," came from my father.

"Why?" I asked. "Because I'm a virgin?"

"No, I'm sorry. You just have to," he said. "Otherwise it's like you're trying to make a statement. People will wonder what's going on."

I sighed.

"You know I don't care about this stuff," he said. "But you have to wear white."

"But I don't look good in white. I look good in lilac."

"Well, do what you want," he said.

But I knew then that I would wear white. If for no other reason than to maintain the mass delusion that I had never had sex.

And, sadly, the Guns N' Roses dress was now long outdated, and seemed somewhat inappropriate, as I was not marrying the abusive lead singer of an eighties hair band. Which meant that I had to come up with a new mental image for my wedding day. And that was the problem. My visit to Kleinfeld had proven to me that I needed to be more specific in my gown desires, that walking into a wedding salon and demanding to see dresses that did not look like wedding gowns was not a good strategy.

After some investigation, I decided to go the Carolyn Bessette route—straight, sophisticated, sleek evening gown. I also decided to ignore the fact that I had merely chosen to be a different kind of princess, that the closest thing we have in this country to royalty is the Kennedy clan, and that I had set my sights on looking like a member of their family. I ran all over SoHo trying on fabulous slip dresses in large industrial spaces. I began to search for the most obscure designers I could find, ending up one day in a third-floor TriBeCa loft in my underwear, shivering as the designer took my measurements, drew a sketch on a napkin, and asked for a deposit of thousands of dollars on a dress that I would never see until it was mine. I stood on line for an hour to gain entrance to a Badgeley-Mischka sale, and, although I had had nightmares about women tearing gowns out of each other's hands, I found a heavily beaded $700 dress marked down from $7,000 that I contemplated for several minutes, hand on hip, fighting for space in the propped-up plastic mirror. Upon reflection I decided the dress made me feel like a lampshade, and put it back. I dragged Kimberly and Ellen around to nearly every bridal salon in New York. When new ones opened I got on their lists and was sure to be the first person in the door. For three months there was barely a waking moment when I was not engaged in some dress-related activity. And yes, I took Ellen and Jami to Vera Wang, where we all stood in a corner staring at a girl trying on a $20,000, ball gown-style wedding dress so covered with beading and embroidery that it looked like it had been gilded. Eyeing the fairy princess in the fitting room next door while I stood in my Carolyn Bessette–like slip dress, the one that Jami insisted did not look like a nightgown, I wondered if I wanted more.

I had, for the most part, gotten what I wanted with the slip dresses. They did not look bridey. They did not look childish. But they also looked like I'd thrown on a sheet after getting out of the bath. They clung in scary places. They managed to simultaneously be unsexy and leave little to the imagination. They looked like my grandmother's lingerie. I suppose that if I had been built like a stick they might have been more flattering, but sadly I have been blessed with what I can only assume were my great-grandmother's proportions, had she not lived on a diet of fried chicken fat and brisket. From the pictures I've seen of her, Bubby (everyone called her Bubby, the Yiddish word for "grandmother") was a woman who had breasts like king-sized down pillows, hips to match, and, mysteriously, a Mae West–like waist. I have the updated version of this figure: queen-sized pillow breasts, matching hips, and a waist three sizes smaller than the rest of my body, which is great if you're a porn star, but not so practical if you're trying to look like Carolyn Bessette.

But body type aside, the biggest problem with the slip dresses was that when I put them on I didn't look like I was getting married. I just looked like I was wearing a white dress. And this was the conundrum. I didn't want to look like a bride, but the un-bridey dresses didn't feel special. Standing there in Vera Wang, I began to wonder if I was passing up my one opportunity to wear a big poofy dress. Because the truth was that I was not a princess and I was not a movie star, and I probably wouldn't see an endless parade of ball gowns and custom-tailored Versace sheaths come through my walk-in closet.

And this, I think, is what most women decide. It's a pretty depressing way to look at buying a wedding dress, but there it is. We know that this is our shot. For many people, their wedding is the only formal event they ever attend. Their social calendars are not filled with awards shows or charity balls. And the lives they imagine themselves having after marriage do not include dinner with Brooke Astor. They spend more on their wedding dresses than on any other garment they ever purchase, and, understandably, they want to make it special. Carolyn Bessette wore a slip dress when she married JFK Jr. *because* she was marrying JFK Jr. She foresaw a lifetime overflowing with poofy ball gowns—there was no need to wear one at her wedding. But for me, was it possible that I would never go to another formal event? Could I admit that this might be the dressiest party of my life? I didn't think so. In fact, no, I couldn't. And so the quest for the slip dress continued.

Compounding my difficulties in finding a gown was the dress purchasing lore, which says that you are supposed to know when the dress is The One. You are supposed to fall victim to some kind of inner feeling—perhaps butterflies combined with heart palpitations—that indicates that this is the dress that you were destined to wear on your wedding day. There is to be no doubt in your mind that you are looking at yourself as you will be on the day that you are married. Never mind that the dress you are trying on was only designed last Tuesday and will be discontinued next year. It was meant for you. And this thought should give you goose bumps.

This philosophy has even made it into print. An ad I saw for the wedding website WeddingChannel.com asks, "How do you know it's the right dress? The same way you know he's the right guy."

Women are used to the whole You Just Know philosophy, as we've been told we'll just know on a whole range of topics throughout our lives. You Just Know when you're in love. You Just Know if you've had an orgasm. And, let's hope, you just know those things before you just know about your wedding dress.

There is such mythology built up around this concept that I discovered a whole range of worried messages on The Knot about the feelings certain women got when they put on different dresses. They want to know exactly what the feeling is they're supposed to feel. They report that their maid of honor cried when they put on a certain dress, but that they themselves did not. Does that count?

"I have tried on approximately 60 dresses and am still waiting for the feeling," reported one bride, adding: "Sometimes I think people watch too many movies—'The sky opened up and angels started singing and I just knew it was the one.'"

Rest assured, other brides told her, you will know when it's The One.

"Follow your heart with the feeling you get in the dress that was made for you," advised one somewhat unintelligible response.

Some women even buy more than one dress. After purchasing the first one, they keep looking, worried that they lack kismet with their dress, perhaps concerned that choosing the wrong garment indicates something about their choice of man, perhaps forgetting their choice of man altogether in favor of this more important choice—this choice of choices, their wedding gown.

A big unspoken factor in dress selection is price. It's something only talked about in whispers, or perhaps filled out on an information sheet when you walk into a bridal salon, not to be spoken aloud. Because the wedding is your perfect day, you should have the perfect gown, and price should not be a consideration. Before my visit to Kleinfeld I called and asked what their price range was. "We start at $1,500," said the woman on the other end of the line, "and go to the moon." I hung up the phone and shook my head, trying to get the information to register in my brain. I wasn't sure I'd ever encountered anything that started at $1,500 before, except maybe rent. But $1,500 for a dress that would only get a few hours of wear and then be put away in a trunk for the rest of its existence?

But much of wedding life is about being over the top, spending included. When I was in the midst of my dress shopping adventures, the New York Post ran an article about a $300,000 wedding gown being made for a bride in Brooklyn, alleged to be the most expensive gown ever made. The bride was reported to have asked for an "over-the-top magnificent wedding dress," so the dressmaker designed a dress covered in diamonds. Pictures of the dress circulated on The Knot, where the vast majority of brides declared it hideously ugly. I thought it looked like just another wedding dress, but heavier.

In recent years, the wedding dress world has been blindsided by David's Bridal, the discount wedding gown retailer ($1,000 and under) that has stolen a large chunk of business. The wedding industry hates David's Bridal—they see the store's large racks of ready-to-wear gowns, fluorescent lighting, and lack of pink decorations as counter to everything a wedding is supposed to be about. One wedding industry website insists that "a chain store may have the styles that look similar to designer gowns, but the fabric is lower quality. Our advice: If there is ever a time when you deserve quality, it's your wedding day."

Sure, we all deserve quality, don't we? But with wedding gowns, quality and price seem to have little to do with each other, because everything has an extra zero tacked on to it. Which meant that some of the $600 gowns I tried on felt like $60 worth of quality. There is nothing quite as strange as standing in a gown that is far more expensive than anything else you have ever owned and feeling that you are wearing something cheap. Along with all my other wedding dress issues, I may have been able to buy a dress sooner had I not also been required to spend two months' rent on it.

I played with the idea of just buying a white dress in a department store, but it was fall and there were no white dresses, and what if I waited until spring and then didn't find one? What then? I went to resale stores that sold once-worn dresses, and discovered that the dresses were so tailored to the previous owners' bodies that I would never find one that fit me, or that I would need to use my imagination to see what it might look like were it retailored to my body, and that I had no imagination when it came to dresses. I went to several discount stores and didn't see anything I liked; or I was unable to find what I wanted because there were no salespeople; or I couldn't tell in the bad lighting what anything looked like, anyway. In the end, I realized that no matter what I did, I was going to be spending a lot of money on a dress because even the inexpensive dresses were expensive. I was going to have to reconcile myself to the fact that it was a stupid waste of money and there was nothing I could do about it.

After a month of gown shopping I began to loathe wedding gowns. I hated the process of walking onto the plush beige carpet of the bridal salon (for nearly every bridal salon is outfitted in a pink and beige rococo-Louis-XIV-meets-the-Playboy-Mansion style), describing the dress I wanted, being told that there was nothing like that in the store, trying on ten other dresses anyway, then leaving—hair disheveled, feeling humiliated by the bridal sales people who could not understand why I couldn't just be happy with a big poofy dress. I hated the pressure of standing in front of the three-way mirror, all eyes on me, feeling that I needed to be beautiful on demand and that I was failing miserably. Because the fact was that as much as I just wanted to buy a dress and be done with it, I still wanted a dress that would make me a beautiful bride. Of course, what I didn't know then is that brides *are* beautiful. The connection between beauty and weddings is so ingrained in our minds that we're not able to see a bride without seeing beauty. I could have worn a barrel; it wouldn't have mattered. People would still have looked at me and smiled at how breathtaking I was. Unfortunately, no one told me that while I was dress shopping.

"I'm going to get married naked," I began telling people. "You won't mind, will you?"

Dress nightmares plagued my nighttime hours. I dreamt that it was the Thursday before the wedding and that I had decided to run the New York Marathon in my wedding gown. I was so relieved in the dream that I at least had a dress, and then panicked when I realized the train would get dirty as I ran, and the dress would be unwearable for the wedding. I told people as I ran by them, my train floating behind me, that it would be okay, the dry cleaner would be able to fix it in time. I had dreams in which I caught glimpses of my dress around corners and through mirrors but awoke before I could touch it. I dreamt that I found the perfect dress but was lost in a labyrinthine bridal salon, unable to find a place to try it on. Other brides were running ahead of me and darting into dressing rooms, then slamming the doors shut. When I told Steven about my dreams, he laughed.

"Gee, I wonder what that means," he said. "I mean, why do you even bother to dream?"

Well sure, why should he be worried? To buy his wedding attire we spent one afternoon in a department store. And I came along and told him my opinion. Whereas here I was buying a dress that in part was supposed to please him, yet he wasn't allowed to see it. (I did bring him to one bridal salon to give me his opinion on a dress, and the sales associates chased him out of the store.)

When I wasn't dreaming about wedding gowns, I was up late at night looking at pictures of dresses online, searching for new bridal shops and unknown designers. Or I was lying awake in bed wondering what was wrong with me that I couldn't buy a stupid dress, going over options in my mind, just wishing the whole thing would be over already. For three months I had done nothing but shop for a dress that I would wear only once in my life for a few hours one evening. The time investment was wildly out of proportion with the amount of time I would actually spend in the dress. Calculating the amount of effort I had expended on looking for a wedding gown, I realized I'd been to 16 stores and had probably tried on in the neighborhood of 123 dresses. The situation was out of control.

And then, while reading *The New Jewish Wedding,* I came to understand that I had been going about the dress shopping the wrong way. I had bought the book in an effort to learn about Jewish wedding customs, having actually attended very few Jewish weddings in my life. The book referred several times to the ancient Jewish tradition of treating the bride and groom like royalty, a tradition that was news to me but sounded interesting.

"The attire and adornment of brides and grooms remain as important as in biblical times," the book explained. "The traditional image of the bridal couple as king and queen invites elegance and display."

I repeated that last part to myself: the traditional image of bridal couple as king and queen. I had been coming at the dress dilemma from the wrong angle! This was not a garment I was shopping for, not in the standard sense. This was not something I was to pick out on the basis of whether it was comfortable, sensible, stylish. No, this was tribal gear for a coming-of-age ceremony. I was to don the tulle headdress and large fluffy skirt traditional in North American twenty-first-century tribal acts for my marriage ceremony. This was an anthropological operation; if I didn't wear the proper attire, I would be exiled from the tribe, I would ruin the ritual of marriage.

And so, what choice did I have? I had to get a biblically poofy dress, a queenly headdress, something regally white.

So I went back to Kleinfeld with Ellen. This time I went prepared. I brought a list of style numbers of dresses I liked and a stack of dress pictures clipped from bridal magazines. I was as close to knowing what I wanted as was humanly possible. It was pouring rain as we walked into the store.

Our salesperson, Donna, came out to meet us. She motioned for us to follow her, and led us through the showroom in front into a small gray cubicle in the back of the store. It was a Tuesday morning, and the store was almost empty.

"I see you've been here before," said Donna, looking over my file as though we were at the doctor's office. I tried to peer over the file to see what could possibly be written on it, but she held it close to her chest.

"Yes," I said. "But I have a better idea of what I want now." I took out my stack of clippings and my list of style numbers.

Donna eyed me suspiciously. "Why don't you just look over the sample dresses on the rack over there," she said.

I looked at Ellen and shrugged. "Okay."

We walked over to the wall Donna had indicated, where huge racks of sample dresses took up one entire side of the store. Sample dresses are big in the bridal industry. They're the dresses that women try on when deciding whether to order their own custom-made version. They're usually in okay condition, but are available for a fraction of the cost of a new dress. We flipped through the dresses for a while, pulling out a few for closer inspection.

"This is stupid," said Ellen. "There's nothing here you want."

"Yeah," I said. Something about Kleinfeld made it hard for me to insist on the things that I wanted. I didn't want to spend the morning looking at sample dresses. I'd already looked at sample dresses all over the city. I wanted to see the dresses that I'd clipped from the magazines, the style numbers that I'd brought. Donna whizzed by us a few minutes later.

"Finding things?" she called out.

"Actually," I said, "I'd just like to see the dresses on my list."

Donna sighed as though this were a major imposition, as though she had a multitude of other better, more interesting, more important things to do. She took the list from me and looked it over.

"No, no, no," she said, ticking off style numbers.

"No?" I asked.

"Don't have it, don't have it. No, no, no." She handed the list back to me.

"You don't have any of them?" I asked.

"I don't think so, no."

I looked at Ellen, who was standing waist-deep in the dress rack. She rolled her eyes.

"There are like forty dresses on that list," she said. "You don't have a single one?"

"Can you just check?" I asked.

Donna took the list back again, scanned it quickly, then walked back down the hall, leaving the list to flutter slowly to the floor. Picking up the paper, I began to walk back to the dressing room, shaking my head. I had finally reconciled myself to the fact that I would have to spend an exorbitant amount of money on a large poofy dress; I had been beaten down by tradition and by the salespeople who gave me dirty looks when I asked to see slip dresses; and now I had come back to the Kleinfeld altar to ask for forgiveness, to tell them I would cooperate with their silly traditions, and I was being shunned. There was no doubt about it: Donna hated me.

"Is it me?" I asked Ellen. "Do I look, like, dirty or something?"

"Something's up her ass," she said.

A few minutes later Donna came back into the room with a dress. "This is the only one we have," she said.

I undressed. Ellen and Donna slid the dress over my head. There was no tulle or beading on this dress, just plain tailored fabric, and the inside felt like a silk parachute against my skin. I spun around to face the mirror.

"Wow," said Ellen. "I'm totally getting chills."

"It's nice," said Donna. She was leaning against the wall, my file in her hand, tapping her foot.

I looked at the mirror. There I was. In a wedding dress. But, as wedding dresses went, it was pretty good. It had a sexy halter top, was fitted through the hips, then flared out very gently through the skirt. It reminded me a little of Marilyn Monroe.

I sighed. "I don't know. It's still kind of poofy."

"You think *that's* poofy?" asked Donna.

"If you think that's poofy, you're high," said Ellen. "It's so not poofy."

"Well, there's this crinoline thing under here," I said, lifting up the back of the skirt. "And this stupid train." I knew I didn't want a train.

"It's not poofy," said Donna. "It looks great on you. And really, you could probably wear it again; it really doesn't look like a wedding dress. You know, dye it, cut off the train, wear it again."

"Yeah, I can wear it when I get invited to the Academy Awards." Ellen laughed. Donna looked down at my file.

I stood staring at myself in the mirror for a while. Was this it? Was this the dress? It was pretty close. Not too bridey. Sexy. I checked my internal signs for heart palpitations, nausea, any sense that this was The One, but I felt nothing. It was just me in a dress. A lovely dress, but still a dress.

"So?" said Donna, as though I was deciding on a pair of shoes at Nine West, and not the most expensive dress I might ever buy.

"I'm debating," I said.

Donna shifted her weight to her other foot, gazed at the ceiling. I stared at myself for another minute.

"Look," Donna said. "If you don't know, then it's not your dress."

I glanced at Donna's reflection in the mirror. In the arsenal of nasty things you can say to a girl in a wedding dress, she had chosen the nastiest. It's not your dress. There could be no greater insult.

"Fine," I said. "It's not my dress."

The next day I called Kleinfeld. I explained to them that they had, in all likelihood, lost a sale. I inquired as to what I had done to insult Donna. I believe that I even cried.

"It's so stressful," I said into the phone. "You spend three months looking for a dress, and there's all this pressure to get the right one, and then you find one you like and they won't even give you a second to make up your mind, and how are you supposed to know, I mean, let me think about it for a minute, you know?"

It wasn't my fault, I was told. Donna was their top sales associate. She had been selling wedding gowns for decades, and some years she sold more wedding gowns than any other person in the entire country. But, she refused to help brides who came into the store without their mothers, apparently operating under the assumption that a bride without a mother in tow was a bride who was not ready to purchase a gown. She had seen me walk into the store, motherless, had sized me up and booted me out. It's a strange view of the world, that all women bring their mothers with them to every bridal salon they visit, that all women have mothers who are interested, accessible, alive, waiting around with nothing better to do than accompany their daughters to Kleinfeld.

Over the next week Kleinfeld called me repeatedly. They offered me discounts, they promised me service like I'd never been served. "We'll treat you like Lady Diana," said one woman. Ah yes, at last I would feel like a princess. An ever-escalating hierarchy of sales associates called me, ending with the Vice President of something-or-other, who promised to personally supervise my visit, and then gave me her home number just in case I should have some sort of dress-related emergency that required calling her after the store was closed. And ultimately, I was sick of looking for wedding dresses. I wanted it to be over. So I went back. Steven's mother was in town, and she went with me, just in case I was called upon to present proof of a motherly presence in my life.

Three people greeted me at the door and escorted me back to a fitting room. Donna was nowhere to be seen. Someone ran off to get chairs for everyone. I gave my list of style numbers to the Vice President of something-or-other, feeling slightly sheepish about the whole thing. I was now expected to try on dresses in front of half of Kleinfeld's senior management. A bunch of dresses appeared, along with the dress I had been contemplating buying. The other gowns were rejected as soon as I put the original dress on.

"I think that's the one," said Steven's mother.

The Kleinfeld entourage agreed.

"Would you like to look at it in the big mirrors outside?" asked someone.

At last, I was being promoted. We all hurried out of the small dressing room, a few people holding my train as I walked. I stepped up onto an empty platform in the hallway, fluffed my dress, looked in the mirror and thought, *This is not important enough for me to expend one more iota of energy on.*

"I'll take it," I said.

Things were anticlimactic after that. The next thing I knew I was standing at the front desk handing someone my credit card, just like any other purchase—I could have been buying groceries or shampoo. I signed the receipt and walked out of the store empty-handed. I wouldn't see the dress again for another six months, as it had to be ordered from the designer in Toronto, and then hand-sewn. I sighed. All of that, three months of stress, and in the end I left the store with nothing, not even a little box for my receipt or an empty Kleinfeld bag.

3

The Great Wall of China

Marry, marry, and
what about the housekeeping?
—*Portuguese proverb*

THREE DAYS AFTER STEVEN AND I ANNOUNCED
our engagement, a fondue set arrived in the mail. Because
married people eat fondue.

It was while we were at Crate & Barrel, exchanging the fondue
set for a wok and a set of steak knives, that I began to see a store
filled with not items that I aspired to own, but row upon row of useless trinkets that would not fit into our tiny New York City–sized
apartment: silver-plated place card holders, stainless-steel avocado
slicers, ceramic butter warmers, a white plastic chip-and-dip set.

"We're going to need to register," I told Steven. "Otherwise more
people might send us fondue sets."

"I don't want to register," he said. "It sounds so stupid."

I sighed. It sounded stupid to me too—"registry" sounded like a
code word for "gravy boat"—but standing there in Crate & Barrel,
suddenly aware of the distinction between gifts that would be nice
to get in the mail and ones that wouldn't, I had begun to understand
the appeal of having a registry.

"If we have to register for something," said Steven, "let's register for something good. Like CDs."

"We don't need CDs," I said. "I haven't seen you buy a CD in years. Name me the last CD you bought."

"Well all right, but there must be something we need."

We were standing in the outdoor entertaining section next to a display of orange acrylic barware.

"Need," I huffed, picking up an orange tumbler. "What do we need? We don't need anything."

Steven narrowed his eyes at me. I was being difficult and I knew it. But the truth was that we needed everything and we needed nothing. We had been living together long enough, and before that, outside of our parents' homes long enough, that we had already acquired all the basics we needed to function as adults. We had a bed, a couch, a television set, an Oriental rug, and assorted knick-knacks collected from remote corners of the world. But a lot of it was shoddy—the sorts of things that you acquire for your first apartment after college, thinking that someday you'll get "real" stuff, maybe when you get married.

It's easy to spend time waiting for your real life, eating off chipped dishes and hand-me-down silverware. It's hard to realize that your real life has now begun. For ten years I had been living a temporary existence, waiting for something to tell me that the time was right to acquire nice, grown-up stuff. Looking down at the orange acrylic tumbler in my hand, I realized that that time was now.

"I want a Cuisinart," I said, with such confidence and force that I almost convinced myself that all along I had wanted a Cuisinart, that somewhere bottled up inside me all these years has been a per-colating desire for a device that would chop food quickly. I am thirty years old. I am getting married. I should own a Cuisinart.

"Oh, yeah," Steven said, perking up. "We could use a Cuisinart."

"And place mats. And maybe some dishes. And our own silver-ware, not that ugly crap I got from my parents. And a roasting pan. And a meat thermometer."

In the end I decided that we should register at Williams-Sonoma, and Steven, partially because he now wanted a nice set of kitchen knives and partially because he wanted the whole registry thing to just be over, agreed. Back at home we went online and picked out fifteen items from the Williams-Sonoma website that were practical and could possibly be classified under the "need" category as well as the "want" category. Breathing out a sigh of relief, I felt that we had narrowly averted disaster. We had fended off the barrage of fondue sets threatening to break down our door, and we had provided our guests with several practical, reasonably priced gift options.

As it turned out, no one else sent us an engagement gift. Perhaps they caught wind of our feelings about the fondue set.

A few nights later, while I was reading a particularly horrific scene in Primo Levi's *Survival in Auschwitz* (where the Nazis beat the prisoners for having unshined shoes despite the fact that no one supplied them with shoe polish), Steven's mother, Marlene, called. She wanted to discuss the registry situation. Apparently overcome with the desire to get a peek at how we planned to set up house, Marlene had driven over to her local Williams-Sonoma the day before and had held an extended conversation with a salesperson who had characterized me, based on my registry choices, as "a sweet and undemanding girl." I tried to explain that this wasn't our complete registry, that we were going to go to the store and register for more items, but Marlene would have none of it.

"Do you have the Williams-Sonoma catalog handy?" Marlene asked.

I hesitated. "Yes."

"Great," she said. "So can you turn to page three?"

I turned to page three, frantically racking my brain for ways to get out of spending the rest of the evening walking through the entire catalog page by page. I should explain here that Marlene is not just a zealous home decorator, she is a zealous home decorator with a degree in fashion and a living room that was once featured in *Architectural Digest*. She is also the kind of person who frequently begins conversations with the phrase, "So the other day I saw this tablecloth . . ."

"Where?" I'll ask. "Where did you see the tablecloth?"

"Oh, just at this store in Atlanta," she'll reply, because Marlene is always just happening by memorable tablecloths in the way that other people happen by interesting graffiti or a new Starbucks.

I had met Marlene a few times since Steven and I had begun dating, and I always felt like she was like a little slice of my childhood that had suddenly appeared in my present life. I felt like I'd known a million permutations of her, and it gave me a nice warm feeling, as though this in some way validated the idea that Steven and I were meant to be together. Because to me she was the mom who drove a Volvo station wagon and ran the carpool. She was the parent who showed up on Visiting Day at sleepaway camp toting a brand-new pair of Umbros, or a six-pack of Jolt, or whatever it was that everyone else's parents somehow knew to bring them, some item of clothing or trendy snack to which my parents were utterly oblivious. And she gardened and sent Hallmark cards and was still married to Steven's father. The first time I ate dinner at her house she served spaghetti and meatballs. Never in my life had my mother served spaghetti and meatballs. Our family dinners were always the latest exotic cuisine that no one else in Connecticut was forcing their child to eat—sautéed bean curd (this was before manufacturers got wise and started calling it tofu), paella, tuna sashimi, several attempts at Szechwan cuisine. Don't get me wrong, I loved eating sashimi for dinner, but everyone else had spaghetti and meatballs. I would have killed for some spaghetti and meatballs. If only I had known Steven then, I could have gone over to his house.

I could hear Marlene rustling the pages of her Williams-Sonoma catalog on the other end of the phone. "You see the glasses here at the top of page three?" she asked.

"Uh huh," I said, reluctantly eyeing a set of bar glasses that were neatly arranged on top of a table as though someone in golf pants was just about to pour in her signature drink.

"You see how there's a range of prices?" Marlene asked. "The problem is that you didn't register for a range of prices. So the juice glasses you chose are really everyday glasses, but you need to get, you know, the nice stuff."

"Well, Steven wanted those juice glasses actually," I explained.

This was not in Marlene's range of comprehension, that Steven might have a preference for one juice glass over another, so she simply ignored it.

"So you see the nicer juice glasses there on page four?"

"Uh huh. The nicer ones, yeah. But Steven wanted the other ones. I mean, I agree with you, these are nicer, but you know that was his choice." We're not even married and I'm selling Steven out to my future mother-in-law. It's not my fault we chose the wrong glasses, it was your son. Your son wanted the big ugly cheap juice glasses and I, your future daughter-in-law, spent much of my early twenties drinking from jam jars and plastic cups, so quite frankly I could care less which juice glasses we get. I said none of this to Marlene. Instead I said, "Steven wanted the juice glasses."

The conversation continued in this circular vein—with me explaining that Steven had an opinion on a household item, Marlene ignoring the explanation. On the one hand, I couldn't blame her. She could paint the house orange and her husband wouldn't notice, so, of course, the idea that a man, any man, and particularly her son, might have some input into a wedding registry was laughable.

The problem was that I wasn't entirely sure she was wrong. She had, after all, a much clearer vision of who I should be than I did myself. I should care about juice glasses. I should know what a table runner is. I should want a set of nice china. I should be setting up a home for her son, never mind that we contribute equally to the household financially, that between the two of us Steven is the one who is most looking forward to having and raising children, that no one I know has a clue what a chafing dish is or why you would need one. Never mind any of that, because, regardless, I am still going to be a wife, and this is what a wife does. And when it comes to being a wife, on some level I trust Marlene. She has, after all, been a wife for thirty years, and I have been a wife never. It is possible that marriages and families and children all depend on having the right juice glasses. It is possible that I'm an inadequate bride who doesn't know how to register, and that as a result I'm going to be a rotten homemaker and a miserable wife and mother, and my marriage will end in divorce and scandal.

The conversation ended with Marlene offering to take me to Bloomingdale's to look at plates over Thanksgiving.

"Sure," I said. "That would be great."

"Just remember," Marlene said. "This is your chance to get stuff, so don't be shy about registering for stuff you want."

I hung up the phone, padded down the hall to the office where Steven was leaned back in a chair still working his way through the early chapters of *War and Peace*, and announced that we would complete our registry by Thanksgiving or die trying.

"If I have to spend five hours looking at plates with your mother, I'm going to begin smashing them over my head," I said.

Steven swiveled his chair around to look at me.

"You just spent an hour on the phone with my mother."

I thought I detected a tinge of horror in his voice.

"Yes. We discussed the registry. Apparently I am bad at registering. She wants me to go to Bloomingdale's with her over Thanksgiving to look at plates."

Steven wrapped his arms around my waist and pulled me close. He was wearing an ancient blue-and-green plaid flannel shirt with huge holes in the elbows. It was a shirt that I loved—something about it felt homey, as though my whole life I had known I would end up with the person who owned this very shirt—but I didn't let on because I didn't want him to think I approved of holey clothing, lest he acquire more of it.

"Do you want me to tell her to back off?" he asked.

"No, it's fine. I can handle myself."

"Okay," he said. "We'll finish registering tomorrow."

Let me make absolutely clear that my loathing regarding going to Bloomingdale's with Marlene had nothing to do with Marlene. If I had to spend five hours looking at plates with Mother Teresa, I would probably behave similarly. I would place my level of plate-related interest at about equal with the outcome of the Poulan/Weed Eater Independence Bowl. And yet Marlene's comment that this was my chance to get the good stuff was a common refrain that I would hear repeated endlessly by registry consultants, salespeople, every facet of the wedding industry.

Here's what *Weddings For Dummies* has to say about registries: "The 'getting' part of getting married is like winning *The Price is Right, Wheel of Fortune,* and *Let's Make a Deal* all at once and then—if you have a wedding registry—personally dictating the prizes you receive. Far from being an unseemly show of greed, registering is the accepted method of making your wish list public to those who care to know."

This was it. I had won the wedding lottery and I was now eligible to purchase that set of Lenox Beaded Majesty china I had always been secretly longing for, for when people talk about "the good stuff," they always mean china.

A year after I graduated from college, one of my close friends, Amanda, got married and registered for china. Although I dutifully bought her some, I couldn't help but feel that it was a remnant of some other era, when people had formal dinner parties and impressed each other with their china patterns. At the time I'd asked her what she'd do with the china.

"Use it for special occasions," she'd replied.

"Like what?" I'd asked.

"Dinner parties."

"In East Lansing?" At the time she and her husband were living in East Lansing, Michigan, where they knew nobody. "Who would you invite?"

"Look," Amanda had said. "I just want the china, okay? Maybe someday you'll want china too."

Ten years had passed since then, so one day in the midst of the registry whirlwind I asked her about the china.

"Oh that," she said. "We never use it. It's funny, though. The pattern we got wasn't actually our first choice. I liked this other pattern better, but we didn't get it because Karen Smith had it."

Karen Smith was a friend of Amanda's from college. She and Amanda haven't spoken in years. Had they both owned the same china pattern it would not have made one speck of difference in their lives. And yet today Amanda is destined to lug crates of unused china around the country—of a pattern she doesn't even like, no less—because that is what one does when one marries. One acquires china.

There was no doubt in my mind that I would never be convinced of the merits of china, that I could very easily live out the rest of my life without ever owning a single piece of china and be very happy. But, sadly, there was no room in the wedding world for a girl who did not want china. Because even though brides may be initially uninterested by china, a variety of sources conspire together to ensure that every newlywed couple has a set of expensive, eminently breakable dishes stored in the closet.

Reading through the discussions on The Knot about registries, I discovered that mothers in particular seem to be a source of china-related pressure.

"We initially just registered for casual everyday china," read one woman's post. "It was a rather expensive brand and it was elegant enough to set a table with if you asked me. But we got so much flack from people (our mothers mostly) that we just succumbed to the pressure and registered for a very plain platinum-band china in addition to our everyday china."

Other co-conspirators in the great china sell-off include the content sides of The Knot and the wedding website The Wedding Channel, both of which not only offer helpful how-to guides on purchasing china, but also partner with a range of retailers to provide one-click access to store registries.

In an article I found entitled "China 101," The Knot provided this sage advice for brides who may be undecided about their plates: "Even if your idea of entertaining is ordering pizza for the gang, there are many pros to registering for elegant tableware. It is the center of any table setting, and it looks great. It can inject loads of style into your home decor. And it's expensive, so why not let others pick up the tab?" At the bottom of the article The Knot had thoughtfully provided a direct link to their online registry. The WeddingChannel.com took a slightly different approach, instead listing the "Top Five Most Romantic Registry Items." China was number four. I guess they couldn't see the romance in a Cuisinart.

Wedding magazines, too, stress the importance of owning china. One article I read in *Martha Stewart Weddings* extolled the virtues of white china as opposed to heavily decorated china: "Colored plates and cups may beckon with their vibrant hues, but you shouldn't overlook the basic beauty of white when registering for your place settings. Simple and adaptable, white china is suitable for almost any social situation."

I can't help but wonder what social situations Martha Stewart has in mind. Most likely not the Rosh Hashanah dinner I hosted last year where by accident I used corned beef to make a brisket, resulting in a twice-cooked fusion of pickled meat and onion-cranberry sauce. Probably not my grandparents' anniversary dinner where my grandmother asserted that my father was trying to poison her and refused to eat. Nearly every bride on The Knot probably has social situations like these in her closet, and yet everyone goes about registering as though they were Princess Diana, Doris Day, Zelda Fitzgerald. In reality most people will eat spaghetti off green FiestaWare plates while watching *Seinfeld* reruns, but just for one moment, just while we can, let us pretend that we might have dinner parties that require a twelve-piece service of Lenox Beaded Majesty.

Because really, the world of wedding registries is all about etiquette and class pretensions, and no one wants to make a horrendous faux pas. Worse, no one wants to be thought of as classless. It used to be, way back in the beginning of registries, that there were a few department stores you could register at and that was it. But today there are a mind-boggling number of options: Home Depot, Target, Bed Bath & Beyond, the Department of Housing and Urban Development (anyone want to register for a mortgage?); even a group of ShopRite stores in New Jersey offer a cleaning products registry basket, because nothing says romance like Brillo pads.

And while many couples may like the option of registering for a power generator or Cheetos, the overwhelming number of choices seems to have thrown Wedding Land into chaos. When you can register for anything under the sun, which gifts are tacky and which are just inventive? One bride posted that she was horrified to discover that a fellow bride had registered for dish soap, causing a whole bevy of other brides to ask if their registry choices were wrong. "Can we register for a vibrator," posted one. "Or would this be tacky?"

Tacky is a big word on The Knot, where women worry constantly over whether the word applies to varying aspects of their weddings.

Is it tacky to have a barbecue for the rehearsal dinner? Is it tacky to register for a honeymoon? Is it tacky to use address labels on invitations instead of calligraphy? In response to the calligraphy question one bride wrote, "Aside from being proper etiquette, handwriting the addresses says you took the time to make the personal touch and not just 'mail merge' your entire address book. . . . The whole paper invitation thing is totally old school, and I say if you are going to do it, do it right. Once the little things are let go of, the bigger things follow. Look how many posts there are about people not even returning response cards, or RSVPing with uninvited guests. These things would be totally unheard of back in the day!"

Back in the day, when the servants hand delivered invitations, people bothered to calligraphy addresses, and everyone was intimately familiar with proper etiquette. Back in *that* day (and for the sake of argument, let's pin down "back in the day" to the Victorian era), most people who are currently on The Knot preaching the gospel of etiquette would most certainly have had things on their mind other than whether people were bringing extra guests to their wedding. Such as, in the case of my family, how many more relatives could be crammed into a one-room apartment on the Lower East Side. In the case of Steven's family, when they might be able to scrape together enough money to get the hell out of czarist Russia. In the case of other families, whether age eight was too soon to send the kids to work. And yet, thanks in part to the great equalizer that is American culture, here we all are today on The Knot lamenting the loss of proper etiquette and lambasting the poor few who haven't yet caught on.

I read up on a little etiquette history and discovered that part of the problem lies in the great classless society that is modern America. Pre–World War II brides had weddings that were in accordance with what they saw as their station. They might have seen Elizabeth Taylor's upper-middle-class wedding in *Father of the Bride*, but unless they could actually afford such a wedding, they went for something more modest. But times have changed, and today every girl is planning her wedding as though she were Princess Diana (albeit on a budget). Because modern brides are all pretending to be society women, we must behave as though we have a firm grasp of the laws of etiquette, as a real society woman would. Unfortunately, the reality is that we haven't a clue about etiquette, have never given it a second thought up until we found ourselves abruptly moved to Wedding Land, and so we grab onto whatever rules are most accessible and shove the rest aside. And the easiest rule of all (and perhaps one of the most antiquated) is that governing the informing of guests about one's registry: any sort of printed material referring to the registry is unanimously regarded—by the brides on The Knot, by wedding magazines, by etiquette books—as gauche beyond belief.

"Tradition still holds that the practice of including lists of gift registries with wedding invitations is considered tacky and inappropriate," chides *Emily Post's Wedding Etiquette*, a bulging volume that explains the proper way to do everything. That is to say, registering for ten thousand dollars' worth of gifts is okay; telling people you've done so is not. Instead, Post suggests providing your mother and maid of honor with a list of stores where you've registered so that they can spread the news. She does not say what to do should you have a mother who is not on speaking terms with the majority of the guest list due to a recent acrimonious divorce, or a maid of honor who doesn't really know any of your other friends.

I found a more dictatorial approach to the registry question in *The New Book of Wedding Etiquette*: "You may *not* print on any part of your invitation, save the date card, or any other wedding correspondence 'No Gifts Please.' To ask guests not to send gifts is to suppose that they will in the first place, which is presumptuous. The way to discourage gift giving is not to register." Rather than discouraging gift giving, it seems to me that this is the way to ensure you receive fourteen toasters, but what do I know?

More than any other etiquette rule, this seems to be the one the brides on The Knot like to torture each other with.

"A woman I used to be great friends with recently got married. I was just informed that she mailed registry cards for all SIX places she registered IN HER INVITATIONS!!!!" cackled one bride. "She was always so bitchy and know-it-all . . . so I was so happy to hear she did the tackiest thing I could possibly think of!"

I couldn't help but wince as I read this post, and I weighed which was tackier: informing guests about a registry or publicly gloating over someone else's social misstep.

Perhaps the strangest thing about etiquette is that it is all in the eye of the beholder. One woman's social blunder is another's polite manners. For example, in reading up about etiquette I came across several pages devoted to the proper way to display checks at the rehearsal dinner. Apparently, in some sections of the country, most notably Texas, it is proper etiquette to display all the gifts the couple has received on a big table somewhere. And checks are to be displayed right alongside blenders and forks, although, as I now know from the etiquette books, the check amounts must be covered up. So, if I did this in New York or Vermont, all my guests would think I'd been smoking crack; but people would think me equally bananas if I *didn't* do it in Texas. Which just goes to show how moronic the whole concept of wedding etiquette is in the first place. This is not to say, however, that I intended to put registry information anywhere within a ten-mile radius of my invitations. I wasn't raised in a barn, you know.

A week before Thanksgiving Steven and I made our way to a Williams-Sonoma store. We were standing on line at the cash register, waiting to receive our barcode scan gun, when I noticed a couple standing by the silverware display. The woman was carefully inspecting a salad fork, holding it up to the light, turning it around, then placing it back down on the display and picking up the next one. A guy standing near her, presumably her husband-to-be, was holding the scan gun like an Uzi, aiming it at a corner, turning around quickly with the gun as though a salad spinner might sneak up on him, then flattening himself against a wall of imported olive oil.

I nudged Steven. "Of course the woman is choosing the silverware and the guy gets to play with the gun."

"Well, yeah," he said. "Darn right."

After filling out a few forms, a sales associate handed Steven the scan gun (there was not even the slightest idea that I might get to hold it) and sent us on our merry way. As we began trolling for merchandise I looked around at the other people in the store and noticed that it was filled almost exclusively with couples who looked exactly like us, lugging guns and brand-new diamond rings, discussing whether or not they really need a bundt pan.

"Check it out," I whispered to Steven. "We're a massive cliché."

"Yeah," he said. "But we're only pretending to be like this. All these other people really are like this."

"How do you know?" I said. "How do you know that they're not exactly like us, and they're all walking around thinking, *Jesus, look at those other morons with the scan guns and the diamond rings. I'm only here because my mom said I had to. But they . . .*"

As we walked by the silverware display nearly an hour after receiving our gun, I saw that the Uzi-fantasizing fiancé and his bride were still there, but now he was on the phone making plans for the evening. As we walked over, he snapped the phone shut, looked up, and met his girlfriend's glaring eyes.

"Sorry," he whispered, and she returned to inspecting forks.

"Okay," I conceded to Steven. "We're not like them."

We passed an hour zapping items in Williams-Sonoma, then turned in our scan gun and headed across the street to Bloomingdale's to pick out silverware and plates. After weeks of mulling over our registry options we had decided to register for regular flatware and regular everyday dishes, but once we got to Bloomingdale's the plan went out the window and I found myself ogling a two-hundred-dollar-a-setting Wedgwood service. I'm not sure how it happened, but it had something to do with the fact that the regular plates were, well, regular, and the china was, well, stunning. When given the option between regular and stunning, particularly when surrounded by people who are all opting for stunning, sticking with regular becomes quite a challenge.

Sparkling demurely under the display lights, the pure white Wedgwood was arranged neatly in a mock table setting for four, complete with a tablecloth and matching napkin rings. The empty plates seemed to ache for a perfectly prepared rack of lamb, pink in the center and crispy on the outside. Or maybe a fan-shaped display of *magret de canard* piled on top of a small mound of cranberry and cassis compote. Looking at the plates, I could almost hear the soft conversation and quiet laughter of a dinner party. My dinner party, filled with fabulous, glamorous friends (whom I would naturally meet once I'd acquired the appropriate dinnerware) toasting the success of . . . well . . . of something. Take me home, the plates whispered, and you will eat well. And, best of all, with a simple wave of a scan gun they could be mine.

And then I tried to imagine the china in our cabinets at home, the plates stacked all on top of each other, piled underneath the plastic Tupperware and cans of Campbell's turkey noodle soup that currently take up most of our cabinet space, the bowls stowed underneath the sink next to the Drano, because in reality we didn't have any room for any of the things we had already registered for, let alone an entire twelve-piece china service.

I turned to Steven for help.

"I don't know," he said. "They're plates."

"They're really nice, though."

He nodded. "They are nice." I wondered if he was humoring me or if he was serious, uncertain as to which interpretation would irritate me more.

Another couple near us was standing in front of a towering display of ornately flowered china, their arms folded, staring intently.

"Do you like the blue? Because if you like the blue, I like the blue," said the woman.

"I like the blue. But I also like the green," her fiancé replied.

"I like the green, but I like the blue too. But I also like the green."

As they wandered away I checked out the display of china they were discussing, and noted that it was priced at four hundred dollars a setting. Who were these people who were so certain that their guests would want to buy them four-hundred-dollar table settings? Because really, that's what the registry is. It's a guess, or maybe a suggestion, as to how much your guests should spend on you. You can register at Tiffany all you want, but if your guests shop at T.J. Maxx, guess what you're getting.

It was this most public aspect of the registry that Steven and I found ourselves struggling with in particular. After spending over an hour examining place settings, we realized that we were incapable of selecting a place setting because we didn't know who we were.

"We're casual elegance," said Steven, rejecting a beautiful Vera Wang set as being too stuffy.

"We're hip, but not that hip," I said, nixing the Calvin Klein set with the square white bowls. It's tough to plan a wedding in the midst of an identity crisis. The wedding guides all say to register for items that will last a lifetime, but standing there in Bloomingdale's, I couldn't even imagine who I might be next week, let alone thirty years from now. Will I like casually elegant bowls when I'm fifty? Will I wish I had chosen something more modern? Less modern? As I wandered through the maze of the registry floor I was suddenly confronted with the terror of choosing silverware and dishes that my children would eat off of. I picked up a bowl and wondered if I would scream at the top of my lungs when a child to be named later broke it ten years from now. Or would I laugh and say, yeah, I never really liked that bowl anyway, but your grandmother insisted we get it.

And what about our immediate needs? We needed wine glasses, but those beautiful handblown Beaujolais glasses with the paper-thin glass, well, realistically they'd be smashed to bits in a matter of moments. Since moving into our apartment a year ago, I'd already broken an entire set of highball glasses. Just because I'm getting married doesn't make me any less clumsy or more patient when it comes to glassware.

Determining our identity was important because a wedding registry is an uncomfortably intimate thing. It gives people the chance to look inside your kitchen cupboards, to see who you are, in a way that they never will again. How often do you walk up to someone and say, "Hi, I own a complete set of All-Clad." Or, even worse, "I aspire to own a complete set of All-Clad. I see myself as the kind of person who should own that sort of thing. I also see myself as the kind of person who has friends who can afford to buy me that sort of thing."

Last year Steven and I went to the wedding of a friend of his from college. Both the bride and groom were lawyers. The registry included every kind of kitchen gadget possible—pasta makers, waffle irons, a tortilla warmer. I said to Steven, "Who the hell is this woman? Is she really going to use a tortilla warmer?" And he said that yes, in fact, she was the daughter of a Chilean diplomat, and that in college she had been known as the Chilean Martha Stewart. Most likely she would be using a tortilla warmer to warm her own homemade tortillas. And so I began to wonder what kinds of questions people would ask when they saw our registry. Would they ask themselves what my selection of Nigella Lawson's cookbook *How to Be a Domestic Goddess* says about my career aspirations? Will they think we're awfully highfalutin if we choose $50 crystal whiskey glasses? Will they think we're cheap and lowbrow if we choose $5 ones?

My friend Cameron, the one who wanted to quit her job to make save-the-date cards, told me that when she and her fiancé went to Williams-Sonoma to register, they got into a fight about muffin tins. She wanted them; he didn't.

"Cam," he'd said, "I have known you for four years. I have lived with you for two. Not once in all that time have you even so much as thought about baking a muffin."

"I know," she'd said. "But I might start."

And yet I wonder if perhaps she thought that muffin tins were the sort of thing that belonged on a wedding registry. That perhaps her public persona, the person she announced she was through the registry, should be a muffin-baking one.

Wedding registries are, in fact, more public than I'd realized that day in Bloomingdale's. Anyone interested in learning what items Liza Minnelli included on her Tiffany registry for her wedding to David Gest can simply go to the Tiffany website and enter her name. (Last I checked they still needed eight silver pasta servers, if you're feeling generous. Although, given that Liza and David are now divorced, the pasta servers might be beside the point.) Not a Liza fan? Then how about Tori Spelling, who is in desperate need of a $1300 clock. The public nature of wedding registries, combined with the fact that, as I read in *Modern Bride*, couples make more buying decisions and purchase more products in the time around their wedding than at any other time in their lives, makes engaged couples highly susceptible to exploitation. Worse than the fact that in a matter of minutes I can know what items Liza Minnelli and Tori Spelling need off their registries is that fact that advertisers and other wedding vendors can know, because the bridal industry is one huge interconnected organism. I took a quick tour of registry websites and discovered that Macy's bridal registry, for example, is affiliated with the Wedding Channel, which also partners with Bloomingdale's, Restoration Hardware, Dean & Deluca, Pottery Barn, Neiman Marcus, Crate & Barrel, Tiffany & Co., Burdines, Rich's, and Williams-Sonoma, among others. This means that any information Macy's has, all these other stores have too.

And, sure enough, after we registered at Williams-Sonoma, we were barraged with phone calls telling us we'd won a honeymoon in Mexico, a registry worth hundreds of dollars, and assorted other items. The phone calls were annoying, but the privacy infringement didn't really bother me until my mother called one day and announced that in a moment of boredom at work she'd gone to the WeddingChannel.com and typed in my name.

"I didn't know you needed a salad spinner," she said.

"What are you talking about?" I asked.

"Your registry from Williams-Sonoma. It comes up when I type in your name at The Wedding Channel."

We agreed that this was creepy, and I spent the rest of the day typing random names into The Wedding Channel and looking at strangers' wedding registries. On The Wedding Channel people can also create wedding web pages to accompany their registries, which meant that I was able to learn that Jane and David from Fredrick, Maryland, met in a bar, are getting married at Ceresville Mansion in a ceremony with a fall theme, and that their registry included a stainless-steel ice bucket and the same salad spinner for which I registered.

We left Bloomingdale's without registering for a single silver spoon. It was too overwhelming: the identity crisis, the public display of consumption, the other happy couples eagerly snapping up blue floral china. And then, we were stuck on that whole issue of what we needed versus what we wanted. I went home and stared inside my kitchen cabinets for a long time, really thinking hard about what I owned. And it occurred to me that everything in the kitchen was mine. Not Steven's, not ours collectively, but mine. I had brought all the furniture, dishes, flatware, wall hangings, and rugs to the relationship. Steven had brought a few boxes of books and a small postcard of Bob Dylan that he'd taped above the desk in the closet we called an office. It might be nice, I thought, to have something that we owned mutually. Something that was really ours. After all, wasn't that the whole point of being married? There would be no more *mine*, only *ours*. Well, maybe a little bit of *mine*, but mostly *ours*. And it made sense. If we were going to stand up in front of all our friends and relatives, all the people in the world who were important to us, and promise to become a unit, a *family*, we couldn't very well then go home and have *my* dishes and *my* silverware.

I picked up a plate from the cupboard and turned it over in my hands. I'd bought these plates eight years ago at a Target in Chicago. I remembered driving over there, back when I had a car and wall-to-wall carpeting. I had just moved out of an apartment I shared with a college friend with whom I'd been engaged in roommate wars (i.e., you didn't do the dishes so I'm going to leave my crap in the living room so you're going to use my soap in the shower so I'm going to eat your special chocolate) and into my own apartment for the first time. The roommate had brought the dishes to my previous living arrangement, so I was dishless. Hence the trip to Target.

I'd stood in the brightly lit dish aisle, picking up patterns and setting them back down, trying to figure out where best to spend my fifteen dollars. Ultimately I'd settled on a red, blue, and yellow-striped pattern that, to my twenty-two-year-old eye, looked hand painted and therefore somewhat hip and funky. A few years later I'd added a second set of solid blue plates that matched the blue stripe in the original plates. Those plates were for when I had company.

Today the plates had a few chips in them, but for the most part they looked pretty good. There was no good reason to toss out perfectly functional plates, except for the fact that I no longer thought that they looked hip and hand painted. Now, really looking at them, I thought they were garish.

I can do this, I thought. I can ask people to buy me . . . *us* . . . new plates.

Later that day my grandmother called.

"Where have you been?" she asked. "I've been calling all day."

"We went to Bloomingdale's to register for the wedding."

"You have to register a wedding?"

"No, Gammy, we were registering for gifts, or trying to anyway."

"I don't know why you're doing this," she sighed.

"Doing what?" I asked, hearing my voice rise defensively.

"This whole big wedding and a big registry, and it's so far away. I don't know why you had to make it so far away."

"Did you want me to get married in Florida?"

"That would be wonderful," she said.

I groaned quietly, then changed the subject. "We had to register because otherwise people will get us stuff we don't want."

"Oh."

Pause.

"Well, I never heard of registering before."

This is my grandmother's favorite phrase. I never heard of this, I never heard of that. She also likes to say, "there's enough food here for an army." She lives in a world of superlatives. Everything is the best, the worst, the biggest, or something so insane, so wild and crazy, that she never heard of it.

"You didn't register?" I asked, not really expecting her to say yes. My grandmother, after all, horrified her orthodox Jewish parents back in 1945 by getting married in her WAC officer's uniform on a Michigan air force base. My guess is that registering was the farthest thing from her mind.

"No, I didn't register," she said. "Nobody registered. I never heard of it."

Or at least, no one she knew registered. I was about to explain that for years people have been registering for gifts (ever since the silver manufacturer Christofle allegedly came up with the idea back in 1856), when I realized that of course I would be the first person in my family to have a wedding registry. Not only did my grandparents not register, my parents didn't register. Nor did any one of my great-grandparents, four of whom married in New York in the early 1900s and could have easily walked over to Macy's and signed up for a trivet or two. But for each of those generations registering was for other people: to my great-grandparents it was for people with money, to my grandparents it was for the country club set, to my parents it was the epitome of squaresville. Not so today, when anyone can register for anything in any price range, when registries need not be limited to dorky items like soup tureens. Today we are all able to participate in the free and equal democracy called a bridal registry.

And so, at a loss as to what to do next, I turned to the brides on The Knot for help.

"We've been to Bloomingdale's, Crate & Barrel and Williams-Sonoma," I wrote. "But everything seems kind of boring. Can anyone suggest a place to register for more off-beat plates, etc.?"

Oddly, a number of brides responded by simply posting where they had registered (a list that usually included at least one of the above-mentioned stores, if not all), but one person suggested we check out a consortium of stores in SoHo, and that is where we ultimately signed up. In the end Steven and I took our rightful place as consumers and registered for an eight-piece dinner service of a highly functional, highly unbreakable, solid white china, funky-looking silverware, and a ridiculously expensive lamp that turned on when you waved your hand over it, which I was sure we'd regret, but Steven found irresistible. At every store the sales people pushed us to register for more expensive items. "It's your wedding," they all said. "You deserve it."

"If I were registering for my wedding these are definitely the glasses I would choose," said the sales woman in a downtown glassware boutique. "Why not get the best?"

4

Who's Afraid of Martha Stewart?

Marry in haste, repent in Reno.

—American proverb

IN LATE NOVEMBER I RECEIVED A SAVE-THE-DATE card for my friend Cameron's July wedding. I had heard of these kinds of cards, which are sent out a few months before the invitation goes out (sometimes up to a year in advance of the wedding) to announce the date and location of the upcoming nuptials, but I had never witnessed one firsthand. Unless you counted the one I had received for Kimberly's wedding several years ago, but that had been a small, ivory card that said simply "Save the date," along with Kimberly's name, her then-fiancé's name, a date, and a location. Cameron's card, on the other hand, had taken her three months to handcraft in her living room.

On the cover of the card was a picture of a couple's legs and feet hanging over the side of a small wooden boat. This image was covered with a piece of see-through vellum paper, on which she'd printed her name and her fiancé's so that it looked like they were the name of the boat. At the bottom it said "Chart your course for the Bahamas," and inside was a paragraph explaining that the wedding would be on a small island in the Bahamas, a few sentences about planned wedding activities, and a list of places to stay.

I had been vaguely aware for some time that I might be required to send out these cards, given that my wedding was going to be on Labor Day weekend and people make plans for holiday weekends far in advance, but I was also aware that it was yet another piece of mis-appropriated wedding etiquette. The evolution of the cards seems to be related to the immutable rule that invitations go out six to eight weeks before the wedding date, in accordance with a custom that originated long before airplane travel and discount airfares that require advance booking. Back then, if etiquette rules are to be trusted, everyone lived close to each other and had totally blank date books, which meant they needed less advance notice. Today, when most guests are not arriving by horse and buggy and have Palm Pilots crammed full of appointments months ahead of time, people need more time to plan. If you want to give people a fighting chance of making it to your wedding, you need to inform them of the date at least six months in advance. And so, instead of just letting people send out invitations earlier, the wedding industry came up with the absolutely brilliant concept of save-the-dates. Because why have one card when you can have two?

And while I thought the whole concept was idiotic, I also knew that I would probably adhere to it simply because to do anything else would require an amount of thought and creativity that I didn't want to spend on paper goods. I probably could have created a more practical combination invitation/save-the-date that went out six months in advance, or I could have sent out the invitations early, but what if etiquette rules were really there for a purpose? What if people forgot about the wedding by the time the date came around because I'd sent the invitations out too early? They would probably need to be reminded, which meant sending out some other kind of reminder card. At which point it just seemed easier to do it the way it was supposed to be done.

But it wasn't until I held Cameron's save-the-date in my hand that it occurred to me that I might actually make the cards myself. Because as I turned the card over, a small voice squeaked inside my head: I can do better. The truth was that I probably couldn't. It was a very professional-looking card, and I didn't have any desire to spend the endless hours of work that clearly had gone into making it. Still, I thought I might try. Not that I'm competitive or anything.

A few days later I found myself at the bookstore flipping absent-mindedly through an issue of *Martha Stewart Weddings*. I just seemed to gravitate toward the wedding magazine section, as though pulled there by the weight of my engagement ring. I would walk into the store to pick up a new book and the next thing I knew I was looking at wedding magazines. The issue of *Weddings* I'd been unlucky enough to stumble across had a big feature on save-the-dates. This being Martha Stewart, the article was accompanied by a center-foldlike spread featuring exquisitely handcrafted save-the-date cards lolling seductively across backgrounds of brightly colored calendars.

"Although your wedding day may be months away, there is no doubt that it is first and foremost in your mind," cooed the article. "Put it in the minds of your friends and family by sending save-the-date cards."

This was followed by four pages of cards, each of which gave the impression that the person who made it had devoted months of her life to coming up with a witty theme and working with an artist and a typesetter. One card included a refrigerator magnet with the names of the happy couple and the wedding date; another was a four-frame photo strip, like the kind you get at the coin-operated photo booth in the mall, showing the couple holding up cards in each frame that spelled out "Save the date." In the last frame they were holding up a card with their wedding date. Other "cards" were actually folders (available at any office-supply store, the magazine explained, implying that, of course, any idiot could just whip one of these up) stuffed full of enough maps, directions, and instructions to orchestrate an armed land invasion.

The most repellent idea was a card that showed a list of one woman's potential married names written in a girlish looping script on lined notepaper:

Mr. and Mrs. John Reynolds
Mr. and Mrs. John C. Reynolds
Ms. Brooke H. Reynolds
Mrs. John Reynolds

At the bottom it read: "Save the date for the wedding of Brooke & John." As I read the card, it occurred to me that if someone sent me a save-the-date like this, I would refuse to go to the wedding on principle. The thought that followed was that my save-the-date card would have to be representative of me, of Steven, of the general idea of our wedding, that it would have to convey the casual, unweddingness of the wedding I imagined we would have. Or, at least the card shouldn't nauseate anyone.

My save-the-date destiny was sealed a few weeks later when an envelope arrived in the mail from Steven's mother. It was a save-the-date card she'd received for a friend's daughter's wedding. This one was simply a typewritten letter on floral stationery. Hell, I knew I could do better than *that*. It might even be fun. I'd always considered myself somewhat artistic and crafty, not that I could point to anything particularly crafty I'd done since making a series of hook rugs in sixth grade, but I liked to think I still had it in me. And anyway, it was getting on to December; I'd have two weeks of cold nothing going on at the end of the month, so what better way to spend that free time than sharing my creative gifts with my friends and relatives? And when I was done, everyone would call me up and tell me how impressed they were with my efforts, and how they knew this was going to be the greatest wedding ever. In my mind, they would do this and then tell me they couldn't come because it was too far and too hard to get to, which would enable me to keep the wedding small.

Up until this point I had been able to sustain the delusion that we would be having a small, casual wedding. This was because we had not yet written the guest list. So one evening Steven and I wrote down a list of our friends, which amounted to about thirty people.

Assuming that our parents both came up with lists of fifty or so themselves, we'd have a total list of around 130. All the wedding magazines assured me that about 30 percent of guests will decline the invitation, but I optimistically bumped the number up to around 50 percent, given that our wedding was going to be an enormous pain in the ass to get to. Which meant that if all went accordingly we'd have about sixty-five people. Small. Casual. Un-weddinglike.

Of course, this number went out the window the minute our parents began compiling their lists. Steven's parents were the first to attempt a list. They came over for dinner one freezing night at the tail end of November, and I offered to do the dishes while they sat with Steven at the dining room table and wrote down names. Standing in our tiny kitchen I could hear the late-fall wind pressing against the windows, making it feel warm and cozy in the apartment. I ran the water in the sink, waited for it to get hot, then slid on yellow rubber gloves, and reached for the first dish. I heard laughter from the dining room.

"We have to invite them," someone was saying.

"That's ridiculous," came another voice. "We can't even remember who they are."

More laughter.

Something about standing alone in the kitchen next to a huge pile of dishes listening to the sounds of family made me feel wifely. It felt both nice and scary. I checked my internal emotions to see if I felt any burgeoning resentment, anything along the lines of a thought like, *why the hell am I standing in here with the dishes while they're all out there enjoying themselves*, which was the sort of fight my parents always used to have. But I didn't. I just felt content to have a house full of people who were all going to be related to me. If they came with lots of dishes, who cared? Someday I'd own a dishwasher.

Another round of laughter brought me back to my sink and the stack of dishes. I peeked my head out the door and looked into the dining room. Steven was sitting at the head of the table with his parents on either side. Marlene was hunched over a piece of paper, pencil in hand, scratching something out.

"Okay," she was saying. "I'll put him as a maybe. But we really should be inviting him."

Steven looks like an exact combination of his parents, as though their genes had split fifty-fifty, and seeing them all together was like witnessing the results of a textbook genetic experiment. Steven has the exact same oval face and watery blue eyes as his father, his mother's dark hair, his father's pale complexion, his mother's angular jaw line. These sorts of similarities always stand out to me because for most of my life I was the odd one out in my family. My father, mother, and brother are all dark-haired and olive-skinned; I am the sole blond-haired, fair-skinned one in the family. When I was a child, people used to ask if I was adopted. As I grew from child to adult my features came to resemble my parents' more, my hair darkened (although, thanks to the wonders of double-process high-lighting, it's now blond again), my lower lip puffed out like my father's, my eyes took on the wide-open shape of my mother's. Watching Steven with his parents, their beautiful little family tableau, I couldn't help but think about my own family. In the six years since my parents' divorce they hadn't spoken once. There was no chance they would ever, not even in my most fantastic dreams, sit down together at a table and write out a guest list.

By the end of the evening Steven's parents had their guest list and it added up to ninety people. His parents put on their coats, wrapped scarves around their necks, pulled on gloves, gave us warm hugs and pecks on the cheek good-bye. Still laughing about inviting Aunt so-and-so or forgetting about cousin whomever, they left the list on the dining room table for further review and were out the door. As I looked at their list full of penciled question marks, crossed out names, and eraser trails, I knew there was absolutely no way I could demand that they cut the list down to my ideal number of fifty. It was their family too. Who was I to dictate who they could and couldn't invite to their son's wedding?

"It's kind of a long list," I said to Steven.

"I know," he said. "Let's hope none of them show up."

❖ ❖ ❖

My head full of visions of Steven's Hallmark-like family moment, I
flew to Florida to sit down with my father and compile his list. But
every time I mentioned the guest list a sudden need would arise to
do something else. "We haven't swum in the ocean yet," he'd say.
"You want to swim before you go, don't you?" Or, "what about a
bike ride?" Or, "have you tried Grand Theft Auto yet?" (He'd
recently acquired a PlayStation.) And so it was with only hours to go
before I left that I finally cornered him and demanded we start
working on the list. He was sitting at his computer in his office—a
book-lined room with floor-to-ceiling windows on one side that
overlooked the pool and a small clump of palm trees. The room was
a new addition to the house, built to accommodate the fact that he
now worked at home most days, and it still had the cold feeling of a
room that hasn't really been lived in yet. It smelled of wood shav-
ings and shellac.

"Papa," I said. "Can we please do the list now?"

"You do it," he said. "Then I'll look it over."

I sat down across the desk from him. It felt like a business
meeting.

"Let's see," I said. "Well, of course we've got all the Schank
cousins." I wrote down a few names.

My father stared at his computer screen.

"And the Meyersburgs," I continued. "What about Aunt Elsie? I
bet you'd like to see her."

"Well, you have to invite her, but she'll never come. She hasn't
left the house in fifteen years."

"How about your friends?" I asked. "I assume you want to invite
Andrew and Arthur."

I smiled at him, pen poised above paper, waiting for him to share
some sort of happy memory involving one of the aforementioned
friends, or perhaps for him to remember a long-lost friend he
wanted to invite.

"I guess," he said.

His computer chirped, announcing that he'd received an e-mail.

"What about, um, Joe and your work people?"

"No," he said. "I don't need to invite any of them. It's not impor-

tant to me to throw a big wedding and invite all my business associates to show them what a big wedding I can throw. Some people
do that. It's not important to me."

"What about your students?" As a professor, my father's life had
always involved a rotating cloud of graduate students, some of whom
had become like secondary family members, showing up at holidays
and making regular appearances long after they'd graduated.

"If you want."

"I only like some of them."

"Well, just invite the ones you like, then."

In the end, I sat silently across his desk and wrote the list myself.

While it seemed that my father didn't want to invite anyone, my
mother went to the other extreme and e-mailed me a long list of
people I'd never heard of.

"Who are these people?" I asked my mother over the phone.
"Why are you inviting people I don't know to my wedding?"

"They're my friends," she said.

"Well, I've never even heard of them, and we've already got too
many guests."

"I just want to have some people there on my side," my mother
said. "I'm sure your father is inviting plenty of people."

"Mama, it's a wedding, not a rumble."

"I just want my friends to be there," she said. "Is that too much
to ask?"

"How can these people be your friends? I've never even heard
you mention them. And I've never met them. I don't want to be
meeting people at my own wedding."

"You're going to be meeting Steven's family."

"That's different."

I sighed. "Let's just wait, okay? Let's just send out save-the-date
cards and see who replies and then if there's room you can invite
these people."

"Has anyone told you they're not coming so far?"

"No! That's my point. Everyone says they're coming. It's insane.
Papa said that even Hortie and the Kuglers said they're coming."

"That's *my* point," said my mother. "Everyone's going to say they're coming *now*. For all you know Hortie could be dead by August."

"Well, if you look at it that way, we could all be dead. There could be no wedding at all."

"Don't be silly. Hortie is eighty-seven, there's a good chance she might be dead."

"Fine, well, when she dies you can invite your friends. Happy?"

I hung up and stared at the phone for a while.

A few days later I made the mistake of telling my father about my mother's desire to invite a whole host of people I'd never met. I don't know why. I guess I was feeling ornery.

"Oh yeah," he said. "Well, did you tell her I'm not inviting Joe? You've known Joe since you were eight."

"I told her," I said. I hadn't mentioned that my father's decision not to invite Joe had more to do with bad business dealings than a desire to keep the guest list short.

"Maybe I should invite him," my father said. "Maybe I should just start adding people. I mean, I've got plenty of people I could invite that we didn't even talk about."

"I know. I think she just feels like she doesn't have anyone on her side, and she's going to feel alone."

My mother didn't have many relatives she was in touch with. She wasn't speaking to her sister; her brother, my Uncle Ted, was a recluse who was unlikely to cross the street, let alone travel to Vermont. Most of the other relatives she would have invited were dead of old age or bad genes. And although it wasn't in the official divorce settlement, my father had unofficially gotten most of their friends. My mother had one high school friend she wanted to invite, and that was it. I could understand her wanting to invite her new posse, a group that would protect her from my father's blond new wife, from the evil eyes my grandmother would probably be casting all night, from the ex-friends who would give her polite, cold smiles as they passed in the lobby of the inn. I could understand it, but I still didn't like it. In an attempt to get her to stop pressuring me to add her friends to the guest list, I told her that I'd gotten a call from Joan, one of my father's first cousins.

"Even she says she's coming," I said. "And she couldn't even remember how she was related to me. She thought she was my aunt. The number of people allegedly coming to this thing is ridiculous."

"Oh yeah?" said my mother. "Well, the last time I talked to Joan she yelled at me for not inviting her to our twenty-fifth anniversary party. And then she hung up on me."

I could hear her voice quivering with anger.

"Well," I said, "I guess that issue is moot."

"Who knows," she snapped. "She's probably still angry about it. Anyway, I'm rooting for her not to come so I can invite my friends."

Because that's what a wedding should really be about: whose side has more guests. I had foolishly thought my parents would be able to set aside their differences and just be happy their only daughter had found someone she liked enough to marry. That wasn't asking too much, was it? I wasn't demanding that they actually kiss and make up. Which is to say, I wasn't demanding that my life actually *be* a Hollywood movie, only that it vaguely approximate one.

I had by now acquired two wedding guides—one from my mother and one from Marlene. After hanging up with my mother I flipped through both of them to see what they said about dealing with divorced parents. It turns out that while the wedding industry likes to flood brides with information on everything from place settings to postage stamps, it is fairly mute on this issue, despite the fact that nearly half of the people planning weddings are children of divorce. A quick check of other guides at my local bookstore turned up a few useless pieces of information along the lines of "don't seat them near each other" or "don't put the fathers in the receiving line," but the general assumption seemed to be that parents will be so overwhelmed with the joyous prospect of marrying off their children that they will behave nicely and ultimately unite in a fantastical celebration of bliss.

Curious to see what actual brides said about the subject, I typed in "divorce" on The Knot message boards, and pulled up a long list of posts. One bride had posted a poll asking how many people on The Knot had divorced parents. A whole host of women had replied with stories of fathers who had left when they were five, or ten, or ten months; of mothers who were unfaithful or had "bizarro" boyfriends. The same women who had bios filled with pictures of wedding cakes and hair styles and engagement rings told their divorce stories to complete strangers, and wrote heartbreaking sentences like: "I have a lot of trust issues. I always expect men to cheat or leave."

One woman wrote that her mother had paid for her sister's entire wedding, "so she had the 'power' over the event. [My parents] are both contributing equally to our wedding expenses, so I'm not sure how the power struggles will play out over toasts, etc."

Others wrote about how their parents' divorce had shaped their own views of marriage.

"I'm determined NOT to end up like my parents," wrote one woman. "To me divorce is NOT an option. I know why my parents split and that's fine, but I'm determined for these things not to happen again."

And yet, despite this outpouring of pain and angst on a site that is normally used for discussions about flower choice, despite the fact that divorce is clearly on the minds of many brides, wedding magazines and guides barely manage to slip in even one sentence on dealing with the emotional strain a wedding can cause for a family that is not Ozzie and Harriet.

Which is not to say that divorce isn't mentioned at all. It is. But generally in one of only two ways: prenuptial agreements and second-time brides. And here the questions are ones of etiquette. How can you make a prenuptial agreement more romantic? Is it okay for a second-time bride to wear white? These questions treat divorce like some annoying little thing that happened in the past, or probably won't happen at all (the general sentiment from the industry on prenups is: don't have one, they're not polite), when the reality is that for most couples divorce is a silent participant in the wedding planning process.

Not only are at least half of brides intimately familiar with divorce thanks to their parents, many of them are divorced themselves. Occasionally on The Knot a bride who was only recently posting on topics like the political ramifications of bridesmaid choice returns a few months later to announce the end of her marriage.

"I have decided to divorce my husband," wrote one former bride. "I told him of my decision about an hour ago, he called me a whore and hung up."

I clicked on the woman's bio just to see what was in it and discovered that she'd gotten married eight months earlier. "We had a perfectly wonderful day for our outdoor wedding!" she'd written in her bio. "My mom did all the flowers and decorations and my aunt did our cake. The napkins were edged in silver, which was one of our colors."

In one instance, a message with the header "I'm back and I'm married" was followed by one that read, "Divorce after 7 months"; in it the recent bride wrote that her new husband had told her that morning he was filing for divorce. She was looking for advice, although it's hard to imagine what sort of words could help her. And at least one woman on The Knot said she was in the middle of finalizing her divorce while planning her second wedding. "I was stupid and young and only married by the court," she wrote. "It's supposed to be over next month. I am still planning all my wedding stuff."

This woman sounded like she was attributing her divorce to the fact that in her first wedding she was married by the court rather than in a white ruffled fantasia—a popular sentiment in Wedding Land. I came across a paper on modern weddings in which the author wrote that the mother of one bride worried that her daughter's marriage was doomed because she "rushed to get married" and "threw it [the wedding] together." In the age of divorce, I suppose that people are willing to hang the blame for a failed marriage on any number of factors, so why not the cost or size of the wedding? And perhaps this is the hidden sentiment behind the obsessions with absurd details like matching napkin colors to bridesmaid dresses, or the desire to handcraft save-the-date cards—perhaps women feel that the more "perfect" the wedding, the more likely the marriage is to last. It's an irrational sentiment, but it's also completely understandable, and one that I suspected myself of sharing. After all, part of the reason I had been against a City Hall wedding was because I wanted something more official. But maybe that was just another way of saying I wanted something that would prove this was a well-thought out, serious decision, not just some hasty Las Vegas–like whim. Maybe it's just another way of saying to the world that this is not a marriage that will end in divorce.

It is, of course, essential to the survival of the wedding industry that it perpetuate the myth that all marriages last forever. Because if you're going to have multiple weddings, then it doesn't make much sense to blow all your money on the first one, does it? The whole selling point for a $5,000 dress you'll wear once or a $1,000 wedding cake that tastes like Styrofoam is that this is the only time you will ever buy these things, so why not go all out? Wedding-related retailers love to play on this notion of the one-time wedding. In one issue of *Martha Stewart Weddings*, a Waterford crystal ad claimed to be "The one and only." A ring design studio called for brides to "Put it on— never take it off!" I saw an ad for Tiffany in the back of *InStyle Weddings* that showed a diamond engagement ring above the words "Only one per customer." The same issue of *InStyle Weddings* featured a discussion of the wedding of Lisa Marie Presley and Nicholas Cage, who at the same time the issue came out were making headlines with their nasty divorce. This is apparently a common problem for *InStyle*, a magazine that profiles celebrity brides and offers tips from luxury wedding planners. The long turnaround time of the magazine and the short length of many celebrity marriages means that on more than one occasion the woman shown as a glowing bride on the cover is filing for divorce by the time the magazine hits the stands. Covers or articles featuring the weddings of Courtney Thorne-Smith, Drew Barrymore and Tom Green, and former *Melrose Place* star Kelly Rutherford all coincided with the couples' divorce filings. But somehow these failed marriages are presented as separate from wedding planning. Divorce, the wedding industry intimates, is what happens to other people. Divorce, it says, has nothing to do with weddings.

No one exemplifies this better than Martha Stewart, whose *Weddings* magazine reads like an obsessive-compulsive manual to planning the perfect wedding circa 1953. Prior to her incarceration, each issue began with a letter from Martha waxing poetic about some aspect of weddings, and occasionally she reminisced about her own wedding.

"When the time came for my wedding," she wrote in one issue alongside a picture of her parents on their wedding day, "Mother helped me make my own dress."

You would never guess, from her willingness to reminisce, that Martha Stewart is divorced.

The save-the-dates were not quick and they were not fun. Well, they were fun for about a day and a half. I dragged Steven to a trendy stationery store in SoHo to pick out paper, a process which he found excruciating, but I enjoyed. There is something lovely about blank sheets of paper, especially fancy imported blank sheets of paper, the kind that look like they should be used for writing adulterous letters in prerevolutionary France. I had fun taking out pieces of paper, holding them up to the light, running my fingers across surfaces that ranged from satiny to dimpled. After about half an hour of this, Steven begged me to please, for the love of God, just pick something. The agreement between us was that we'd split the wedding chores fifty-fifty, but the unspoken agreement was that the save-the-date project was my thing.

As it happened, over time most wedding-related tasks would come to be "my thing." In theory everything was evenly divided up—Steven was in charge of booking the band and the ceremony musicians, I was doing the photographer and the flowers—but the truth was that I was also responsible for the five billion little things that needed to be done, like picking out save-the-date paper. I'd been rationalizing this to myself by saying that I worked at home and could easily get these things done, while Steven was cooped up in an office all day and had less time to make phone calls or brainstorm ideas for hors d'oeuvres, until I read some interviews with brides about how they'd split the planning tasks with their fiancés. Almost every single bride said something like, "We're splitting it fifty-fifty, but I just have more time."

Groom guides, the male equivalent of wedding planners, make this division of labor painfully clear. I had the misfortune to absent-mindedly pick up a book called What the Hell is a Groom and

What's He Supposed to Do in the bookstore, and opened the book to this endearing passage:

> *If you really want to get involved with something maybe she'll let you handle the invitations (most guys can't screw that up too badly). However, are you going to write the mushy gobbledygook in the invitation asking your guests to 'attend the loving nuptials of the beloved bride Mary Jane and her handsome and dashing stud Joe Blow'? Stay with what you know . . . put the stamps on the envelopes and the return envelopes.*

And as much as this made me want to hunt down the book's author and shoot him, or ask Steven to write the invitations just to prove that, one, invitations didn't need to be constructed of mushy gobbledygook and, two, a man could write invitations just as well as a woman, the reality was that when it came to divvying up the wedding tasks, I ended up taking on most of them. Part of this was due to the fact that a tremendous amount of wedding planning involves choosing colors, and Steven is colorblind. Which meant that when we were looking at save-the-date paper, I would pick out a card, ask him what he thought, and his response was always, "What color is that?"

"It's gray," I'd say. "It's green. It's slate. It's the color of the sky on a snowy day. Does it matter?"

It didn't matter. It was all shades of gray to him.

I found that over the course of our relationship I'd come to master a color lexicon that I'd never needed before. Who really spends time thinking about whether a color is more like dull moss or sea foam green? Steven liked to have these differences articulated to him, I think so that he could learn to identify colors by their proper names, not because knowing the specific shade of green or gray or taupe would help him see the color any more clearly. Of course, the only question that really matters when it comes to color is: do you like it? And this was the question that Steven could never answer. He liked colors he could see. He liked yellow.

But to say that I took on most wedding tasks because I didn't want everything to be yellow isn't exactly fair. The fact was that most of the wedding stuff just mattered to me more. As much as I didn't want to admit it, Steven was not going to die if the save-the-date cards weren't breathtaking. I couldn't say the same for myself.

Eventually I picked out cream-colored cards and burgundy ribbon and a hole puncher. My master plan was to create à la Martha Stewart, a little booklet filled with information about the inn, travel details, and wedding weekend activities. I had already written the inside pages (which I'd begun referring to as "copy" from my advertising days). All that was left was to dust off my Photoshop disk and get to work on designing the cover.

A few days later I sat down at my computer, opened up Photoshop, and waited for inspiration to come. I put on some music, loud (one needs loud music to be artistic, I think), and started moving things around on my computer screen. I'd found a sepia print of the inn a few days earlier and had decided to put it on the cover. I spent the better part of an afternoon playing around with fonts and colors, then decided I was good to go and hit print. My computer made some grinding noises and promptly froze. At this point, the fun stopped. Two days later, I had managed to get the cover to print horizontally across the page (it was supposed to be vertical). Thoroughly disgusted with my computer skills, my printer, and this whole stupid crafty idea, I e-mailed all my files to Ellen, who once upon a time had been a graphic designer, and said I'd be at her store in an hour.

It was a gray, slushy day, so I pulled on my snow boots, wrapped myself in layers, and trudged down to the subway, grumbling the entire way. By the time I got to the store, Ellen had figured out the problem.

"You didn't set the resolution properly," she explained.

"This sucks," I said. "This was a stupid idea."

"They look nice," she said.

"I can't believe this is how I'm spending my time."

"So why are you?"

"Martha Stewart said I had to."

Ellen shrugged. "I saw you put a web address on the bottom," she said.

"Well, I figure I have to have a website. I mean, it is what I do for a living."

Ellen just looked at me.

"Is that insane?" I asked. "I figure that way I can put directions and information and stuff up there, and hopefully I won't get, like, ten thousand people calling me the day before the wedding saying they need directions."

"It's not insane," she said. "It's just funny how into this you are."

"I'm not into it," I said. "I'm just trying to save myself a headache later on."

"Sure."

I sighed. "Of course, the whole website thing is turning out to be a pain in the ass too."

"How so?"

"Well, I thought I would just use one of the premade ones. You know, you just fill in the text and stuff. But they're all ugly. Or at least, the colors don't match."

Ellen's eyes widened. "The colors don't match what?"

"The save-the-date cards," I explained patiently. "I want the website to look like the cards. So they're in keeping with the brand."

This was an expression everyone used at the advertising agency where Ellen and I used to work. It meant the TV ads had to be the same general idea as the print ads and the website and the online ads and so on. And I had just used it in reference to my wedding. I clapped my hand over my mouth.

"Omigod," I mumbled through my hand.

"Okay, *that's* insane," Ellen said.

I stared at her for a minute. I knew that this wedding planning stuff was already going too far. I also knew that I would get my save-the-date cards and my wedding website to match, or I would die trying.

Once Ellen had fixed the graphics and made the cover printable, it took a few days to print everything. The paper was thick so it had to be hand-fed into the printer, which meant I had to stand next to the printer and hold each individual piece of paper as it loaded. Early on the printer ran out of ink, which necessitated a long, cold walk to Staples in the rain. And then, there were a lot of cards to print. Between my parents' competitive inviting and Steven's extended family the guest list had ballooned to two hundred and fifty. Another few days passed before everything was ready to be assembled. It turned out that the hole puncher I'd bought was too big and made the cards look like they should be clamped into a Trapper Keeper, so I had to go to an art supply store for a smaller hole puncher. There was another trip to buy more ribbon. And still another trip to buy envelopes, which somehow I'd forgotten. Finally, everything was ready to be assembled. Steven and I sat on the living room floor one weekend with a pile of covers, a stack of paper printed with information about the wedding, three rolls of ribbon, and four rented movies. We got up for meals, but other than that, we did nothing but punch holes, fold paper, tie ribbon, and watch movies. It was a save-the-date assembly extravaganza.

When we finished, I have to admit, I thought the cards looked pretty good. I sat in the living room by myself for close to an hour just looking at them while Steven went off to the bedroom to lie down with *War and Peace*. They looked just like the little booklets I'd envisioned in the beginning—antiquey yet modern with the combination of sepia and cream on the cover and burgundy ribbon tying the whole thing together. I ran my thumb across a stack of them, pleased with the fact that I had actually created something. So rarely did I make anything physical anymore—for my job I just created air and ephemera—that I couldn't take my eyes off this pile of something that had come from my own hands. And then I was struck by the realization that after all that time, this was what I had created: a frilly pile of paper.

After that weekend it was a while before I could look at the save-the-date cards again, let alone think about mailing them out. This was partially due to the fact that I was missing the majority of addresses for my guests, and this was in turn due to the fact that when my parents divorced, my mother, who had always been Keeper of the Addresses, threw out her address book. I kept picturing that address book: it had pastel flowers on the front, and the little tabs for each letter were stained with coffee or tea or some other dark liquid. I knew exactly where it had been in our old house—in a white kitchen drawer under the phone—and couldn't shake the feeling that it would still be there for me to take if only I had keys to the house. It was hard to imagine the address book where it probably was—buried under tons of garbage somewhere, rotting, maybe already moldered into earth and dirt. My mother still had addresses for her guests, but the majority of guests were on my father's side (even though he didn't care who was invited and who wasn't, he still had the larger family), and he had never kept an address book in his life. The only person who might still have all the addresses was my grandmother. So I called her. She was able to give me a few, but quickly became confused as to who people were and which addresses she'd already given me.

"Do you need Klari?" she asked.

"You already gave me her address, Gammy."

"I did?"

"Yes, like two minutes ago. Now I need her son, George."

"What's his last name?" she asked.

"It's the same as Klari's." I tried to sound patient.

"Oh, right."

I heard her fumbling with the address book.

"Everything is so scratched out in here," she said. "I can't tell who lives where anymore."

It was true. I'd seen her address book. It was a mess. Finally she located George and gave me his address.

"Okay," she said. "I'll talk to you later."

"Wait!" I yelled. "I need more addresses."

"Well this is going to take all day," she said.

"What, you've got somewhere better to be?" I asked. "You've got a hot Mahjong game to get to?"

"No, but I'm tired."

I put the phone down for a minute, rubbed my forehead, and considered the situation. I was trying to get addresses for guests from her side of the family, whom apparently nobody cared about inviting. I remembered back to past family affairs—anniversaries, birthday parties, my bat mitzvah—where there had been heated discussions over guest lists and excitement in the planning. I didn't think it was too much to ask that at least one person in my family enjoy the fact that I was getting married. But between my parents' bickering and my grandmother's slowly decaying mind, there was no one left.

"Okay," I said, picking the phone back up. "Let's just do a few more, and then I'll call you tomorrow to get the rest."

"Oh great," she said bitterly. "I have to do this tomorrow too?"

We went through the slow process of finding a few more names before I decided it was enough.

"Is there anyone else you want to invite, Gammy? Anyone I forgot or anything?"

"No. You've got too many people as it is, and none of them are going to come."

I took a deep breath, then stated the obvious.

"How can I have too many if none of them are going to come?"

"I don't know," she said. "But you do."

When you join a new family, you never know what sort of peculiar habits you are going to be subjected to for the rest of your life. When Steven met me, for example, I am sure it never occurred to him that a life with me would involve receiving bimonthly answering machine messages from my grandmother that always say the same thing: "Hana? Hana!? It's Gammy." Click. When I met him, I had no idea that it meant I would never need to buy stamps again. His father, it turns out, is a stamp collector. For some reason this means that every few months we get an envelope in the mail stuffed full of stamps. At first I wondered if this was some sort of effort on his father's part to encourage letter writing, but Steven assured me that his father simply figured we needed stamps (who doesn't?) and he had some. So when it came to collecting 250 stamps for the save-the-date cards, Steven's father was only too happy to oblige.

These were not, of course, your normal flag stamps, or the invitation-friendly "love" stamps. These were a random assortment of stamps that honored everything from floral diversity to Enrico Fermi. I've always been a little obsessed with invitation stamps ever since my bat mitzvah, when every other girl in my class used "love" stamps on their invitations, and my mother decided that for my invitations a stamp honoring Sojourner Truth, the former slave and abolitionist, would be more appropriate. I think I never quite got over the fact that while everyone else had cute little hearts on their invitations, I had a picture that recalled one of the more horrific eras in our country's history. And so as I sat at the dining room table with Steven, licking first a Statue of Liberty stamp, then a Kwanzaa stamp, then a stamp celebrating Arab heritage, I wondered vaguely if my guests would think I was trying to send them some sort of message (be it patriotism or cultural diversity). The same *Martha Stewart Weddings* magazine that ran the four-page spread on handmade save-the-date cards had also included an article on stamp choice and how it can help to enhance your invitation envelopes (in summary, they were pro–"love" stamp). But as my saliva ran low around stamp 50, I flexed my fingers, still sore from last weekend's ribbon-tying, hole-punching festivities, and decided that at this point I had ceased to give a shit what anybody thought about anything.

It took a day to get all the envelopes stamped, and another day to finish organizing the addresses and print them out onto labels. And then another day to stick all the address labels onto the envelopes. We did a final check of envelopes against the guest list, making sure no one had been accidentally omitted. Then, just to be certain, I alphabetized the envelopes and checked again. And, finally, we loaded all the envelopes into two shopping bags and put them by the front door.

"Thank God," I sighed.

"Go team!" Steven yelled, holding out his hand for me to high-five.

I smiled and high-fived him. "Go team."

"So that's it, right? We're done."

"Yup," I said. "Nothing left to do but mail them. No turning back then."

"Nope. People will be expecting a wedding, damn it. And we're going to give it to them."

"So you wanna mail them now?" I asked.

"Let's do it later. I'm exhausted." Steven flopped down on the couch to indicate just how exhausted. "My hands are still red from that stupid hole punch."

"Me too," I said, flopping down next to him and putting my feet up on the coffee table. "It's Sunday anyway, so waiting a day won't make any difference. I'll do it tomorrow."

A week later the envelopes were still sitting patiently by the front door, wondering if they were going to be mailed or if they were going to spend the rest of their days as a doorstop.

Every day on my way out the door I would look at the bag full of envelopes and decide it was too wet, or too cold, or too annoying for me to mail them at that particular moment.

"I might be having some issues with mailing the envelopes," I told Steven one night as we were preparing dinner. "It's, like, a serious commitment."

"Gee," he said. "I thought it was a serious commitment once you said yes."

"I know, but I didn't mail my 'yes' to 250 people. I mean, once we mail them, the wedding is on."

"And . . . ?"

I looked up at Steven from where I'd been seasoning pork chops. "And nothing," I said. "It's fine. I'm just getting nervous."

"Now? You're getting nervous now?"

"I'm not nervous about getting married," I explained. "I'm nervous about having a wedding."

"Don't worry about it," he said. "It's going to be great."

I sighed. "Sure it will."

"Do you want me to mail them?"

"No. I'll do it."

The next day it was sunny and clear. I took the bag of envelopes down to the corner mailbox and stood by the box, opening the mail slot, then closing it.

"This is ridiculous," I said aloud, then looked around quickly to see if anyone nearby had noticed me talking to myself.

I took a deep breath, then opened the slot and dumped in the envelopes. What will be will be, I thought, then walked home and waited for what I imagined would be an onslaught of excited replies and congratulatory phone calls.

The first response came the following evening. It was an e-mail from my reclusive Uncle Ted. The e-mail stated that his name was no longer Ted. It was now Theo. His save-the-date card had been addressed to Ted. He had been Theo, he explained, for quite some time, and was hurt and angry that I refused to call him by his new name. Given that I had seen him maybe twice in the last ten years and in that time had most likely not called him anything, as one generally doesn't address people by their first names when speaking directly to them, I found this accusation a little strange. And that was the end of the e-mail. No "congratulations you're getting married." No "what a beautiful card it must have taken you weeks to make it you must be such a talented designer." No any of that.

The next response came from my cousin Elizabeth. Elizabeth is my closest cousin agewise, and for a brief period of time about twelve years ago, when we'd both been living in Washington DC, we'd hung out a few times. We were also each other's only female cousin, so we had some kind of a special bond, I suppose—as much a bond as one can have with a second cousin one rarely sees. In her e-mail, Elizabeth congratulated me and asked where Steven and I were registered. This was then followed by a detailed listing of all the food allergies on her side of the family, to assist me as I planned the wedding menu.

I am allergic to capers, cloves, bananas, avocados, kiwi, aspartame, carnations, and chestnuts. As for meat, I only do seafood and snails. My mother has the same allergies as me; however she eats meat except for veal and rabbit. My father won't eat rabbit. Uncle Murray is on a very strict heart healthy diet. Katherine may be a fishetarian—she has some sort of ulcer-thing I think, because I know that eating much in the way of tomatoes is a no-no for her. Aunt Linda is allergic to corn and citrus fruits.

I was tempted to write back that I had planned a meal consisting exclusively of rabbit, chestnuts, and aspartame, and that all the flowers would be carnations. Instead I thanked her politely and quickly deleted her e-mail.

This should have been a lesson to me. The wedding magazines and guides all claimed that the wedding was My Day, and I had begun to believe them. I had believed that my parents would stop being petty, that my relatives would put aside their weird narcissistic tendencies and perhaps decide that the wedding wasn't in fact about them and what they like to be called any given week or what random food items they couldn't eat, but the truth was that no one was going to become a different person just because I was getting married. The industry has to hype your wedding day so you'll buy more stuff, but your extended family doesn't care. Or at least, mine didn't. For my family, my wedding was just another reason to gripe. Somewhere in the back of my mind had been the idea that if I made the save-the-date cards absolutely breathtaking, they would cover up the cracks and fault lines that divided my relatives, they would hide the infighting and the crazy cousins and the general strife that most people call family.

I had also expected that once I unleashed the brilliance of my save-the-date cards upon the world, it would stop spinning and all nations would come together to praise my creative genius. Although my mother called to say that the cards were beautiful, Marlene said a few of her guests had asked if they were professionally done, and Kimberly e-mailed that she thought they set the perfect tone for the wedding, I kept holding out hope that someone would leave me a message on my answering machine saying that they had practically fallen over once they witnessed the sheer beauty of the cards, that they had run screaming around the neighborhood, "OH MY GOD, THIS IS THE MOST FANTASTIC THING I'VE EVER SEEN AND IT'S COMPLETELY CHANGED MY LIFE!" I guess after you slave over something for weeks, obsess about choosing just the right color paper, make countless trips to countless stores, you want some type of response that will justify the effort.

Still holding out hope of receiving praise and adulation, I asked Steven if anyone had said anything to him about the cards.

"Well," he said. "My friends wanted to know if I tied the bows myself."

"They're not bows," I snapped. "They're square knots. I spent a whole afternoon on the Internet researching how to tie a square knot. They're goddamned square knots."

"I know, but my friends don't know that."

I pouted for a minute.

Steven sighed. "They're just joking."

"I know," I said.

I thought about it, and then I started to giggle.

"It is kind of funny," I said. "'Did you tie the bows yourself.' That's cute. They think you're girly."

"Whatever."

"And you have a wedding website too."

"Shut up."

"Ha ha," I sang. "You have a wedding website."

"Well, so do you," Steven said.

I stopped singing.

"Okay. Let's just forget it," I said. "After the wedding is over, we'll never speak about bows or the wedding website again."

"Okay," said Steven. "Deal."

5

Waiting for Cha Cha

If a young woman says no to marriage
just wait until her breasts sag.

—*Burundian proverb*

"I PROMISED YOUR GRANDMOTHER THERE WOULD
be great-grandchildren in three years," my father announced
over the phone.

"Who's producing them?" I asked. "Because it's not me."

"Oh I'm not worried," he said. "There will be grandchildren.
After all, that's why you're really getting married. That's what we're
really celebrating. Not the marriage, but that you've decided to have
kids."

"When did I decide that?"

"I don't know. But you did."

I never thought the world would demand I begin reproducing
before the ink on the marriage contract even existed, but a surprising number of people seemed to be in agreement on this point.

Shortly after we announced our engagement, Steven and I went
out to our local dive bar with a group of friends. This was a gang of
people we'd been hanging out with throughout many stages of
life: the cheap-beer-and-sleazy-bar years, the five-martini-evening
years, the barbecue-on-the-roof years, and now, the glass-of-wine-
and-early-bedtime years. We were the first of this group to get

engaged, and that night several people suggested starting a betting pool as to how long it would be before I was pregnant. I guess I shouldn't have been shocked. First comes love, then comes marriage, then comes Junior in the baby carriage. We've all known that since we were old enough to skip rope. Even so, the baby equation (marriage + 30-year-old woman = baby) caught me by surprise. I had no idea if I wanted children. I guess in the abstract it sounded like the right thing to do, but I certainly wasn't ready to just skip right into procreation.

This, apparently, was not appropriate behavior. As a woman, particularly as an engaged woman, I was supposed to want babies, find baby clothes cute, gaze enviously at the pregnant women I encountered. And no one communicated this to me better than my own family. They had been fairly quiet on the subject for the first few months of my engagement, but lately there had been rumblings. My father would drop comments on the phone about how the longer I waited to have children, the harder it would be. Steven's mother informed me that she would never buy her grandchildren Barbies. And then there was Passover.

Somehow the collective decision had been made that Steven's parents should fly to my father's house in Florida for Passover so they would have a chance to meet before the wedding. Steven and I had been so eagerly anticipating this meeting of the parental minds that we managed to miss our plane out of Newark. (Technically, the airline gave away our seats. Technically, this was because we were two minutes late.) So instead of spending the day suffering through awkward silences, fearful of which parent might open his or her mouth and say the most embarrassing thing, we passed the time arguing with airport supervisors and feigning hysteria after being turned down for flight after flight. Or at least, that is how I passed the time. Steven had taken a heavy dose of antianxiety pills just before we arrived at Newark, in the hopes of timing the effect to coincide precisely with what he saw as the highly improbable and therefore terrifyingly dangerous taxi and takeoff of our airplane. Which meant that while I was screaming myself purple at the mindless bureaucracy known as the airline industry and bursting into dramatic tears at the customer service desk in the hopes of scoring us a seat, Steven was staring vacantly at the wall.

The problem was that we were not the only people flying from New York to Florida for Passover. In fact, we were formulaic: a young couple adrift in a mass exodus of tri-state area Jews, all of whom had gathered their belongings and children and overbooked every single flight out of the New York area. We were only two of hundreds of people in the airport shrieking sentences that consisted of the words "Miami," "parents," and "before sunset," as though the airport had been invaded by a flock of vacationing vampires. Twelve hours after we arrived at Newark we finally found ourselves on a flight south—Steven frantically gripping the arm rests of his seat (because when the plane crashes, *that* will help), my eyes red and swollen from too many overly theatrical fits of hysteria.

We staggered into my father's house to find the Passover seder already in progress. A quick check of the occupants of the room revealed, to my immense relief, that no one appeared upset or emotionally disheveled. Steven's parents seemed to be smiling. My father and brother were laughing. My grandmother was quietly sipping wine, her blond puff of cotton-candy hair sprayed extra high with Aqua Net for the occasion. The Gershman family—two parents, who were friends of the family, and their teenage boys—were at the end of the table as they were every year. Everything seemed to be running smoothly. The proceedings straggled on as Steven and I slipped into our seats—two empty chairs strategically positioned next to my father and across the table from Steven's parents.

A Passover seder, or at least, my family's Passover seder, can be a somewhat chaotic affair in that there is some sort of religious proceeding going on, but almost none of the seder participants are paying attention at any given moment. So it was completely normal for Gammy to call me over to talk to her while my father was in the middle of loudly blessing the matzo.

"Hana dear," she announced to the table. (My grandmother's range of vocal tones does not include whispering.) "Hana dear, I have something for you. Come over here."

I pushed my chair back and leaned over to her.

"I have this for you. To get married with." She pushed a ring into my hand, a plain gold band. "It was your great-grandmother's ring," she said.

I looked inside the band and read the engraving: *December 12, 1907*, followed by something written in Hungarian, which was my great-grandparents' native tongue.

"Gammy, that's so great," I said. "I love it."

"It's for you to get married with," Gammy said, in case there had been any confusion.

"Right. To get married with."

"Now, Hana," she continued.

By this point the seder had more or less ground to a halt. The Gershman boys were arguing over the meaning of the bitter herb at the far end of the table, the result of too much Jewish education; my father was thumbing through his Haggadah, the prayer book used for the Passover seder; and everyone else was pretending not to listen to my grandmother. I glanced across the table at Steven's parents, pleasant smiles frozen on their faces, clearly at a loss as to whom to pay attention to. My grandmother, since she was the oldest person at the table? My father, who was allegedly running the seder? The inane argument over the bitter herb?

"Hana, I want to know," my grandmother continued. "Will I live to see great-grandchildren?"

This was not a new question. In fact, it was a question she had been asking since long before there was a Steven. To be fair, the original question was "*When* will I have great-grandchildren," followed by much cooing and the miming of holding a baby, as though I might be unsure as to the form that said great-grandchildren would take. After my grandfather died a few years ago, the question morphed into its current "will I live to see" format.

"I don't know, Gammy," I muttered. "How long are you planning on living?"

"I don't know," she replied. "I'm pretty old."

"I'll see what I can do," I said, and pulled my chair back towards the table.

My father had reached the part of the seder that involved reciting a translated song called "Who Knows One." He had made it into a sort of quiz game when we were kids, and out of tradition, or lack of any better ideas, we still play it. He would ask, who knows One, and the right answer was, One is God in heaven and earth. Who knows Two? Two are the tablets of the commandments. Who knows Three? Three are the patriarchs. You got extra credit if you could name them: Abraham, Isaac, and Jacob. It was essentially a random association of numbers with elements of Judaism that you had to try and remember from Passover to Passover. The associations grew more obscure as the numbers got higher, concluding with thirteen, which stood for some Judaic minutiae that no one ever remembered or understood.

That night my father's audience was fading by number eight. With the exception of Steven's parents, we'd all sat through this exercise so many times it was about as exciting as watching VH1 count down the top songs of the eighties.

"WHO KNOWS EIGHT?" my father bellowed. Bellowing is his favorite mode of communication at Passover, partially because it is the only way to be heard over the constant din of the other conversations and transactions at the table, and partially, I think, because he likes bellowing.

Someone knew eight. One of the Gershman boys, perhaps, or maybe my brother, who tended to jump in with answers when he detected that everyone else was ignoring the counting. Eight are the days before circumcision. (We're such a happy people—always know how to celebrate the joyous occasions.)

"WHO KNOWS NINE?" came next.

No one knew nine. Steven's mother began a quiet conversation with someone next to her. My brother was picking dried food off his Hagaddah, my grandmother was trying to surreptitiously pull the wine bottle closer to her, the Gershman boys were arguing loudly over who knew ten.

"WHO KNOWS NINE?" my father yelled again, looking at me.

"Nine," I said.

"You don't know nine?" he asked.

I shook my head.

"Steven, do you know nine?"

Steven grimaced. "Nine is the number of glasses of wine I'm going to have tonight."

My father took a deep tornadolike breath, almost as though he were about to suck up the whole table, seder plate and all. "CHILD-BIRTH!" he screamed. "NINE ARE THE MONTHS OF CHILDBIRTH." As his face turned red from the exertion of all that screaming, it reminded me of cartoon drawings of the wind—just a big face with lips pursed, blowing itself out.

I threw a horrified glance at Steven, who was carefully studying the tablecloth, then turned and looked at my father. When people meet my father they always say they imagined him bigger. He's got a big personality, a big voice, and big opinions, but he's smaller than he used to be. He used to have a big woolly beard, big hair, and a big belly, but these days the beard is gray and close-cropped, the hair has given way to a shiny Michael Jordan-like dome, and the big belly is a little smaller thanks to the Zone diet. He's still a big presence, though, and most people find him scary. Sometimes I find him scary too, and the only thing to do is act scary back, which was what I did now.

"For God's sake," I snapped. "Give it a rest. We're not even married yet."

"Well you're not getting any younger," he said in a normal voice.

I looked at Steven's parents. I had no idea how to interpret their neutral expressions. Were they as appalled as I was by my father's decision to introduce my reproductive capabilities, and by extension, their son's sex life, as a topic of discussion at the Passover seder? I had, in that moment, a vision of everyone else imagining Steven and me having sex on the seder table—seder plate crashing to the floor, bitter herb and roasted lamb shank flung against the wall, my hair dangling in the red wine set aside for the prophet Elijah. Was this what they were thinking? Worse, were they picturing my uterus? Sperm? Mitosis?

But there was a larger problem inherent in the topic my father had raised at the seder table, taste and appropriateness aside: I wasn't so sure I wanted children. I had never had anything that, as far as I knew, could be identified as a maternal instinct. Where other women cooed over babies passing by in strollers, I had always smiled and thought, I'm so glad that's not mine. I had never liked babysitting, and, in general, small babies made me uncomfortable. Between the two of us, Steven is far more child-oriented. I had watched Steven in the airport earlier that day come out of his antianxiety haze to discover a two-year-old who was babbling incoherently sitting next to him. He had smiled and waved politely at the baby.

"Ablalofuasdoiaelkrj," said the baby.

"Pardon?" said Steven, sending the baby's mother into a fit of giggles.

"You don't say pardon to a baby," I whispered.

"Oh," he said.

And yet "pardon" was a hell of a lot more than I'd said. I'd been trying to ignore the baby, to tune out its incessant babbling.

But what I hadn't realized until that moment at the seder table was that hidden in the sparkle of every diamond engagement ring is the whispered promise that there will be children, there will be a family. Because, the thinking goes, why else would you get married?

The two are so intertwined, in fact, that The Knot recently created a Baby Talk message board (categorized strategically under Newlywed Boards, lest anyone think of having a baby without being married) so that women can move from comparing wedding gowns to comparing ovulation kits without having to find a new website. Just as the rest of The Knot has its own language, so does Baby Talk, where women say they are TTC (trying to conceive), have stopped BCP (birth control pills), and unfortunately, have AFNW (aunt flow not wanted). The result is a strange mixture of women with screen names like DancingBride describing bodily fluids found in their panties in just as much loving detail as they described their flower arrangements only months earlier.

And cultures around the globe incorporate fertility rites in their wedding ceremonies: Malaysian wedding guests each receive a decorated hard-boiled egg (what could *that* mean?), in Korean weddings the groom's father throws red dates at his daughter-in-law to bring her fertility, and one of my least favorite interpretations of the

Jewish tradition of breaking the glass maintains that the tradition represents the breaking of the bride's hymen.

"We're doing it in two years," said Cameron when I called to ask her about babies. "After Dan's finished with grad school."

"We have a plan like that too," I said. "Like, maybe in three years or so. But can I ask you, do you have any, um, maternal urges?"

"No," said Cameron. "I'm just assuming I will."

The truth is, yes, Steven and I have a plan, but it is entirely based on my age, not on any kind of mutual desire we have to create life. Every now and then I get something that could be construed as a maternal urge. I feel the desire to hug something; I think about how nice it might be to hold something warm and small close to me. But I'm not entirely convinced that these symptoms indicate my desire for anything other than a cat, or maybe an electric blanket.

When I was a teenager, my father explained the biological clock phenomenon to me. I think someone who worked for him was pregnant at some time that he found inconvenient and annoying. "When you hire women they always say they're not interested in having kids," he said. "And then, when they hit thirty, they get this internal thing that says, 'Baby. Baby. Baby.' And they try to ignore it but it just gets louder. BABY. BABY. BABY." This sounded to me like the kind of thing that would be hard to ignore. I mean, my uterus was going to be screaming. But so far—silence. While I was in Florida for Passover I turned thirty-one. Shouldn't there have been at least a little whining by then?

Sometimes I think that my lack of maternal desire draws from the fact that I spent much of my adult life living in a babyless world. My twenties were lived out exclusively in neighborhoods inhabited by other single twenty-somethings: Chicago's Wrigleyville, New York's East Village. Weeks, months, sometimes even entire seasons, passed between baby sightings. The enormous apartment building I lived in for most of my late twenties in the East Village had only two children in it, and on Halloween you were given the option of signing up to hand these two underprivileged kids candy. Which meant that if you opted in, you had to buy an entire bag of Halloween candy, knowing full well that you would dole out only two pieces all night. I never signed up—I was always too busy doing some other non-child-related activity like consuming mass quantities of alcohol in a nearby bar while wearing a purple wig.

As the wedding drew closer, though, it was as though some higher power had turned on the baby faucet. My friend Amanda became the first of my close friends to actually produce a baby, giving birth just a few days after Passover. I had just gotten used to the idea that she was pregnant *on purpose*, that this was cause for celebration, not hushed late-night talks about ruining one's life; and now here she was with an actual living, breathing baby on her hip.

"Did it change your life?" I asked her on the phone after she came home from the hospital, hoping she would share some maternal revelation that would turn on my internal baby voice.

"Not really. Sometimes Paul and I will be in the kitchen after she's asleep, and we're just doing dishes or something and we'll look at each other and go, hey, we have a baby," she said. "We're just like us but now we have this baby."

She then went on to describe the various fluids her body was secreting, and how the pain of labor was like nothing she'd ever experienced before. Needless to say, none of this quickened my desire to reproduce.

And then there was my neighborhood. When Steven and I had moved in together two years ago, we'd decided to leave Manhattan for a roomier place in Brooklyn. The neighborhood we'd chosen turned out to be Baby Central. By late spring the neighborhood baby parade was out in full force; every third person on the sidewalk seemed to be wearing one of those contraptions that suspends the baby in front of the parent's chest, facing out. SUV-like strollers began to take over the sidewalks, their girth and thick-tread tires edging me into the street.

But the biggest baby pressure came from real estate. Steven and I had decided to buy an apartment, since it had begun to look like we'd be staying in New York for the foreseeable future, and since we were getting married and all. And, speaking in quiet and calm tones, we had decided to buy a two-bedroom. Yes, there were only two of us, but we would need an office since I worked at home and Steven was about to become a graduate student. Yes, there would definitely have to be an office. And yes, we both knew that "office" was code for "place to put the potential baby, should there be one," although we never said it. Instead we said, "you'll be up late studying," and, "what if I want to watch TV and you want to read," but we both knew that the rooms we were looking at had to be big enough to fit a crib and a changing table.

As our apartment hunt progressed, it became increasingly hard to ignore the semi-obvious, given that all the apartments we looked at were being sold by people moving out because their kid had outgrown the tiny nursery with the cute yellow walls and bunny stencils. I'm not exactly sure how it happened, but at some point we began referring to our nonexistent progeny as Cha Cha, as in, does Cha Cha really need all this room in here? How loud do you think Cha Cha will be? Is it better if Cha Cha is near us or on the other side of the apartment? This would have seemed less disconcerting were it not for the fact that Cha Cha was the name of our recently deceased Japanese fighter fish. After a few weeks of apartment hunting, Steven declared Cha Cha a royal pain in the ass. Were it not for Cha Cha, we could get a great one-bedroom instead of the miniscule two-bedrooms our budget could afford. Stupid Cha Cha.

"Does it bother you that we're calling our potential spawn the same name as the fish?" I asked. "Do you think that's cause for concern?"

"Well," said Steven. "I don't think we should seriously consider having a child until we stop viewing its name as a source of amusement."

"I'm not the one with the funny names," I pointed out. "I like Max, after my grandfather."

"I like Boom Boom," said Steven. "Or Oedipus."

But if I didn't hear any yelling from my biological clock, I was beginning to get the sense that the rest of the world did. At one apartment showing, the realtor and I were standing in the second bedroom, when I said something like, well, I guess this would be fine for an office. I work at home, my fiancé is a PhD student, we need an office.

The man smiled at my words. "Not to be too blunt," he said, "but it would make a fine nursery too."

I smiled back at him. "Right," I said. "It could be a nursery."

Later that day I dropped by Ellen's store and recounted what the realtor had said.

"Is it me?" I asked her. "Do I just look that fertile?"

"You do look pretty fertile," she said. "Although I'm looking pretty fertile myself these days."

And the baby parade went on.

In April, my yoga teacher showed up to class visibly pregnant. She had always been curvy, especially compared to all the other ultra-toned, board-straight teachers in the yoga world. But now, suddenly, her body had just exploded. Her breasts were as big as her head, and in her body I saw my future. I'm curvy too, and now I imagined breasts so big they needed to be carried around in a sling, hips that couldn't fit through a door, an ass like a hot air balloon. The yoga teacher just oozed maternity. In four short months she'd been transformed from a shapely fitness queen into Mother Earth. It did not make me want to be pregnant.

Steven came home that night to find me sprawled out on the couch watching *Maternity Ward* on The Learning Channel, a show that broadcasts video of difficult births, and usually ends with mother and baby cuddling in a hospital bed.

"What the hell are you watching?"

"Shh," I hushed. "They're about to induce."

Steven stood behind me on the couch, watching for a moment.

"Babe, is this about you trying to, like, stimulate some kind of maternal instinct?" he asked.

"Shut up," I said. "I'm trying to learn something."

"You know, we don't have to have babies just because everyone says we do."

I grunted.

"It's our decision," Steven said.

"I know," I said. "I'm just trying to be informed."

The woman being induced on TV began to scream.

"See, like stuff like that," I said. "I should know this stuff."

"Oh God," said Steven. "Turn that off."

A few weeks later, Kimberly, whom I had asked to be my matron of honor, announced that she was pregnant. Several months earlier, Steven and I had decided to keep the members of the wedding party to a minimum. I had initially thought about asking all the friends who had forced me to put on ill-fitting bridesmaids dresses and act happy that they were getting married to do the same at my wedding, but the more I thought about it, the more I realized that I had a true loathing of the entire bridesmaid concept. I didn't want to run around town picking out dresses for other people, I didn't want my friends pretending that they were delighted with my choice of dress, my choice of earrings, my choice of shoes. I'd always hated being a bridesmaid, so why should I subject anyone else to the horror?

Steven had struggled with a similar decision, although of course his thought process didn't include the issue of making his friends purchase dresses. His problem was that he had in the neighborhood of 486 close friends from college; and if he invited one of them to be in the wedding, he'd have to invite all of them. So in the end I chose my oldest friend as my matron of honor, he chose his former roommate as his best man, and we called it a day. And now, my matron of honor was going to look like a small balloon as she walked down the aisle.

When Kimberly called to share her joy, my first thought was how this would affect my wedding. That was probably wrong. I should have rejoiced in her maternal bliss. So it was probably worse that I was pleased this would cause Kimberly to look inflated at the wedding. But then Kimberly was always the friend I hated going to bars with because the men all wanted to talk to her. She's that friend all women have who is a size two, smart, pretty, friendly. I thought a little catty pleasure at her expense was justified.

Other people weren't as pleased, though. My grandmother insisted I'd have to find a new matron of honor.

"How can you have a pregnant matron of honor?" Gammy squawked into the phone. "That's the silliest thing I ever heard."

"She's not going to stop being my friend just because she's pregnant," I explained.

"But a pregnant matron of honor . . . I never heard of such a thing."

"It'll be funny," I said. "She'll be like a fertility god walking down the aisle." I imagined tiny Kimberly, five foot one and all belly, clunking her way through the guests.

"It'll be funny all right," said Gammy.

Despite the baby onslaught happening all around me, I'd still been unable to tap into my maternal desires. I began to wonder if there really was such a thing as a maternal instinct that causes women to want to reproduce. Perhaps I could have mine checked to make sure it was on. I decided to do some research, and it turns out that quite a bit of literature exists on the subject of the maternal instinct. But, despite much study, it has never actually been proven to exist. Maternal instinct was a hot topic in the sixties-era women's liberation movement, which pointed out that the idea of an innate desire to have babies had been used throughout history to keep women in the home and out of the workforce. Although this idea didn't get much play until the sixties, it's been around for a while. I came across an article from a 1916 issue of *The American Journal of Sociology* that described maternal instinct as "an all-consuming desire for parenthood regardless of all personal pain, sacrifice, and disadvantage involved." I doubted this was the modern interpretation of maternal instinct, but I was pretty sure that I'd never felt an all-consuming desire for anything beyond chocolate, a beach vacation, or, more recently, a pink handbag. But certainly not for babies.

In general, when people talk about maternal instinct they are referring to one of two things: an innate desire in women to procreate or an innate desire to nurture. I have no doubt that I possess the second. I used to have a cat, and I loved him madly from the second I picked him up from the animal shelter. I even loved our dead fish Cha Cha, who expressed his love for me by biting my fingers and eating the fish food I gave him. It is the first that I think I might be missing.

❖ ❖ ❖

A few weeks later Steven and I went to meet with the rabbi who was going to perform our ceremony. Steven had asked the rabbi from his childhood synagogue if he would officiate, and despite the fact that the rabbi hadn't seen Steven in at least fifteen years and would have to drive five hours to get to Vermont from his home in the New York City suburbs, he'd agreed. The only caveat was that we'd have to go out to his synagogue to meet with him before the ceremony; so one warm spring day we boarded a train out to leafy Pleasantville. Yes, Steven grew up in Pleasantville.

The synagogue was a soaring modern building filled with shiny blond wood and muted browns and taupes. A short, slight, middle-aged man dressed in khakis and a blue oxford shirt came out to the hall to greet us. As he hugged Steven hello, it dawned on me that this was the rabbi. I guess he looked somewhat rabbi-esque—he had the broad smile and warm hellos that I always associate with members of the clergy—but for some reason he didn't quite look the part.

Our train had arrived late, and the rabbi hurriedly explained that unfortunately we only had a little bit of time before his next appointment arrived, so we'd just have to get done what we could, and then we'd have to come back some other time. He ushered us into his office and motioned for us to sit on the couch. Aside from the pictures of Jerusalem on the walls and the assorted Judaica on the bookshelves, the room felt like a therapist's office. There was a desk to one side that looked like no one ever sat at it, and a leather couch and chairs in a little sitting area behind the desk. I felt tears threaten to gather in the corners of my eyes. I always cried at the therapist.

"So, why do you want to get married?" he asked as soon as we were seated on the couch.

I was slightly taken aback. I had imagined that the meeting would involve us listing off the elements we wanted him to include in the ceremony. I had also imagined how pleased he would be when he discovered what a laid-back bride I was, and how I didn't care if his yarmulke matched the color scheme. But, no matter. I knew the right answer to his question.

"Because I want to be a family," I said. Other people might

answer they wanted to marry for love, but being the child of a psychologist and a professor of, among other things, psychology, I knew that love was never the answer.

"But you would be a family without being married," said the rabbi.

"Because we want it to be official," said Steven.

I nodded at him. This, I thought, would certainly be the right answer.

"Why?" asked the rabbi.

Steven and I looked at each other. We were now out of answers.

"I don't know," Steven said.

"It's okay," said the rabbi. "You don't have to know. Getting married isn't always a rational decision. We want to marry, but we don't always know why."

"Whew," said Steven. "I was worried that we'd failed."

"Now," said the rabbi. "Do you want to have children?"

"I don't know," said Steven, answering for me.

"Probably," I said, answering for Steven.

"Hmm," said the rabbi. "You haven't discussed this?"

I laughed, and explained that we'd given each other's response.

"Well, it's fine if you don't want to have children, but if you do, let me suggest that you do it sooner rather than later." He looked at me. "How old are you?"

"I just turned thirty-one."

"Well, I'd say you should do it soon if you're going to do it. Let me tell you a story." He then went on to tell us about a couple who had waited too long, hadn't been able to conceive, and who had ended up adopting two disabled children with life-threatening diseases.

"They're very happy and they have a great marriage," said the rabbi. "But listen to me: please, just have kids soon."

Steven and I sat in silence, not wanting to look at each other.

"Unfortunately, that's all the time I've got today," said the rabbi, glancing up at the window in his office door.

I followed his gaze and saw that his next appointment was waiting outside. We said quick good-byes, made an appointment to see him again in two weeks, and were out the door.

"That wasn't exactly what I was expecting," I mumbled to Steven as we made our way out of the synagogue.

"I know," said Steven. "I mean, what the fuck was that about hurry up and have kids. Can't we just worry about getting married first?"

I rubbed my forehead. "It's everywhere, you know."

"What is?"

"This whole thing about the evils of waiting too long. It's all over the fucking media all of a sudden."

Sometimes it seems like whatever you're obsessed with at the moment the whole world is also obsessed with. Just before Steven proposed I felt like it wasn't possible to turn on the television without seeing an ad for De Beers, or to get on the subway without having women shove their ringed fingers in my face. When I'd been shopping for a wedding gown a few months earlier I couldn't open a newspaper without seeing articles on wedding gowns or ads for gown sales. But with the baby issue, I didn't think it was just me. Around that time a book called *Creating a Life: Professional Women and the Quest for Children* put the issue on the cover of every magazine and every news show with the assertion that 49 percent of women earning over $100,000 a year are childless after forty. The media love stories about how women can't have it all, and this was no exception. *Sixty Minutes* ran an episode that featured twenty-something female Harvard Business School students announcing they were certain they'd be able to reproduce into their fifties, followed by a cluster of sad-eyed forty-something business executives who had Waited Too Long. *Time* ran a cover story about infertility after thirty-five, showcasing a different group of women who had Waited Too Long.

I decided that if I was going to drive both Steven and myself crazy obsessing over my reproductive capabilities, then I at least wanted to have my facts straight; so I looked around for some statistics that would give me some insight. But it turns out that there is a statistic for every side of the story: 43 percent of women of child-bearing age are not having children, but 71 percent of *Fortune*'s Most Powerful Women in Business have children; the childless percentage among women in their forties has increased by more than half in twenty-eight years, but the Census Bureau says that "childless levels are approximately the same now as they were a century ago." The National Organization for Women argues that women are being purposely scared into having kids, citing TV ads and billboards produced by an unknown source telling women to reproduce sooner. And still others worry about population growth, which in the United States is sinking precariously close to an "even replacement rate"— meaning the number of births that must occur for the population level to remain where it is. With the exception of a few groups who are proponents of zero population growth, most people in the world see an even replacement rate as a bad thing, ostensibly because we are all in favor of the continuation and growth of the species, which becomes less of a sure thing the lower the birth rate sinks. I for one think that zero population growth might not be such a bad idea, particularly when one considers the effect it might have on New York real estate prices.

But even though I'd learned both sides of the story, the infertility maelstrom left me adding numbers late into the night. *If I'm thirty-three when I go off the pill, and it takes us three months to conceive, and then another nine months of being pregnant, will that give me enough time to really establish a career and perhaps buy a house? What if I'm thirty-four, but it only takes us a month to conceive . . .* Was this any way to have a baby?

And while I didn't know if I wanted kids or not, what I did know was that I didn't want to be one of those women who Waited Too Long. Because other women know who they are. We whisper about them in hallways at work, we smile and offer helpful hints. (I know them all, even though I've never tried to conceive: Just relax, take your mind off it. Have you bought an ovulation kit? Is it him? Is it YOU?) And all along we think, that will never be me. Look at me! Look at this body! Look at these hips, which must have been made for childbearing because they sure as hell weren't made for low-rise jeans. No, it would be far better to just decide one way or the other.

✦ ✦ ✦

A few weeks later Steven's parents called to ask about Tay-Sachs, the genetic disorder prevalent in Eastern European Jews that causes convulsions, blindness, paralysis, and eventually death before age five. Steven's father knew he was a carrier. If it turned out that both Steven and I were carriers, we'd have a one-in-four chance of having a child with Tay-Sachs. Steven's parents were both frantic that we get tested for the disease before we got married.

"I don't get it," I said. "Like if we're both carriers, we're not going to get married?"

"Right," said Steven. "I have no idea."

"Then why?"

"In case you get pregnant, I guess?"

"But if I got pregnant, we could test then. And anyway, I'm not getting pregnant any time soon."

"Let's just get tested and get it over with," said Steven.

"Fine," I said.

But we didn't. We were too lazy or too busy to deal with an issue as abstract as our genetic makeup.

Later that day my father called.

"Don't get pregnant before you go to India," he said.

We were going to India for a month on our honeymoon.

"You think it's going to happen that fast, do you?"

"It might," he said. "And you don't want to be pregnant in India."

It wasn't enough to worry about whether I wanted to create life. I wasn't even pregnant and I had to worry about the health of a nonexistent fetus.

After we hung up I called my mother.

"Mama," I said. "How did you know if you wanted children?"

"It's a totally irrational decision," she said. "You just know."

It wasn't until a few weeks later, when Kimberly and I went makeup shopping, that I began to understand what my mother meant. We were standing at the chaotic intersection of Fifth Avenue and Fifty-seventh Street, the epicenter of the Manhattan shopping world, trying to cross the street. The traffic slowed on Fifth Avenue, and I stepped off the curb, ignoring the Don't Walk sign flashing on the other side of the street. Most New Yorkers take Don't Walk signs to be a mere suggestion rather than an edict, and I expected Kimberly to step off the curb with me.

"Wait," Kimberly said, lightly grabbing my shoulder.

I looked at her, puzzled, then looked back up Fifth Avenue. There was a bus in the distance, but we certainly had time to cross.

"Let's wait for the light," Kimberly said. "Since I'm pregnant." She touched her flat stomach, patted hello to the little grouping of cells swimming inside her.

"Okay," I said. And for a moment I glimpsed the allure of babies. How amazing it must be to value someone else's life over your own. Someone that you don't even know yet.

After several months of apartment shopping for a version of our family that didn't even exist yet, Steven and I gave up. There were too many variables. Would there be a child? If so, what would it be like to have one? What floor plan would be best? I'd heard that children needed to be taken outside, for airing or something. So would it need a backyard? Would a cement alley do? A balcony? Would we have to move to the suburbs?

"You promised me that we would be Hip Married Couple," Steven said accusingly after a day of apartment hunting in Riverdale, a suburban section of the Bronx. "How can we be Hip Married Couple and live in Riverdale?"

I *had* promised him we would be Hip Married Couple. Our engagement had been partially contingent upon my insistence that being married didn't mean being boring, or becoming someone else. That we could be married and continue living just as we had before. We would stay in the city, we would have interesting jobs, we would go out with our friends. Being married, I had explained, did not mean moving to New Jersey and working for AT&T. But somehow in the midst of the wedding talk and the baby talk, we'd lost sight of that promise. After all, we had a wedding registry that included fancy place settings, I had a big white dress, I'd designed my own Martha Stewart–inspired save-the-date cards.

"You're right," I said. "What the hell are we doing?"

A few days later we settled on a three-bedroom rental two blocks from our apartment in Brooklyn. Or at least, the realtor called it a three-bedroom. Really it was more like a one bedroom with two small rooms. Rooms that would be perfect for an office. Or a nursery. Or shoes. Or a new fish. Or whatever we decided to do with them.

And as I sat in the realtor's office and signed the lease I realized that getting married, having a baby, and finding a new apartment were all intricately interwoven events. Because in getting engaged, Steven and I had unknowingly announced to the world that we might reproduce at some time. And yet, our one-bedroom apartment with its tiny kitchen and a bathroom so small I had to step out into the hall to towel-dry my hair, felt to me like living a lie. We had told people that we were ready to reproduce, should the urge arise, but I knew that there was no way that was possible, not with our current living situation. But now with the new apartment, the assumptions matched up with reality. Even if we didn't want to have kids, even if my maternal instinct never turned on and our office remained an office, at least now the story we were telling people through our marriage would correspond with the story we were telling ourselves.

"Did we make some kind of decision?" I asked Steven as we walked out of the realtor's office.

"About what?" Steven asked.

"You know," I said. "The baby thing."

"I thought we had a plan."

"Which one?"

"Get you pregnant at thirty-four."

"Yeah," I sighed. It all seemed so abstract, though. And Steven seemed so abstract about it. He tended to change the subject when I brought up babies, or to just shrug it off and say we'd talk about it later. "I feel like we need a more concrete plan than that. I mean, we have no way of knowing if we'll want babies then, but we're just planning on having them."

"Well," said Steven, "look at it this way. We know we don't want them right now, right?"

"Yeah."

"What about a year from now?"

"I don't know."

"Okay then. So why don't we wait a year and see how we feel about it then."

"Okay," I said.

And with that, I felt we had resolved something. We had decided not to decide, which seemed, for the moment, like the best possible decision.

6

Tradition!

No marriage contract is made without a quarrel.

—*Hebrew proverb*

"EVERYONE HAS A FUCKING STRING QUARTET," my brother grumbled over the phone.

I had made the mistake of asking his opinion on the ceremony music. It was getting on toward mid-April and Steven and I had been struggling with the ceremony music for the better part of a month. We'd finally narrowed down the choices to a wind trio or a string trio.

"It would be a string *trio*," I explained. "Not a quartet."

"Whatever."

Joshua had been going to a seemingly endless parade of weddings ever since graduating from college four years earlier; for some reason his friends were more eager to rush down the aisle than mine.

"Everyone has strings," he said. "And a perfect little choreographed walk down the aisle, and a perfect little string quartet, and it's all so perfect and lovely it makes me want to puke. I mean, what, not one person can have, like, a trumpet or something? An accordion? A harmonica? I hate weddings."

My brother is not usually a bitter person. He generally thinks that whatever he's doing is the greatest best most wonderful thing ever, that his friends are the greatest best most wonderful friends ever, and that the events he goes to are the best most fun thrilling events ever. I think he'd just watched one bride too many walk down the aisle. In any case, after that conversation there was no way I could even consider hiring a string combination of any kind, so the wind trio it was. Wind instruments were a little hipper than strings. Sort of. (See we're being different! No violin!)

As with everything else, I felt slightly stupid hiring the usual musicians for the usual stroll down the aisle. But there seemed to be no other option. One can't walk down the aisle in silence, and I didn't have any musically inclined friends or family who might want to contribute to the ceremony, so the choices were classical music or the wacky route. The wacky route being walking to, say, the theme from *Star Wars* or the baseball stadium favorite, "Another One Bites the Dust," but I didn't really see myself using my last walk as a single woman to express my sparkling sense of humor. Steven and I had briefly discussed using something from our CD collection, but the only groups we had in common (aside from classic stuff that everyone on the planet listens to, like the Beatles or the Rolling Stones) was Elliot Smith, the singer-songwriter, who sang mostly about death, loneliness, and the general misery of humanity; and, although we didn't know it then, he was only a few months away from committing suicide. The standard classic rock stuff was out by virtue of the fact that my parents had used it at their wedding. And not many people use "Here Comes the Bride" anymore, unless they're being smugly ironic. So classical music it was.

One Saturday afternoon Steven and I holed ourselves up in our office with the wind trio's repertoire and the computer, and trolled the Internet for the songs listed on the repertoire. We quickly eliminated anything that sounded like it might be used in a church service ("Jesu, Joy of Man's Desiring," "Ave Maria," "Panis Angelicus"), anything that might be construed as even remotely anti-Semitic (Wagner's Bridal Chorus and everything by Mendelssohn), and anything used in an AT&T commercial ("Canon in D"). That left about half the list. I had a vague idea that we could add some personal touches to the wedding by incorporating Jewish music into the ceremony, so we listened to some of the selections on the repertoire list, but every-thing sounded like the *Schindler's List* soundtrack. The problem with coming from a culture that has a centuries-long history of persecu-tion is that it's hard to find a Jewish song that doesn't sound like peo-ple being tortured or suffering intense emotional trauma.

"Oh well," I said. "At least we can use "Mazel Tov" for when you break the glass."

This, I assumed, was a given.

"Blech," said Steven. "I hate that song."

"Well it doesn't have to be that song. It can be some other kind of happy klezmer music kind of thing."

"I don't know," he said warily.

I reached across the table for the mouse and clicked onto a song titled "Sisu et Y'Rushalayim." Bouncy clarinet sounds filled the room. Okay, it sounded a little like *Fiddler on the Roof,* but I liked it.

"No," said Steven, pushing his chair back from the desk. "Absolutely not."

"But that's what you do at a Jewish wedding," I said. "People will be expecting it. They're going to shout *mazel tov* after you break the glass, and they'll be expecting Jewish music."

"It's cheesy and I don't want it at my wedding."

"But you can't have the glass breaking without it," I reasoned. "It's part of the glass-breaking thing."

"It's like everything I hate about Jewish weddings. That song honestly makes my stomach turn."

"You've never even been to a Jewish wedding, how can you hate it."

"Well I've been to synagogue and it's that whole thing. It's the same thing."

"So, what, our kids aren't going to go to Hebrew school then?" I huffed.

"Oh no, they're going," he said. "But you're taking them."

"Great," I said. "I'm taking them."

He nodded.

"So I'm going to be the religious one in this relationship. I don't want to be the religious one."

"Well," said Steven. "You have to be because I'm the funny one. I can't be both the religious one and the funny one."

"We know who's really the funny one, but that's okay, you can think you're the funny one."

"I don't just think I'm the funny one, I am the funny one," Steven said, folding his arms and leaning back in his chair.

"Sure you are. You're the funny one. And what am I, the organized one? The religious one? That sucks. Who wants to be that?"

"You're the cute one."

"Great."

We glared at each other.

"Let me play this one song for you that's Jewish that's great, okay?" I said, trying to steer the conversation back to the music choices. "I found it the other day when I was looking around on the Internet."

Two bars into the song Steven announced, "I hate this."

"You hate it? You hate it? This is what I was planning on walking down the aisle to."

"It is?"

"You hate it? How can you hate it?"

"I hate it. Quite frankly, it's cheesy. It's schmaltzy."

I was near tears. "Well, it's what I'm walking down the aisle to."

Steven's chair squealed as he stood up abruptly and left the room.

I sat by myself for a few minutes, staring at the computer screen. At a loss as to what else to do, I checked my e-mail. No one had sent me anything. I heard Steven moving around inside the apartment. A minute later he appeared at the office door.

"I'm sorry," he said. "I don't hate it."

I sighed.

"How can I walk down the aisle to something that you hate?"

"Well, I don't hate *you*, I love you."

"Yeah but now I'm going to be walking down the aisle and you're going to be thinking, God I hate this song. You're going to be standing there thinking about this very conversation, and how you told me you hated this song and I used it anyway. How can I use it now? I can't use it. You hate it."

"I don't hate it. Let me listen to it again."

He leaned over to the computer and clicked the play button.

"There are two versions," I said. "Maybe you'll like the other one."

We sat quietly listening to the first version, then the second version, then the music stopped and there was no sound but the whirring of the computer.

"You know," Steven said, "I think it's just with the strings that it's cheesy. I like it with the solo cello."

"We're not having strings. We're having a wind trio."

"Oh right, we're having a wind trio. I think it'll be fine then. I forgot. I thought we were having strings."

"You really think it's cheesy?"

"I think it just sounded cheesy with the strings. It'll be fine with the wind."

There was, of course, no way I could use the song now, and possibly no way there would be any Jewish music in the ceremony at all. It wasn't really an idea that made much sense, using Jewish music, as I wasn't familiar with anything but the few stupid songs we learned in Hebrew School, several of which had accompanying arm movements and were sung in rounds. It had just seemed like a quick and easy way to make the wedding more personal, more us. These songs were supposedly our heritage, our cultural traditions, although of course after years of Americanization the bulk of our musical culture had been reduced to "Sunrise, Sunset" and Barbra Streisand. So while these ancient Jewish melodies were supposed to be evocative of a traditional Jewish wedding, I'd never actually been to a Jewish wedding that used them. Kimberly walked down the aisle to "Jesu, Joy of Man's Desiring," and beyond that, well, I guess I hadn't been to any other Jewish weddings. My close cousins were either still single or had been married in secular ceremonies; my friend Lynne had married a Jewish man, but it was right after college and, not knowing any better, she'd walked down the aisle to "Here Comes the Bride." So I had no idea what Jews actually did on the music front. But the wedding industry had a few helpful suggestions. All the wedding magazines and books I read were big on personalizing your wedding, and what better way, they asked, than reaching back into history and rummaging through the great toy chest of traditions.

I read an article in Martha Stewart Weddings on the ancient English tradition of incorporating horseshoe motifs into your wedding. An accompanying picture showed a couple getting into an old-fashioned car; in the bride's hand dangled a fabric horseshoe. The caption said the photo had been taken in 1964 in London, England (if there is one thing better than being quaintly old-fashioned in the American wedding world, it's being English). Despite the fact that I had never heard of this tradition, nor known anyone to use horseshoes, the article insisted that "brides have been wearing pretty satin ones, looped around their wrists, for nearly a century." This was followed by detailed instructions on how to sew your own felt horseshoe. "Revive an age old custom," the article advised breathlessly.

And then there are the traditions that refuse to die, despite the fact that their meanings and origins have been long forgotten.

"Is it any wonder that the color of the infinite sky has inspired brides for centuries?" asked an article counseling brides to include blue in their wedding attire. Never mind that no one has any idea what the whole blue thing is about or where it comes from. Don't ask. Just wear it.

Curious to see if I could find out the origin of some of the traditional elements of the modern American wedding, I poked around a bit and discovered that most of our traditions don't even bear much resemblance to their points of origin. Bridesmaids, for example, were originally dressed like the bride in order to confuse any evil spirits that might be hanging around. The tradition has mutated into its current state—where bridesmaids dress like each other—serving no purpose at all, other than making the bridesmaids feel ridiculous. The origins of the best man stem from the days of marriage by capture. Back in the day, a man would tear into a neighboring village and haul off a wife. Sometimes, as you might imagine, the woman didn't so much want to be captured, and she put up a fight. So the man frequently brought along a friend to help him with the struggling maiden. And today, we honor the beautiful spirit of this tradition through the best man. Isn't that sweet?

On the other hand, some traditions have barely changed at all. I'd always thought that modern wedding vows sounded, well, modern, now that the whole bit about "honor and obey" had been gotten rid of. But according to the wedding history books, here's what people were saying back in the late 1300s:

> *Ich M. take the N. to my wedded wyf, to haven and to holden, for fayrere, for fouler, for bettur for wors, for richer for porer, in seknesse and in helthe, for thys tyme forward, til dethe us depart . . .*

Then, at the conclusion of the vows, all the woman's property went to her new husband, who immediately went off to rape and pillage in the Hundred Years' War, leaving his bride at home to die of the plague. It's creepy that today's wedding vows are only a few odd spellings away from sounding like a passage out of *Beowulf*.

The concept of a honeymoon dates to even earlier than the vows, a sequence of events that makes sense once you know that the honeymoon was originally a month spent hiding after the groom dragged off his captured bride, a woman with whom, one can safely assume, no vows were exchanged. Some versions of the origin of this tradition have the newly married couple hiding from the bride's enraged father and then appeasing him with gifts upon their return, as though a nice vase could make up for some silly raping and pillaging. Other versions say that the month away also included forty straight days of drinking mead, a honey-based wine, hence the term "honeymoon". If you think forty days of drinking sounds like a lot, you're in good company. Attila the Hun, who also went by the cute nickname The Scourge of God, is said to have died on his honeymoon from too much mead.

Equally exciting as dredging up long-dead traditions or incorporating ones that have lost their original meaning, is borrowing a tradition from some other ethnicity. Gloria Steinem made headlines a few years ago when she got married. It was a big story because she'd always said she'd never wed, but a less-reported side to the story was that she'd gotten married in a traditional Cherokee ceremony. Neither she nor her husband is Cherokee.

But the wedding industry would have been pleased; it encourages a little tradition borrowing here and there. Not happy with your own cultural traditions? Why not take someone else's? I found an entire section of The Knot devoted to wedding customs (tagline: "embrace your heritage or rejoice with traditions from around the globe"). Another wedding website recommends borrowing a tradition that "Turkish brides have been practicing for generations," which involves having single members of the wedding party sign the bottom of the bride's shoes. The person whose name is not rubbed off by the end of the wedding festivities will be the next to marry.

But in choosing which traditions to borrow and which traditions to leave alone, most couples are universal in omitting the painful ones. While there may be brides out there having single guests sign their shoes, I doubt there are many who are incorporating the other ancient Turkish tradition of pelting the groom with footwear. It turns out that many wedding traditions have a sharp edge to them—in early Roman weddings the groom broke a loaf of barley bread over his bride's head; in Northumberland, England, the wedding cake was thrown into the air, along with the plate, to determine the fertility of the couple. Today some couples retain the tradition of having guests throw things at them, but the airborne objects have become less painful. Rice has given way to birdseed, which in turn has been replaced with confetti, glitter, or soap bubbles. Similarly, few couples adhere to the ancient tradition of no-sex-before-marriage. And with Jewish weddings, not many people rush to conduct the traditional wedding day fast. On the other hand, when I asked Steven if he planned on breaking the glass, he looked at me wide-eyed and said, "Hell, yeah." Why? Because that's fun. A twenty-hour fast, not so much fun. People like their traditions, they just like them easy.

Of course, I was as guilty of rummaging through traditions as anyone else. I'd thumbed through The New Jewish Wedding and I'd picked out my own dead tradition to follow: yichud. In English this meant that Steven and I would spend fifteen minutes alone after the ceremony. Originally the fifteen minutes were allotted for the groom to bring his new wife back to his tent, where they would consummate the marriage. Some versions of this tradition had him leaving the tent waving a bloody sheet. The modern incarnation of the ritual has the couple doing, what else, eating. When I heard about the tradition I thought it sounded like a good idea to have some time for just the two of us right after the ceremony, and Steven agreed, although not without the obvious barrage of consummation jokes. (Is fifteen minutes enough? Where will we get a bloody sheet?)

A few months later it was made embarrassingly clear just how removed I actually was from this tradition. Steven and I were meeting with the (non-Jewish) photographer, and my mother happened to be there. I told the photographer we would be doing "this fifteen minutes alone thing" after the ceremony, so she wouldn't wonder where Steven and I had disappeared to.

"Oh," she said. "What's that called? It's something like, um, *likud.*"

"Yeah," I said. "I think that's it."

"No," said my mother, annoyed. "*Likud* is a political party in Israel."

And then there was my great-grandmother's wedding band. The one that my grandmother gave me at Passover. I'd been thrilled at the idea of having my very own heirloom to use in the wedding ceremony, and best of all, it was inscribed in Hungarian, a weird and bouncy-sounding language of which I knew one sentence (I love you, grandmother). How very ethnic and cultural and all that good stuff. A few weeks after Gammy gave me the ring I brought it to the jeweler to have it resized to fit my ring finger. Steven and I were sitting at a long table in the jeweler's office as he examined the ring, magnifying lens clipped onto his glasses.

"Hmm," he said. "There's an inscription in here."

"I know," I said excitedly. "It's in Hungarian and I have no idea what it says. I need to get it translated or something."

I had mused for quite a while on what the inscription might be, and had come up with all sorts of intriguing possibilities—the Hungarian translation of a Hebrew prayer, a secret joke between my great-grandparents, something beautifully romantic my great-grandfather had said to my great-grandmother.

"Well," said the jeweler. "It says . . ."

I stared at him.

"From Joe to Helen."

I gasped. "You speak Hungarian?"

"No," he said. "It's in English."

"What?" I snapped.

He handed me the ring and the magnifying glass. "See for yourself."

I held the ring under the glass and, sure enough, that's what it said. In plain English. I guess I'd been so excited by the possibility of my own mysteriously ethnic heirloom, my own little element of traditionalism, that I'd completely overlooked the fact that it wasn't all that mysterious or ethnic. I had looked at the engraving and just assumed it was in Hungarian. But with the English words staring me in the face, it occurred to me that of course my immigrant great-grandparents would have been trying to be more American and less ethnic. They would have seen an engraving in English as modern and trendy.

So why this desperate attempt to incorporate random traditions into modern weddings? Part of it is related to the whole personalizing-your-wedding mania. One book I read about lavish weddings claimed that the biggest fear most brides and grooms have on their wedding day is not that they will eventually get divorced, but that their wedding won't be memorable. I can't say that this didn't cross my mind. In our conversations, Steven and I repeatedly talked about how we wanted our guests to have a great time, how we wanted people to come away feeling like our wedding had really been something special. And what better way to personalize your wedding than to dig up some long-dead tradition from another culture and incorporate it into the ceremony? It may not be meaningful, but it's sure to be memorable.

Sociologists generally agree that tradition is all about dealing with change. When things get too scary in the world, people revert back to the things they see as safe, comforting. I remember reading an article shortly after 9/11 on how the TV show *Friends* had suddenly become popular again. The writer attributed this to the fact that people were looking for solace in the routine. They wanted to convince themselves that everything was okay, and as long as the usual gang was hanging out at the usual coffee shop talking about the usual nonsense, they could pretend that the world was normal again. And so it is with wedding traditions. As marriages have become more precarious, as social norms about what it means to be married or a couple or a family continue to shift and change, people seek refuge in traditions. It just happens that the traditions they choose aren't always traditional.

Bucking tradition can sometimes be as hard as deciding which arbitrary dead traditions to resurrect. When I informed Marlene that there would be no cake at the wedding, she said, "Oh."

Silence.

Then: "That's interesting. Don't you think people will be expecting cake?"

"Maybe," I said, "but I hate cake. I like crème brûlée."

And my mother was even less pleased to learn that there would be no hora, the circular dance that always involves having your Great Aunt whomever drag you by the hand and force you to perform hernia-worthy kicking motions while smiling.

"No hora?" she gasped. "What kind of Jewish wedding doesn't have a hora?"

"The hora is a new tradition," I said. I'd researched it for just this argument. "People only started doing it in 1946 after they formed Israel."

"Really?" she said.

I'd known this would blow her mind. Cultural traditions seem to play on our inability to remember things over the long term. As far as she knew, as far as most Jews know, the hora has always been a part of Jewish celebrations. People have been hora-ing for centuries. Turns out it's not true, and I gloated with my knowledge.

"Still," she said. "I mean, no hora . . ."

When I mentioned the lack of hora to my father a few days later, he was more to the point.

"If you don't do the hora," he said, "it won't be a Jewish wedding."

"It's two Jews getting married," I countered. "How much more Jewish can it be?"

"Hmph," came over the phone. This is what my father says when he's run out of other things to say, but feels he hasn't adequately expressed his displeasure.

"Hmph to you," was all I could think to say back.

There are a lot of traditions that people accept as being old and venerable that were practically invented last week. Invitation format is another example. Most etiquette books and wedding guides I read talked about invitation wording as though it had been written by the hand of God. I was under the impression that there was only one way one could possibly word an invitation, that all invitations since the beginning of time had contained the words "request the pleasure of your company," that to write anything else would be sheer folly and would cause all your guests to immediately check "no" on your response cards. Then in one of my wedding history books I happened across the invitation to President Grover Cleveland's wedding in 1886. It had been handwritten, and was dated five days before the ceremony (so much for his save-the-date cards). The invitation read:

My dear Mr. ——

    I am to be married on Wednesday evening at seven o'clock at the White House to Miss Folsom. It will be a very quiet affair and I will be extremely gratified at your attendance on the occasion.

Yours Sincerely,
Grover Cleveland

And this was a wedding at the White House. So, those ancient, unbreakable traditions—not always so ancient or unbreakable. But one's parents won't always see it that way. The hora issue came up again months later, long after the wedding, when I happened to mention to my mother that if I had children I would probably want to give them traditional Jewish names.

"I'm so surprised," she'd said. "I mean, you guys didn't have a hora."

There were a whole range of traditions Steven and I had decided not to follow. There would be no first dance. There would be no bouquet toss or announcing of the bridal party. In fact, there would be no bridal party, only a matron of honor and a best man. But no matter how many traditions we easily agreed to cast aside, there were still others to argue over. The music issue was only the first in a series of battles over our allegedly shared cultural heritage.

"So are you going to wear a beanie thingy?" Steven's friend Sasha asked him one night while we were out to dinner.

"A yarmulke?" Steven asked.

Sasha nodded and took a sip of wine.

Steven threw me a quick glance. I thought I glimpsed worry.

"I dunno."

"You're not?" I asked.

"I hadn't really thought about it. Probably not."

I stared down at my plate. I had just assumed that he would wear one. And right then, it seemed very important. It seemed like if he didn't then we couldn't get married. If he didn't, I knew my entire family would demand to know why. Wasn't he Jewish, they would ask. Jews got married in yarmulkes, didn't they? Was he a self-hating Jew, then? What kind of anti-Semite was I bringing into the family, for God's sake?

Sasha coughed uncomfortably, and somehow the topic of conversation changed. I tucked away the yarmulke issue in my mind for discussion later, and stewed through the rest of dinner. When we got home, I pulled the topic back out. I was standing by my dresser, taking out my earrings. Steven crawled into bed with *War and Peace*.

"Can you put your book down please?" I sniped.

"Are we going to argue about the yarmulkes?"

"Yes."

Steven snapped the book shut. "I don't want to wear one."

"Why not?"

"It's stupid. I hate that shit."

"It's not stupid. It's what Jews do when they get married. You know I don't feel strongly about most of this stuff, but I do about this. This I actually care about. I'd really like it if you wore a yarmulke."

"Why? I don't get it. You're not usually into this religious stuff."

"It's not the religious part of it. I could give a shit about the religion. It's just that it's tradition. I'm proud that I'm marrying a man who's Jewish. That makes me happy. I want to show it off."

Steven fiddled with the cover of his book.

"Plus, my family will drive me nuts about it if you don't," I added.

I pulled back the covers and slid onto my side of the bed.

"And besides, I was planning on getting yarmulkes for the guests. I mean, my family will certainly want them, and most of my guests will want them. So it'll look pretty weird if all the guests are wearing them and you're not."

"I don't care how it'll look. I don't want to feel stupid. I don't want it to feel like it's my bar mitzvah."

"You'll look cute in it," I said.

"The hell I will, because I'm not wearing one."

I felt my heart starting to beat quickly, my face felt hot. I wasn't sure why this was so important to me, but it was. I had to get Steven to wear a yarmulke or the whole thing would be off. Ordinarily I didn't care about practicing Jewish traditions. We paid twice-yearly visits to synagogue on the high holidays, and those were under duress. Worse, I knew that the traditions we'd chosen to keep and the ones we'd chosen to discard were completely arbitrary. Jewish grooms are supposed to get married in a *kittel,* a long white robe that they're also supposed to be buried in, but you don't tend to see a lot of those around. And if you looked at it that way, we weren't supposed to be living together before being married, we weren't supposed to be eating pork chops for dinner, and Steven was supposed to buy me for something equal to the value of one shekel. But the further away you get from your own culture, the harder you try to grasp onto the few things that remain. And wearing yarmulkes was the tradition that had remained; it was a tradition that I knew my family would see as unbreakable.

It shouldn't have been a surprise to me that Steven didn't want to wear a yarmulke or walk down the aisle to ancient Jewish melodies.

This sort of thing had come up in our relationship before. The very first Chanukah we'd spent together I'd been astounded to learn that he didn't want to light the menorah with me. Ever since my weepy teen years I'd looked forward to the day when I might have a Jewish boyfriend who would want to light candles with me—not that I'd lit candles since high school, but I could start. For most of my twenties I'd dated a long string of Catholic men who all encouraged me to light candles in front of them while they watched, which always gave me the feeling that I was participating in some sort of anthropological study—Ways of the Urban Jew or something along those lines. Of course, I didn't have plans to light candles in the first place, but these non-Jewish boyfriends always seemed to feel that if I wasn't going to celebrate Christmas, the least I could do was to observe Chanukah. The end result was that I usually dragged out a beat-up menorah my mother had mailed me one year and self-consciously lit candles in silence. But that first Chanukah with Steven, when I pulled out the menorah, I had all sorts of romantic visions in my head of us quietly singing together in the candlelight. Instead he sat in a chair and ignored me while I lit candles and sang the prayers to myself. It was almost as though he found my Chanukah observance embarrassing. For a year or two after that I just ignored Chanukah altogether. But the December after we got engaged I'd dug out the menorah again, and finally Steven had indulged me and sang along and even lit a candle or two. So I guess I'd been under the impression that his lack of Chanukah observance was just a passing phase. He knew the prayers, after all.

I lay back on my pillow, stared at the ceiling and thought about crying, which I knew would probably make Steven feel guilty enough about the issue that he would begin to waver. But it felt dishonest. I wanted him to wear one, but had it not been for my family, I wouldn't have insisted. Because when I thought about it clearly, I saw what an irrational request it was, that he should adhere to one random tradition over any other random tradition.

"It's really important to me," I said, finally. "I'd really like you to wear one."

Steven grunted. "I'll think about it."

+ + +

The fact was that even our families were confused as to which Jewish traditions to uphold and which to ignore. This became abundantly obvious when it came to picking the menu. On the first go-around Steven and I had chosen ribs and chicken for the rehearsal dinner on Saturday night.

"I don't know," said my mother when I told her about the menu. "Maybe they should be beef ribs."

"But pork ribs taste better," I argued.

"But what about people who keep kosher?"

"Who keeps kosher?" I asked.

"Your father's friend Arthur."

"He's not coming and anyway, I don't think he's kosher anymore."

"What about the rabbi?"

"He won't be at the rehearsal dinner. And, you know, he could have the chicken."

"I don't know," said my mother. "I don't think it's a good idea."

"Well, then it's probably an even worse idea to have prosciutto at the cocktail hour."

"Oh, Hana," my mother gasped into the phone. "You're having *prosciutto*?"

"No good?" I said.

"On the night of the wedding?"

"I like prosciutto," I argued.

"I know, but, you know, usually I don't give a shit about this kind of stuff, but to have pork at a wedding just seems like flaunting it. Like you're just doing it because you can. I just think it's not right."

After I hung up with my mother I called my father for his opinion.

"Absolutely not," he said. "You can't have prosciutto."

"But I like prosciutto," I whined. "Why can't I have it?"

"Because the wedding is like a religious holiday and you can't have raw pig on a religious holiday."

"Argh."

"Sorry," said my father.

"Well, what about the pork ribs the night before? It's not actually on the night of the wedding, so it's not really a religious holiday. There's nothing religious going on that day at all."

"Well," he said. "I guess that's okay."

"What about crab cakes?"

"When?"

"Instead of the proscuitto."

"Look," my father harrumphed. "Have crab cakes some other day."

And so it was decided: pork ribs were in, prosciutto and crab cakes were out. We would all be delusional together.

One tradition Steven and I both agreed on was getting married under a chuppah, the Jewish wedding canopy. The Vermont inn had no idea what a chuppah was or how to get one, so it was up to us to find one and get it to Vermont. A chuppah is supposed to consist of a piece of cloth suspended by four handheld poles, but of course, like everything else in Wedding Land, it's become a lot more than that. Most chuppahs these days are freestanding and covered with decorations. Some are made entirely of flowers. Some are wrought iron or gilded or God knows what else. And the piece of cloth can be made from some heirloom something-or-other, from your grandfather's prayer shawl, from your duvet cover, from a piece of cloth you picked up at a street fair in Guatemala—from anything, really.

I wanted to go as simple as possible with the chuppah. My parents had been married under a handheld one, which was considered very retro and ethnic back then. I didn't really care whether it was handheld or freestanding, I just wanted it to be simple and cheap, so I went on The Knot and typed in "chuppah" to see if anyone had any suggestions. What came back, mixed in with a long list of postings about where one could rent or buy a chuppah, were a handful of brides asking if it would be sacrilegious to get married under a chuppah if neither the bride nor the groom were Jewish. They really liked the symbolism, they said. They thought the chuppah was pretty; it made for lovely wedding day photos.

So whereas Steven wanted our wedding to be not-so-Jewish—he didn't want to walk down the aisle to Jewish music, he didn't want to dance the hora at the reception, and he didn't want anyone yelling *mazel tov*—other non-Jewish couples seemed to find our discarded traditions endearingly ethnic. Today ethnic is hip—Americans wear nose rings and eat *nuevo* Latino–Chinese fusion and buy tribal handicrafts imported from remote regions of the globe—but one's own ethnicity is never hip.

I sorted through the chuppah postings on The Knot and found some that said there were a few Judaica shops in Manhattan that rented chuppahs. Well, officially they're called Judaica shops, but I always think of them as Jew Stores. They're the places you go once a year to buy Chanukah candles, or if you're feeling particularly religious one week, you might pop in for a box of Shabbat candles. So for secular Jews, they're basically big candle shops. For more heavily practicing Jews, they're a lot more, but to me it's the place I go when I'm feeling like making my old Hebrew School teachers proud. And now it's the place you go when you're getting married.

One cold Sunday that April, Steven and I trudged up from Brooklyn to a shop on the Upper West Side. The Judaica stores in the city, with the exception of a few super-fancy ones that sell menorahs designed by famous artists and silver Christofle *kiddush* cups, are run by the orthodox Jewish population. So for your average bacon-eating, mini-skirt-wearing secular Jew, a visit to the Jew Store is a little bit like stepping back in time.

I had forgotten this, but was reminded the instant I opened the door. The store was swarming with children, and the volume level was at the rock concert end of the decibel scale. A cluster of women in dark pageboy-style wigs and long skirts hovered up front by the cash register. Bearded men in yarmulkes stood together in the aisles, deep in conversation or huddled over various books. When Steven and I walked in, everyone instantly ignored us. It felt like we'd walked into someone's living room, where it just happened that some stuff was for sale. I glanced down at my hip-hugging jeans, my tight low-necked sweater, suddenly feeling overtly slutty and large-breasted, and buttoned up my jacket, even though it was stuffy and hot in the store.

We made our way over to the cash register and stood silently next to the cluster of women, who glanced sideways at us and then carried on their conversation. I imagine that stores like this existed all over the Jewish ghettos of Eastern Europe at one time, that the ghetto streets were filled with women in long skirts and hats and pageboy wigs and a whirling tumbleweed of children. And suddenly I felt very not Jewish at all, and all the arguments we'd had over which remaining fragment of our traditions to clutch on to felt absurd.

I cleared my throat. The women continued to ignore me.

Eventually, a bearded man came over and asked Steven what he wanted.

"We're looking to rent a chuppah."

"Yeah," said the man. "We've got one." He spoke with a slight accent. "It might be out. Lemme check."

He pushed his way through the narrow aisles, past the children, and called out to some other unseen person in Yiddish. I picked out the word "chuppah" in his sentence, but nothing else. Little white strings peeked out from under his sweater, swinging as he walked. I knew they were called *tzitzis*, and that they were attached to some larger garment that Jews were supposed to wear, but standing there in the store aisle I suddenly had no idea what the garment was. I thought maybe a prayer shawl, but was that right? Or was it a belt? A sash?

A moment later the man returned.

"Okay, today it's out, but tomorrow it comes back. When do you need it? Tomorrow?"

"No," said Steven. "Not till August."

"Oh, well," the man rolled his eyes, as though this were the most ridiculous thing he'd ever heard. "In August you can certainly have it."

"What does it look like?" I asked.

"What does it look like?" asked the man. "It looks like a chuppah."

"I mean, um, what color is it?"

"What color? I don't know. Hey, Shlomo," he called across the aisle to the invisible man. "The chuppah, what color is it?"

"Blue," came the answer, floating across stacks of Shabbat candles and prayer books. Shlomo poked his head around the aisle and looked at us.

"It's blue," he said again. "Velvet. With a *magen David* on it. In gold, I think."

He walked down the aisle toward us, holding a stack of books. I gave a mental nod of thanks to my parents for torturing me with six years of Hebrew School, without which I wouldn't have known that a *magen David* is a Jewish six-pointed star.

"You know, it's got poles," Shlomo explained.

"The cover has hooks," said the first man. "You attach it to the poles. We've got handheld and also the other ones."

"Or you can attach it to your own poles," said Shlomo.

I'm not sure what it is about Jews and their love of blue velvet, but religious items are always blue velvet. The Torah scroll covers in most synagogues are blue velvet, the little bags people use to store their prayer shawls in are blue velvet. And not just blue velvet, but always blue velvet with either silver or gold embroidery. The Jewish people are not, for the most part, known for our visual artistry, with the notable exception of Marc Chagall, and I believe that a good portion of our failure to excel in that area stems from an obsessive reliance on blue velvet. There is not a lot of fine art executed on velvet.

"How much is it?" I asked.

"Fifty dollars," said the first man. "You pick it up, then you bring it back the next day or a few days later, it doesn't matter when."

"So, you want it?" asked Shlomo.

I looked at Steven. I didn't want it, and I would have bet the cost of the wedding that he didn't want it, for one simple reason: too Jewish. There is a fine line in cultural Judaism between embracing your heritage and shouting "I'm a Jew" from the rooftops, and this chuppah was shouting. I didn't want to get married under something with a gold embroidered Jewish star. And I didn't want to get married under blue velvet. Of course, there was no way to explain this to the bearded man with the yarmulke and *tzitzis*, for whom there was no such thing as too Jewish. There was no way to explain that blue was not in the color scheme for the wedding, that getting married under a chuppah was Jewish enough, I didn't need a big ass Jewish star above my head. To this man, this was a chuppah, this was what we had asked for. We wanted a chuppah, no? Well, here you go. And cheap too.

"Do you want to think about it," I said to Steven.

"Yeah," he said, nodding. "Thank you very much. We'll think about it."

The two men looked at each other and shrugged. I knew what they were thinking: damn secular Jews. You offer them a perfectly good chuppah and it's not good enough.

A few weeks later I found a place in the garment district that would sew me a plain ivory chuppah for seventy-five dollars. Now here was a place that was used to dealing with your garden variety secular Jew. When I walked in they handed me ten different fabric swatches. They said they could match any wedding colors I threw at them. They wanted to know what color my dress was, what color the flowers would be, whether the wedding would be indoors or outside. And best of all, they could sew it in a week and mail it to Vermont.

I stopped by Ellen's store one day in the midst of the music-yarmulke controversy. She was reorganizing the store windows—as far as I could tell the windows were in a constant state of reorganization. I think this had to do with the fact that she sat in the store all day and stared at the windows, and after a while she got sick of looking at them and had to take everything down and put up something new.

"I'm thinking," said Ellen, "that the music thing is not such a big deal."

She stood, hands on hips, in the storefront and examined a clay pot overflowing with small rugs. "I think this pot thing needs to go.

What would happen if we put it in the corner over there, and then we put that chair here with that rug draped over it? Would that look hip and cool or would it look stupid?"

I picked up the rug Ellen was pointing to, a big fluffy white thing that looked like it had once belonged to an enormous sheepdog, and dragged it into the window.

"It's just that I spent, like, weeks looking for a song to walk down the aisle to, and I finally found one and he hates it, and he doesn't want to have any Jewish music at all. Granted, I can find a different song, okay, fine. But, I mean, you tell me, what the hell are we going to play after he breaks the glass? 'Celebration'?"

"What's 'Celebration'?"

"You know, 'celebrate good times come on!'"

"Oh for God's sake. I'm sure you can find something that you both agree on that's not Kool and the Gang."

Ellen walked to the back of the store and got a wooden chair.

I moved a large porcelain plate out of the way and helped her put the chair into the window. "It just seems so ridiculous that two people who don't really even care that much about religion and are the same religion in the first place can find so much to argue about, you know?"

"Okay," said Ellen. "Here's the thing. You know my friend Murtazah?"

"The art student guy?"

"Yeah. So he's a Shiite Muslim, and his fiancée is a Shiite, but they can't get married because their parents are different kinds of Shiite and they can't agree. And so they have to have all these negotiations in India and they're probably not going to be able to get married."

"Wow," I said. "Religion sucks."

"Yeah. So, just be thankful that you guys can at least get married."

I lifted the white rug on top of the chair and tried to drape it artfully.

"I'll do that," Ellen said, elbowing me out of the way.

❖ ❖ ❖

That night I decided to approach the music discussion from a different angle.

I was sitting at the dining room table staring at the wind trio's repertoire list when Steven walked in the door.

"Hi babe," I said.

"Hi." He walked over to me and we kissed hello.

I gave him a minute to put his messenger bag down on the floor and take off his shoes. I had just read an article in some bridal magazine that advised against launching straight into wedding crap the instant your fiancé walked in the door. It had seemed moronic when I read it—as though women are so crazed by wedding planning that it's the first thing that comes out of their mouths the moment they see their fiancés. But. This was important.

"I've been thinking about the music situation," I said.

"Mmm." Steven walked over to the fridge and took out a beer.

"Why don't I just walk down the aisle to whatever I want to walk down the aisle to, and you can walk down to whatever you want to walk down to, and for the rest we don't have to use any Jewish music."

Steven popped the top off the beer, let it clatter quietly on the kitchen counter and came over to the dining room table. He peered over my shoulder at the repertoire list, took a drink from the beer bottle.

"Okay."

"But," I said, "I'd really like it if we could find something Jewish to play for when you break the glass. We can look around at other stuff, if you want, but I just think it's going to sound silly."

Steven sighed.

"And I'm not going to walk down to that song you hated."

"I didn't hate it."

"Yes you did. I'm not going to use it. I'll find something else."

It took another few days to get all the music selected. In the end I chose a different Jewish melody for my walk down the aisle, and for everything else we settled on Bach. In the final struggle over the glass-breaking music Steven relented and agreed to use a Jewish song, so long as it wasn't something he'd learned in Hebrew School.

We looked around for some modern alternatives, but everything sounded equally silly, and I guess ultimately he decided it was more important to me than it was to him. And so we went with the song I'd wanted in the first place, the one with the bouncy clarinet sounds.

As for the yarmulke issue, I came to understand Steven's point of view better when we went back to meet with the rabbi a second time. We took the train out to Pleasantville again on a cold and rainy day, and when we arrived at the synagogue, the rabbi was sitting at his desk. As he ushered us into his office it dawned on me that he wasn't wearing a yarmulke. I don't know how this had passed me by at our first meeting, but I'd never seen a rabbi without a yarmulke, and now I couldn't stop staring at his head.

We sat down in the same spots we'd sat in on our earlier visit— Steven and I on the leather couch, the rabbi next to us in a chair, as though we had assigned seats.

"So," said the rabbi, opening a folder. "Let's see where we were."

He read over some notes in his folder.

"Right, okay, we were really just at the beginning. So," he looked up at me. "Are you Jewish?"

I nodded.

"Really?" he wrote something in the folder. "Both parents?"

"Yes."

"Any Jewish education?"

"I was bat-mitvahed," I said curtly. I wondered if he was also going to ask me to name all the original tribes of Israel.

"Wonderful," he said, and made some more notes.

Apparently I had passed.

"Now," said the rabbi. "Is there anything you want to ask? People usually come in with lots of questions."

"Actually, we do have some questions," Steven said. "Are there any specific dimensions for the chuppah?"

"You're going to have a chuppah?" asked the rabbi.

We both nodded.

"That's wonderful," he said. "The chuppah can be any size, it just depends who you want to put under it. You know, it needs to be big enough to fit whoever you want under there."

"What about the *ketubah*?" I asked.

The *ketubah*, the Jewish marriage contract, was an old tradition that had lately been resurrected. My parents had a *ketubah* somewhere once, but it was just a little piece of paper and nobody paid much attention to it. I'd never even known such a thing existed until recently, but *ketubahs* are a huge business. My friend Kimberly had an enormous one hand-painted by an artist. After the wedding she framed it and hung it in her living room, over the sofa, proclaiming it art. I'd been poking around online a little looking at sites like ketubah-ketubah.com, and had found most of the *ketubahs* to be garish and wildly expensive. I was hoping the rabbi would just have a small one to give us so we could circumvent the whole fake-new-tradition thing.

"You want to have a *ketubah*?" the rabbi asked incredulously.

"I thought we had to," I said.

"Well, it's your choice," he said.

"But I thought that otherwise it's not a legal Jewish wedding or something."

The rabbi shrugged.

I was completely confused. I had grown up in a more conservative synagogue and was used to being told what to do when it came to religion. But this rabbi seemed to indicate that we could pick and chose whatever we wanted from the supermarket of Jewish traditions. We could take a chuppah and pass on the *ketubah* and who knew what else.

"We were also thinking about doing that fifteen-minutes-alone thing," I said.

"The *yichud*," the rabbi nodded. "That's terrific. In that case, maybe you guys would like to do an *aufruf*."

Steven and I looked at each other, slightly panic-stricken.

"That sounds painful," said Steven.

The rabbi smiled pleasantly. "No, it just means you come to a Friday night service before your wedding and you do an *aliyah* and then there's a special blessing for the bride and groom. It's a way of being blessed by the congregation."

I stared at the floor. I wasn't interested in the least in making yet another trip out to Pleasantville, and even less interested in sitting through an entire Friday night prayer service. I also knew that Steven would rather do just about anything than go to synagogue.

"Sure," said Steven. "That sounds great."

"Are you kidding?" I said.

The rabbi looked at me like I'd just stolen his new red balloon.

"I just mean, um, it's not really your kind of thing."

"Well, why not?" said Steven. "Why not do it?"

I looked back at the rabbi. He was smiling at me patiently.

"It was just a thought," he said. "It's not required that you do it."

"No," I said. "I'll do it."

"Yeah," said Steven. "Let's do it."

"Great," said the rabbi, writing in his folder.

We discussed a date for the *aufruf*, spoke briefly about what would happen at the wedding ceremony, and then were quickly ushered out the door, as the rabbi's next appointment was waiting in the hall. As Steven and I pushed open the synagogue's double doors and stepped outside, I turned to him.

"Who *are* you?" I said.

"What do you mean?"

"You hate synagogue. You hate religion. You don't want to wear a yarmulke."

Steven shrugged. "I got caught up in the moment."

I shook my head.

"And I thought you'd want to do it," he added. "You like that crap."

"I was worried you thought that. I don't care, really. But if you want to, I'll do it."

"I think we're doing it anyway," he said. "We're all signed up."

We stood quietly in the rain. It smelled great out there in Pleasantville, all green and leafy and wet, the sweet smell of rotting grass and fresh dirt mixed with the last chill of winter. It smelled like my own suburban childhood. I shivered a little and Steven put his arms around me and kissed my forehead.

"So," I said. "Now I understand about the yarmulke."

"Why?"

"Because even your rabbi doesn't wear one. I've never met a rabbi without a yarmulke, but I guess for you it's normal."

"Well," said Steven. "I was talking to Scott about the whole yarmulke thing." Scott was Steven's best man and former roommate.

"Uh huh."

"He *wants* to wear a yarmulke."

I laughed. "Well of course he does, because he's not Jewish, so it's all cool and ethnic and he wants to, like, respect our weird ethnic traditions."

"Yeah, he was pretty excited about it. He was like, ooh, do I get to wear one of those yarmulke things?"

"Right. He doesn't know enough to think it's dorky."

"Right."

Steven leaned back from me a little and looked into my eyes.

"So," he said. "I think that if it's that important to you and that important to your family, I don't want to make anything more difficult than it already is. We've got enough things to worry about."

I smiled. "You'll wear one?"

"I'll wear one."

"Aw, thanks, sweet. I love you."

"Yeah, yeah."

An old beige car pulled into the parking lot entrance a few yards away and drove around to the front of the synagogue where we were standing. I brushed my hair from my eyes. It was damp from the rain. Steven and I slid into the back seat of the car, the suburban version of a taxi, and rode silently over winding hills, past wooden houses and front lawns and freshly painted white fences. Sitting back there against the stained cloth seat, watching the suburbs pass through the car window while someone else drove, it was, for a moment, like being a child again.

7

These Colors Don't Run

He who wants a rose must respect the thorn.
—*Persian proverb*

ACCORDING TO THE WEDDING WORLD, I WAS SUP-
posed to have a favorite flower. This theoretical flower was
supposed to go in my bouquet and be incorporated into
the table arrangements. And the bouquet and table arrangements
were, in turn, supposed to guide my choice of wedding colors, which
the wedding magazines indicated were the key to successful wedding planning. But the whole flower concept was a difficult one for
me. Sure, I like flowers as much as the next person. They're pretty.
They smell nice. But women are presumed to have a kind of relationship with flowers that I've just never had. We're supposed to
demand roses on Valentine's Day (and they'd better be long-
stemmed) and expect dates to occasionally surprise us with a bouquet or a loose grouping of hand-plucked blooms. But I've always
felt uncomfortable with this presumed floral intimacy. This is in part
due to the fact that I know the names of perhaps six flowers (roses,
daisies, carnations, lilies, violets, tulips), and even those I can't
always tell apart. And I guess I've always had different floral expec-
tations of my boyfriends than most women. Generally, if they
brought me flowers, I broke up with them. I didn't want anyone
pigeonholing me. After a boyfriend sent me two dozen roses on

Valentine's Day, I called him up and explained the principles of markup and supply and demand.

"Do you understand economics at all?!" I cried into the phone. "If you have to send me roses, at least do it the day after Valentine's Day when the price is reasonable." But I knew at that point it was a lost cause. The relationship was over. How could I be with someone who understood me so little as to think I wanted roses on Valentine's Day?

So, as all the wedding magazines said I should start my floral adventures by figuring out what colors would be in my bouquet, my first step was to convince myself that I actually wanted a bouquet. The bouquet was yet another one of those silly wedding traditions that I didn't really see the point in. I'm getting married, so I have to walk down the aisle holding flowers? What for? I don't usually walk around with flowers. But then it occurred to me that if I wasn't holding something, I wouldn't know what to do with my hands. So then I thought, well, what about a book. That would be different, and more me. I could carry a favorite book. This thought was immediately followed by intense angst as I tried to figure out what book could possibly be appropriate for a walk down the aisle. The dictionary? My journal? A Sylvia Plath anthology? And what would I do with the book once I got up to the chuppah? Read it? And if I didn't read it, everyone would want to know: why is she carrying a book? What book is it? No, it would have to be flowers.

Which brought me back to the color issue. If there was a bouquet, then there would be colors in it, and these, ostensibly, would become the wedding colors. I didn't know at the time that choosing wedding colors was actually the first step in a long, dangerous descent into wedding obsession. Because once you've chosen colors, you become a color fascist, and demand that everything be colored baby blue, or celadon green, or burnt sienna. I'd seen this happen to women on The Knot, who wielded their assorted hues like gang colors, with the periwinkle and sage contingent wanting nothing to do with the light pink and espresso brown posse.

"Those who have their bridesmaids wearing rust/cognac . . ." began one Knottie's post about coordinating bridesmaid dresses and bouquet colors. Another bride declared orange "the most hated color." And I remembered one of the first posts I'd come across, back when I was just starting down the bridal planning path, demanding that someone find the bride Victorian Lilac ribbon, damn it, because she couldn't get married without it. I recalled articles that had seemed strange back in those halcyon days, suggesting that brides "match your cocktails to your color scheme," or ads for color-coordinated accessories that asked, "Working within a wedding color scheme? Our Color-Coordinated Collection lets you customize to your heart's content." But, like all horrors beyond one's comprehension, I thought: *that will never happen to me.*

So I decided to go about choosing wedding colors in the simplest way possible. I picked up the latest issue of *Martha Stewart Weddings*, which, as luck would have it, had a big picture of an antiquey-pink, champagne and gold-colored bouquet on the front that month, and tore off the cover. Voilà. Wedding colors.

I informed both my mother and Marlene of my color choices, and they immediately ran out and bought the same issue of *Martha Stewart Weddings*. Somehow it was then decided that they would both dress in the wedding colors. I can't say exactly how this arose, other than they had both been asking me what colors they should wear. Initially I had told them, I don't care, wear whatever you want. But they didn't believe me. They asked again. Both of them. And so, finally, they decided to coordinate.

For Marlene, this was easy. She's got dark auburn hair and olive skin and looks great in both gold and champagne. For my mother, with her salt-and-pepper flyaway hair, this was cause for major drama.

"I don't look good in any of those colors," she said over the phone after reviewing the color choices.

"There are three," I said. "You mean you don't look good in any of them?"

"No, they wash me out."

I sighed. This was supposed to be easy. And she was the one who had wanted to dress in the wedding colors in the first place.

"What about teal?" she asked.

"Teal isn't one of the colors."

"But what if it was one of the colors? Teal is a nice color for a wedding."

"Yeah," I said. "In 1953."

"Why, teal is so dated?" she snapped.

"Look, Mama. I picked out the colors. Teal is not one of them. And anyway, Kimberly and Marlene already got their dresses so, you know, feel free to wear teal, but I think it'll look silly."

I closed my eyes for a moment and marveled at the fact that somehow I had now been thrown into the position of insisting on wedding colors that I didn't care about in the first place. I suppose I could have simply capitulated and said, sure, wear teal, but I suddenly had a mental image in my mind of the wedding party dressed in muted late summer shades standing next to my mother in a glowing teal dress. She was already going to be removed enough from the rest of the wedding, between her small number of guests and my father's tendency to dominate whatever situation he's in. She didn't need to be dressed completely differently on top of that.

"What about a nice chocolate brown?" my mother offered. "I look good in brown."

"Mama. Come on."

"Well," said my mother. "I don't know what I'm going to do."

A few days later she e-mailed that she'd found an ivory dress that was perfect. I forwarded it to Kimberly, who had been following the color drama from the beginning.

"Is it weird for my mother to wear ivory?" I wrote in the e-mail.

Kimberly's dress had been decidedly less hassle. I'd told her to just go out and buy whatever she wanted. I couldn't be bothered with picking out a bridesmaid's dress for her, and given that she was going to be six months pregnant at the wedding anyway, I didn't see that it mattered much what she wore. Minutes after I forwarded the e-mail, my phone rang.

"Are you kidding me?" Kimberly yelled into the phone. "She can't wear ivory! You're wearing ivory!"

"That's what I thought," I muttered. "It's weird, right?"

"It's ridiculous. It's the most ridiculous thing I've ever heard, I mean . . ." I heard sputtering on the other end of the line. In Kimberly's book, there was no bigger breach of etiquette.

"You're supposed to stand out," she finally managed. "How can you stand out if you're both wearing the same color?"

I agreed, then hung up the phone and flung myself on the bed.

"Auuugghhh!!" I yelled. "I'm so sick of this wedding! And it's only June!"

Steven was in the living room reading. He'd made it more than halfway through *War and Peace*, and he chose to ignore me.

"Did you hear me?" I yelled. "I can't take it. I mean, do I care what the wedding colors are? No. But Kimberly says my mother can't wear ivory."

"Mmhmm," said Steven.

I picked up the phone and dialed my mother's number to break the news that ivory was out.

"Hmm," she said. "What about silver?"

"For God's sake, Mama. The wedding colors are champagne and pink and gold. Is silver champagne or pink or gold?"

"Well you don't have to be nasty about it," she said. "What about brown?"

I sighed. It was clear she wasn't going to budge, and I'd had enough.

"Fine," I said. "Wear brown."

My grandmother was equally unhappy.

"I have to get a new dress?" she complained when I told her the color scheme.

"Only if you want to be in the wedding colors, Gammy. But you're walking down the aisle, so it will look nice if everyone's coordinated."

"I'm walking down the aisle?"

"Yes. I told you. You're walking down with Joshua." I didn't mention that she would also be walking down with my other grandmother, my mother's mother, a woman with whom she'd had a barely civil relationship even before the divorce.

"Ooh, I'm walking down with my grandson," she squealed. "That's wonderful."

"Okay, so you're going to get a dress?"

"If that's what you want, I'll get a new dress. It's a stupid waste of money, but I guess that's what weddings are about."

"That's right, Gammy," I said. "That's what weddings are about: a stupid waste of money."

What the wedding industry, busy rhapsodizing about color coordination, doesn't tell you is that once you select colors, it becomes easy to just make every aspect of the wedding be in those colors. Which in turn spurs you on to become obsessive about every aspect of the wedding. Coordinating your cocktails with your colors is a great example. Who would even think about which cocktails are going to be served at the cocktail hour? A cocktail is a cocktail. But once you're thinking about how cute it would be if the cocktails were blue, or pink, or whatever, then you're thinking about the cocktails. Then you're worried that if you don't have a signature cocktail, everyone will think you're a huge failure, and at the cocktail hour, behind their randomly colored drinks, they will whisper about how they give your marriage four years at most.

The industry benefits by egging brides on to care insanely about every little thing. A bride who worries about the tiniest detail is more likely to buy more magazines to help her figure out what to do with all the tiny details. She is more likely to order personalized confetti in a color that matches her bridesmaids' dresses and chocolate bars with her and her fiancé's names spelled out in chocolate. And along those lines, a bride with a theme is more likely to buy personalized votive candles for her "candlelit" theme, personalized hot sauce for her "hot 'n spicy" theme, or personalized golf tees for what one can only assume is her "boring sports" theme.

One article I read in *Modern Bride* offered creative wedding ideas sent in by readers. Culled from hundreds of responses, by far the most startling idea came from Jackie, who wrote that her "fantasy butterfly theme" would include "ice-blue dresses, pastel pink-and-yellow flowers and silver vests and ties for the men."

Just stop and visualize that for a moment.

Because there's more.

"We'll decorate the room with silk and feather butterflies and also tie them to the bridesmaids' bouquets with silver twine," continued Jackie. "The flower girl (our two-year-old daughter) will have white wings to look like a fairy princess. Each table will be named after different butterflies, with beautiful centerpieces to match. The cake will be decorated with small sugar butterflies on each tier leading up to the floral cake topper."

Think about the amount of planning, energy, and time spent running around town looking for silver twine involved in pulling off a fantasy butterfly theme. I couldn't help but wonder what sort of acid-induced trip had even spawned this idea, and what other drugs would propel poor Jackie through the remainder of the planning process.

But *Modern Bride* loved the theme enough to feature it in their magazine, right next to another bride who was planning a wedding luncheon reception that would recreate exactly the picnic where her fiancé proposed, and a third bride who wrote, "I bought 150 mini treasure chests made of wood for my favors. I'm going to stain them and attach place cards with a ribbon, then I'll fill them with Hershey's kisses and add a note that says: 'A few kisses from the Mr. and Mrs.'"

The wedding history books say the personalization craze began in the 1950s, when couples began putting their names on matchbooks or cocktail napkins, and today has evolved to the point where couples create a total wedding world for themselves. That world can be entirely robin's egg blue and lime green, sports-themed, or populated by butterflies, but no matter what, it is a totalitarian state where the bride and groom issue edicts and the citizen-guests must obey.

The stereotype that dominates today is the obsessive-compulsive bride, the Bridezilla who demands that her bridesmaids dye their hair to match their dresses, or file their nails the exact same length. But of course most women don't start out this way. They are shaped slowly over time, after repeatedly being bashed over the head by article after article like the one in *Modern Bride*, by an industry that tells them repeatedly that their weddings must be perfect. That to have anything less means utter failure as a woman, as a wife, as a human being.

Perhaps the best illustration of this is the change in the number of wedding tasks. Most wedding magazines come with some type of checklist of organizational tasks that need to be completed when planning a wedding, things like "find a ceremony site," "decide on a caterer," or "choose a wedding cake design." And these lists have been growing astronomically. In 1959 BRIDE'S magazine told brides they needed two months to plan their weddings and listed twenty-one tasks to be completed. By 1970, the recommended planning time was six months and the number of tasks had grown to forty-seven. Today, a year is the generally accepted planning period, and the checklist that I used on The Knot lists 187 tasks. Granted, some of these tasks were probably combined in the past under one task (for example, "start working on invitation wording," "finalize your invitation wording" and "order your invitations" could just as easily be called "get invitations"). But even so, tasks like "begin envisioning your wedding," "start taking better care of yourself (eat right, exercise)," and "practice walking in your wedding shoes" could have only arisen out of a quest for perfection.

And even though I wasn't worried about having a "perfect" wedding, I heard the word endlessly drilled into my head. Lots of wedding retailers used it as a selling point. When I had been sorting through ceremony musicians back in March, I called one booking agent to tell him I had chosen another, less expensive group, who admittedly were not as good, but really, it's ceremony music— who the hell is going to notice. The booking agent was, of course, horrified.

"The music is going to set the tone for the whole wedding," he huffed. "Skimp on something else, but you want the ceremony music to be perfect."

Just once I would have liked to have a vendor say, "You know, you're right, $1,000 for three musicians to play four songs really is exorbitant, I wouldn't bother," or, "Yeah, no one will really notice if the clarinetist is a little sloppy, go for the cheaper group." But no, every vendor has to sell you on how, for this once in a lifetime occasion, it is necessary to hire the Boston Pops.

"It has to be perfect," demanded a Men's Wearhouse ad for tuxedos in one wedding magazine.

"Complexion Perfection!" screamed a *Modern Bride* article on skin care. "Whether you're dancing cheek to cheek with the groom or smiling for the camcorder, you want your skin to be clear, baby-soft, and radiant."

I don't think I fully believed the complexion perfection hype until I was personally accused of having less-than-perfect skin. My mother was in town visiting, and we'd decided to go to a bridal store in an attempt to locate an appropriately colored dress for her. She'd just come out of the dressing room in her eighth dress of the day, and we were standing in front of the three-way mirror in the main area inspecting it. It was the best option thus far—it had a jacket-like top and a long, straight, floor-length skirt, and best of all it was champagne.

The saleswoman came over to inspect my mother.

"What a beautiful dress," she said, and then turned to me.

I smiled at her a little warily. She had a big black poof of hair sprayed into a beehive of sorts, and long French-manicured nails.

"You're such a lovely girl," she said. "You're going to make a beautiful bride."

And then, she reached over and lightly brushed what I had always considered until that moment to be a barely visible scar on the top of my left cheekbone. It looked like an extra puff of skin or a small wrinkle, and it tended to become more visible when I was tired or stressed out. The scar was the result of the delusional belief, at age four, that whatever Mary Lou Retton could do, I could do. Which meant I was thoroughly surprised when my attempted back flip off a table ended with the corner of my face meeting the corner of the table.

"You're going to cover that up for the wedding, no?" she said.

Well, I wasn't. I didn't even know how I would begin to attempt covering up something like a puffy piece of skin. And anyway, I'd always thought of my scar fondly. It made me me. It reminded me of what it was like to be four and think I could do anything.

But then a few weeks later, a funny thing happened. In the midst of trying not to get obsessed about my skin, I became fixated on my teeth. Some years earlier I'd gone to a dentist who seemed to be involved in a kickback program from the tooth-whitening companies. I'd gone in for a cleaning and had been greeted with a color chart that gave my current tooth color a number (seven) so I could see just how far it was from the ideal tooth color number (one). I'd then been asked if I was interested in investing in a long and costly process of tooth-whitening. I hadn't been then, but of course that was in the era before Crest Whitestrips and extra-strength whitening toothpaste. It was possible that the rest of the world had also developed a sudden tooth-whitening fixation (perhaps everyone else had been shown the same dental chart), but it suddenly seemed as though white teeth were everywhere. Which meant in turn that my teeth had to be as unnaturally white as could be achieved using over-the-counter products. I decided to buy not only the tooth-whitening strips but also tooth-whitening toothpaste and a tooth-whitening liquid for extra measure. So I guess it should have been no surprise that about three weeks into the whitening experiment my teeth began to hurt. And they still weren't white. I took to staring at my teeth in the bathroom mirror for long periods of time. Not since the long-gone years of braces had I found my teeth so fascinating. I examined them in different lighting situations, compared them to white pieces of paper and manila folders. And despite the strange dull aches in my front teeth, I kept slapping on the strips. Pain or no pain, my teeth would be, dare I say it, perfect.

The bridal industry doesn't allow for someone who wants to have less than perfect anything, be it skin, teeth, or, as I discovered, shoes. I had decided to save time and money by ordering a pair of $30 white satin shoes from a bridal shoe website. There are a lot of shoe-obsessed women out there, and many of them were forking over $250-odd dollars for white shoes they'd wear once and throw away. For some reason this rationale made sense to me when it came to the dress, but for the shoes it seemed like an even dumber waste of money, especially given that with a floor-length gown no one was even going to catch sight of my shoes. Not once. But the wedding industry didn't care that I'd bought cheap footwear. When the shoes arrived, they came with a huge note inside, printed all in caps: YOU MUST ABSOLUTELY LOVE YOUR SHOES!! I must? What if I don't want to? What if I don't give a shit about my shoes? But it didn't matter. Even my $30 shoes that no one would lay eyes on had to be perfect.

Oddly, the two nuptials that the wedding industry holds up as the pinnacles of bridal perfection are those of Jackie and John F. Kennedy, and Princess Diana and Prince Charles. Neither of which, in reality, even approximated perfection. Princess Diana, the woman whom millions of people worldwide watched walk down the aisle, admitted to being utterly terrified at her wedding and worried that she was making the wrong decision, which, as we all know, it turned out she was. And at the Kennedy wedding, Jackie's father turned up too drunk to walk his daughter down the aisle, an event which would certainly send any Knottie into hysterics and years of therapy. At the very least, no bride would call a wedding with a falling-down-drunk father "perfect." And yet, brides are all encouraged to seek out this alleged perfection, to match our weddings up to the two most perfect weddings in the world, neither of which was actually perfect in the least.

Perhaps the scariest fact is that this quest for perfection has actually changed the way people now think about getting married. Planning a wedding that coordinates cocktail colors with bridesmaid dresses takes time. Lots of time. As a result, engagement lengths have been steadily stretching out beyond one year and sometimes beyond two. And I know that for Steven and me, we actually planned our engagement based on when we wanted to get married. I had heard that we would need to reserve a wedding location a year in advance, and we both agreed we wanted to get married over Labor Day weekend. So, he proposed in August. It wasn't exactly that cut and dried, but that was the general train of thought.

And no matter how much I told myself that perfection was silly and unimportant, the constant barrage of demands that I be a perfect bride with perfect skin and perfect shoes started to get to me. Not only that, it started to get to some of the unlikeliest of people. One beautiful, warm spring day in May, the kind of day where you're just happy to be outside and in Capri pants, my mother accompanied me to Kleinfeld for my final dress fitting. She wanted a chance to see the dress before the actual day of the wedding, and so I had arranged a fitting on a weekend that she would be in town.

Unlike a regular dress, once you purchase a wedding dress, it's not the end of the story. The dress lives at the store, and you have to make appointments to go back and visit it every few weeks. These are ostensibly for fittings and measurements, but I secretly thought of them as visits to some expensive folly I'd purchased, as though I had special privileges to view a painting at the Museum of Modern Art all by myself, in a little all-white room. I think it's also about getting more face time with the dress. Because the fact is that unless you're somehow able to figure out a way to use the dress after your wedding, you're really only going to spend eight hours max wearing the thing. But these visits, these little appointments where you put the dress on and have someone fuss over you and then take the dress off, make it feel like you get more wearing mileage.

We were running late by the time we got to Kleinfeld, because I always underestimated the time it would take to get there (I'm in Brooklyn, the store is in Brooklyn, how long could it take?), so we tore into the fitting room and I immediately began stripping. Rosa, the seamstress who had been assigned to me, arrived with the dress, her arm extended up in a futile effort to keep the long train from dragging on the floor. She slipped off her shoes—no shoes are allowed in the fitting area, lest they dirty the plush cream carpet and, in turn, dirty a dress—and pulled the fitting room curtain closed behind her. I had bought a tummy-sucking contraption to wear under the dress, which I pulled up with a fair amount of effort, as I was sweaty from rushing. Rosa stood back and watched me as though I was nuts.

"Why you wear that?" she asked in an indeterminate accent.

I shrugged. "So it's all smooth under the dress, I guess?" Someone along the way had suggested I get a fat-smoothing garment; I could no longer remember who.

"You don't need it," Rosa said.

I looked at myself in the mirror, tummy-sucking device glued to my ribs, and saw that she was probably right. In the course of planning the wedding over the past few months, I had forgotten to eat. Which was somewhat ironic, given that early on in the planning process I had made the radical decision not to go on a diet. Dieting brides seem to be a big business, with lots of gyms offering bridal workouts; and there is at least one for-brides-only company called Bridal Bootcamp, where brides spend a week starving themselves and doing push-ups while surrounded by other hungry women in a setting that must closely approximate the fourth ring of hell. The pressure to diet, yet another aspect of the pressure to be the perfect bride, is in fact so great that several months after my wedding, an acquaintance who was in the process of planning her wedding pulled me aside and asked if I'd been on a prewedding diet. Not because I looked so skinny, but because she was trying to decide if she should go on a diet, despite the fact that she wasn't overweight.

"I get the feeling that everyone in the world goes on a wedding diet," she said. "I really don't want to, but I just feel like it's what I'm supposed to do, you know?"

I did know. But I had decided to be different. Mostly because I didn't want to look back at my wedding pictures and think, wow, look how skinny I was then. I figured, Steven loved me the way I was, extra-five-pounds or no extra-five-pounds. He was going to marry me either way, so in the meantime, why not eat chocolate?

Back in the Kleinfeld fitting room, I considered my reflection.

"Whatever," I said. "It can't hurt to wear the thing."

Rosa hoisted the dress over my head and I slipped it on. As she smoothed down the skirt and zipped up the back I turned to look at my mother.

She was looking at me a little strangely—not exactly grimacing, but not wild with pleasure either. All the wedding magazines had indicated that upon seeing me in my wedding gown she would cry, or scream with joy, or maybe even tell me she hated it, but she just stood there watching.

"So?" I said, finally. "What do you think?"

"What do I think?" she said. "I think it's perfect. I can't imagine a more perfect dress. I mean, it's just perfect."

Where she got that word, I have no idea. Perhaps it was over the transom, through which the sounds of the woman in the next dressing room kept floating in. It sounded like she'd brought her entire wedding party to her fitting. For the last half hour they'd been having a conversation about earrings, which I'd been absentmindedly tuning in and out of. And then there was shrieking, and oohing and aahing coming through the carpeted divider, and someone kept saying over and over, "It's absolutely perfect. It's absolutely perfect."

Back in my silent dressing room, Rosa kneeled on the floor with a mouthful of pins and began pinning up the hem and taking in extra fabric around the waist.

"All done," Rosa said finally. She leaned back on her heels and admired her handiwork. I did a little twirl to check the length of the hem, and all the pins on the bottom glittered under the bright fitting room lights. If I'd had an idea of perfection in my mind, this might have been it.

But this is the problem: once you embrace the idea of perfection, it holds you in its grasp and refuses to let go; and even though I was not using the word "perfect" I had the sense that I wanted things to be "right," which is more or less the same thing—and by that, I meant that I wanted the little things to be right. I wanted menus and I wanted them to look nice. I wanted little floral arrangements in the bathrooms that told my guests I had tried extra hard to make things nice for them. I wanted what I wanted. End of story.

And the end result was that, as much as I tried to fight it, as much as I tried to shut the wedding out of all the little crevices of my life, it crept in anyway, like grout. Because once you're thinking about all the million little things that you want to be right, you can't stop. It's ridiculous, really. Here you are making this huge life decision to spend the rest of your life with someone; and instead of thinking about love and marriage, you are tormented by retailers demanding that you have perfect tuxedos, that your skin be not just clear but radiant, that your cocktails match your lipstick. And the truth was, no matter how revolting I had found the industry's demands that I become obsessed with my wedding, in the end, I became obsessed. One lazy Sunday morning Steven and I were rolling around in bed, snuggling, kissing, thinking about going to Chinatown for some dim sum. Steven had just rolled me over for some more kissing when, midkiss, his lips on mine, I mumbled, "Don't let me forget to give the final okay on the invitations."

"Ohhh yes," he whispered, "I love it when you talk about the invitations. Are they going to be engraved or letterpress?"

Horrified by the words that had come out of my own mouth, I pushed him away and buried my head in a pillow.

"Uhh, yeah," he breathed into my ear. "Tell me they're going to be regular postage, tell it to me now."

But it wasn't until my brother called to ask about the softball T-shirts that I realized just how much the whole fascist color scheme had spun out of control. Steven and I had planned a softball game for the day of the wedding—there was a softball diamond right behind the inn, and it seemed like a fun thing to do with a big group of people—and I had come up with the idea of making T-shirts for the teams. It started as a joke. I'd seen shirts for sale on The Knot that said "bride" across the middle in small blue letters, which I guess are for women who are really excited about being brides and want the world to know they're getting married. They also had shirts that said "groom," and since the natural division for the softball teams was my family versus Steven's family, I thought it would be funny to get "bride" and "groom" shirts for the teams. I had delegated the entire softball project to my brother, who seemed to want to be doing something for the wedding, and he'd gotten a little carried away. He'd ordered bases, bats, and had now taken on the task of buying T-shirts. He wanted to do something more than the T-shirts on The Knot, so, in a moment of distraction, I'd said fine, do whatever you want.

"So," said Joshua. "Should the softball shirts be in the wedding colors?"

He was trying to be helpful.

"Oh God," I sighed. Had he heard from my mother that I was being a fascist about the wedding colors? Did my whole family think I had gone temporarily insane? Or was he just trying to be nice?

"No," I said. "The shirts don't have to be in the wedding colors."

"Well what colors should they be?"

I stared at the phone. I didn't want to be talking about softball T-shirts. I didn't want to be talking about the colors of softball T-shirts, or the style of softball T-shirts, or the cost or the quality. I was getting married. I wanted to be thinking about love and marriage and life changes. Instead, I was madly regretting that I'd ever come up with the softball idea in the first place.

"I don't know, Joshua, whatever colors you want."

"What about Mets colors?"

I groaned. "Electric blue and headache orange?"

"No good?"

"Okay," I said. "Do the wedding colors."

There then followed a brief conversation wherein I attempted to explain the meaning of the color champagne to my brother, who is not colorblind, merely male, and therefore not always aware of the names of shades in between the primary colors.

"Look," I finally said. "Just go with yellow."

As I hung up, I figured the color discussions were nearing a close. I was wrong.

Whereas all the women in the wedding wanted to wear coordinating colors (or, at least, they had started out that way), the men weren't so cooperative. Early on I had made an executive decision that all the men in the wedding party, which included the two fathers, Steven's best man, my brother and Steven's brother, would wear solid gray suits. Steven and I both disliked the look of having everyone in matching tuxes, and anyway, it was an outdoor wedding in the mountains—tuxes seemed wrong. But what about the ties? was the next question on everyone's lips. Once the women were wearing pink and champagne (I was still pretending in my head that my mother was going to finally end up with a dress in one of these colors), it made sense that the men's ties be some variant on pink and champagne.

When I informed my father about the gray suit decision, he was annoyed.

"Why do I have to match everyone else?" he complained.

"It's not really matching everyone else," I explained. "You can wear whatever suit you want."

"But I thought you said it has to be gray."

"Okay, you can wear any gray suit you want."

"What about the gray suit I have with the pink pinstripes?"

"Um."

"It's a nice suit," he said. "It's Versace."

My father has always been the clotheshorse of the family. He loves weird fabrics and bright colors. He went through a phase in the eighties when he wore enormous hats, causing me one of the more embarrassing moments in my high school career, when he strode across the softball field where my team was practicing one afternoon wearing an ankle-length black leather coat and a wide-brimmed felt safari hat. He also owns a black-and-white double-breasted thirties-gangster-style suit. Which is not to say that he doesn't look stylish. He does, but he also looks funny, which he says is the point.

"Don't you have a plain gray suit?" I asked.

"I thought you said I could wear any suit I wanted."

"As long as it's a plain gray one, you can."

Pause.

"Okay."

I hesitated. "And I bought the ties at Barney's, so I'll mail you one. You can have either a pink one or a champagne one. Everyone's wearing either pink or champagne."

"Why?" he demanded. "We all have to look alike? We all have to be in uniform?"

"You're not in uniform."

"Why don't we all wear epaulets? And brass buttons?"

"Fine," I said. "If you don't want to wear the tie, don't wear it."

"I'll wear it," he said. "I just don't understand why we have to be in uniform."

I didn't want to be obsessive-compulsive about the colors, I really didn't. But once I'd made a decision, I expected my family to comply.

After all, they'd expressed fairly minimal opinions up until that point, so I figured that they'd just be happy to wear whatever I asked them to. And in the grand scheme of wedding culture, I wasn't really asking all that much. I hadn't insisted that anyone wear an exact shade of puce, or dye their shoes gold, or wear rhinestone chokers. I hadn't made anyone go to Gingiss Formalwear to get measured, hadn't written one of those horrific Bridezilla letters to members of the wedding party that seem to float through my e-mail every now and then. Kimberly had even declared that I was "the coolest, most laid-back bride ever."

For her wedding I'd been one of six women swathed in identical golden hues of thick floor-length satin, in a backless dress that required a major hydraulic system of lingerie to keep my breasts in place. I had purchased satin shoes that adhered to the one-and-a-half-inch heel that Kimberly specified. (She didn't want to look short in pictures, she'd explained, so the bridesmaids should all wear low heels. Given that Kimberly tops out at around five foot one, one would think it unnecessary to point out that she *is* short, no matter what heel height her bridesmaids wear.) And I wore the little pearl drop earrings we were all asked to put on before the wedding. I had asked none of these things of her nor of anyone in the wedding party. All I had asked was that people wear one of three colors. Colors that initially I hadn't even cared that much about, until people started objecting.

A few days later my brother sent me mock-ups of the softball T-shirts. One featured a bright pink bride in a poofy wedding gown holding a baseball bat on a field of bright yellow. In an arch over the bride were the words "Schank Shaklan Wedding," written in a looping cursive—the same sort of script you might expect to find on the back of a leather jacket reading Mom's Bikers From Hell. The other showed a yellow groom in a top hat and tails in the same batting stance on a pink background, with the same wording. I immediately picked up the phone.

"So," I said to Joshua. "Um."

"Aren't they funny?" he said.

"Well, I guess I'll give them funny."

"No good?" he said.

I tried to be delicate. "They're a little, um, bar-mitzvah-ish."

Joshua said nothing.

"I like them," I added. "But, you know, they'd be better for your wedding. I was thinking something more, um, understated."

"Okay," said Joshua.

A few days later my father called.

"You're getting ridiculous," he said.

"What do you mean?"

"Joshua told me you're making him change the shirts."

"Did you see them?" I demanded. "They were awful!"

"Who cares," said my father. "He liked them."

"It's not his wedding."

"You just have to control everything," said my father. "Joshua can't have his shirts, I can't wear the suit I want to wear."

"Well for God's sake, if it's so important to you to wear your stupid pink suit then wear the stupid pink suit. Everyone else is going to be in plain gray, but if that's too hard for you, then do whatever you want."

"I want my daughter back," my father yelled.

"What are you talking about?" I yelled back.

"I used to have a daughter who didn't care about who wore what suit or what color whoever's nails were or any of that garbage."

"I never said anything about anyone's nails. I don't know what the hell you're talking about. I'm not allowed to say that I didn't like Joshua's shirts? I mean, did you see them? They were truly horrible."

"So what?" yelled my father.

"This is ridiculous," I said. "I'm hanging up."

I slammed down the phone.

Yes, the wedding was taking over my life, but I didn't think it was making me into a different person. In the grand scheme of things, I still thought I was being pretty laid back and easy.

8

A Ribbon Runs Through It

Marry a mountain girl and
you marry the whole mountain.

—*Irish proverb*

IF CHOOSING WEDDING COLORS HAD BEEN BOTH mind-numbing and maddening, it was nothing compared to the weekend-long planning trip to Vermont. For weeks before the trip I stressed. The more I thought about it, the more I feared I'd made a monstrous mistake. I had, after all, been the one to make the somewhat sadistic suggestion that both my mother and Steven's mother accompany us up to the inn for a weekend chock full of wedding tasks, but it turned out that the trip wasn't difficult for the reasons I had assumed. I'd worried that the mothers, who had never met, would hate each other, that they would hate the inn, that they would hate the entire state of Vermont. None of that turned out to be the case.

The mothers got on great. They yakked the entire six-hour drive from Brooklyn to Vermont. In preparation for the trip I had created a wedding binder, which was essentially a big black plastic folder. It had started out as a place to put receipts and had grown into my own scrapbook of obsession. I had filled it with torn out magazine pictures of floral arrangements, hairstyles, table settings. But perhaps the scariest binder items were the spreadsheets: I had one spreadsheet that estimated the cost of each item based on the total budget, and another that listed all the guests we'd invited, with columns to check off who had replied, which gifts they'd sent, and if we'd sent a thank you note. The fact that I'd not only created such a binder but also come to rely on it was so beyond the pale that I simply chose not to think about it. The mothers, on the other hand, thought my binder was fabulous and spent most of the drive bonding over its contents. They discussed hairstyles, table decor, dishes, and floral schemes. Somewhere in there Marlene offered to draw upon her years at the Fashion Institute in New York and sew us fifty gold table runners, and my mother volunteered her services in assembling seventy in-room baskets. But by the time we reached Vermont, they had both agreed it would be better to leave these things in the hands of experts, and instead do what they did best: supervise.

When they ran out of wedding topics they shifted to the difficulties of raising children in what sounded like nearly identical suburbs. Steven and I grew up about an hour apart as the crow flies, on opposite sides of the New York–Connecticut border. I liked to think about us as children sometimes. I don't picture chance meetings in Stop & Shop or passing in the backseat of cars on the highway. Instead I just see myself going through the activities that peppered my childhood—playing softball or picking the wild blackberries that grew behind the house, or pretending to be the last Mohican while tiptoeing as silently as I could manage over a wooded trail rumored to be an old Mohawk footpath. And then I pull back my mental camera and see the dotted line of the state borders, and on the other side of the border I see a little version of Steven playing soccer or being driven up and down the hills of suburbia. Somehow it makes me feel good. I like to think that all that time I was busy living out my childhood there was someone else living out his just a few miles away whom I was destined to meet and marry.

It was late by the time we reached our destination, and a sleepy silence had settled over the car. In the dark the inn looked beautiful. It was an old white three-story colonial building, gently floodlit in front. Just looking at it made me feel calm and rustic. Each story had its own balcony lined with rocking chairs and potted plants. It was the sort of structure that looked like George Washington had slept there only yesterday.

The mothers stirred in the back, then peeked their heads through the gap between the front seats.

"Oh," said one, "it's lovely."

"Beautiful," said the other.

"Just perfect."

"Wonderfully restored."

They seemed to be in some sort of superlative compliment competition.

The inn consisted of a main building and several outbuildings, little white clapboard houses along the main road that had once belonged to the more prominent citizens of the town. Since it was only May, the inn had yet to get too busy, so they were generously allowing us to stay in one of the houses for free. Well, sort of generously, given the amount of business we were about to hand them.

As we stepped out of the car I felt the heavy silence you only find deep in the country. I always think the sky feels incredibly close up in the mountains, as though if you could just make it to a high enough mountain you could reach out and grab a handful of slate-black night sky. A few stars peeked through clouds, but all around us was a thick darkness. We made our way in silence into our house, chose our rooms, and quickly wished each other good night.

Steven and I had ended up in the largest bedroom in the house—a suite with a large sitting area and a big, canopied four-poster bed. Steven fell asleep immediately, but I lay awake, looking at the dark shapes the furniture made and the slashes of starlight that shone in through the gaps in the blinds. Years of living in New York mean that sometimes when I get out of the city I find the rest of the world too quiet to allow me any sleep. I have come to expect drunk people yelling beneath my window at three in the morning, or techno coming up through the floorboards just as I've turned out the light. But it wasn't just the quiet. I was up all night tossing as various flower combinations and colors ran through my head. I compulsively went over my list of things to accomplish on the trip (pick hairstyle, pick flowers, pick food, get mothers to like each other), silently ticking off the items in my head, then starting again at the beginning. Wedding Land had pushed me toward the brink of obsession, and now, in the quiet Vermont night, I acquiesced. I was ready for whatever the wedding world would deliver. Bring. It. On.

In the morning I woke to the sound of a large truck lumbering up the gravel driveway in front of the house. I nudged Steven.

"Mmmph," he said, then opened his eyes.

"Babe, there's a large truck outside the window."

I propped myself up on one elbow and studied his reaction. Steven sleeps on his stomach with his face buried in his pillow. He closed his eyes. "Okay," came from the pillow.

"Did you sleep?" I asked, flopping back down onto the pillows.

Steven made some waking up noises, then rolled over onto his back. "Sort of," he said.

"Yeah. I didn't. I'm anxious."

Steven stared up at the ceiling. "I'm anxious too. It's hard to sleep with two mothers in the house."

"They seem to be getting along, though."

"Yeah."

We stared silently at the ceiling for a moment.

"I guess we should get up," I said.

Steven sighed. "I guess so."

A little while later I made my way downstairs while Steven finished getting ready. My mother was already waiting for me at the bottom of the stairs. She was sitting at a little desk with her small leather address book in front of her. She looked stressed out, but she usually does, so I wasn't sure how to interpret the stress. Was it just anxiety from meeting Marlene and having to be nice and get along with everyone?

"Good morning," I said hesitantly. "How'd you sleep?"

"I slept okay," she said. Apparently there hadn't been much sleeping getting done in our little house. "But there was no hot water this morning. They had to send a maintenance crew to fix it."

"What happened?" I asked. "You turned on the shower and there was no hot water?"

My mother nodded.

"Did you let it run?"

"I let it run and I let it run, and then I knocked on Marlene's door and she said she had no hot water either, so I called the front desk."

I felt a flash of annoyance cross my brain.

"That's weird," I said. "Because we had hot water." How just like my mother to cause drama in the first few minutes of our trip. Okay, if there was no hot water then there was no hot water, but still.

I took a deep breath and told myself I was overreacting. Marlene and Steven came downstairs a few minutes later and we all went across the street to the inn to have breakfast.

By nine A.M. my mother and I were on the road heading for the hairdresser. Steven and Marlene had stayed behind so Steven could give his mother a tour of the inn and the town. The hairdresser's was like a salon straight out of *Steel Magnolias*. It was on the first floor of a little wooden house with rickety floorboards. Old-fashioned hair drying chairs were positioned at random intervals across the floor, and the whole place seemed to be on a slant. It felt like someone had just decided to open a beauty salon in her living room. There seemed to be a bunch of women there just hanging out. Or at least, there were a bunch of women in the place, and no one was doing any hair cutting. Some were sitting beneath silent hair dryers, leaning forward on the vinyl seats to make a particularly important point. Others were leaning up against racks of nail polish. None of them looked like they'd recently purchased any of the beauty salon's services. Or at least, if they had, then I was in trouble.

Everyone turned to stare at us as we walked through the door.

"Hi," I said to the woman behind the desk. "I have an appointment for a wedding hair consultation thing."

"Oh," she said. "I don't work here. Does anyone know where Joanne is?"

After some mumbling and shuffling a heavyset woman wearing a faded turquoise sweatshirt appeared and introduced herself as the owner of the salon.

"We spoke on the phone," she said.

I smiled and nodded.

"Did you bring pictures?" she asked.

I held up my wedding binder. Joanne didn't even blink. I bet she'd seen worse. We walked over to a yellow vinyl chair positioned in the middle of the room. I sat down in it, and Joanne pulled up a chair for herself and my mother.

"Now," she said. "Let me see your pictures."

I began pulling them out. First a picture of my dress. Then a swatch of fabric from the dress, as though that might somehow influence my hairstyle. Then three pictures of different hairdos. My mother and Marlene had sorted through the fifteen or twenty hair pictures I'd pulled out in the car and had narrowed them down to these three, all of which were variations on a theme. I have long hair that had been stick straight until I turned fourteen, at which point it decided to attempt curliness and only mildly succeeded, leaving me with hair that can be coaxed into curls or straightened flat, but that when left to its own devices chooses a happy, frizzy medium. Despite the recent craze for straight hair, I usually wore it curly because I still thought of myself as a girl with stick-straight hair who had only recently been blessed with curls. And so all the hairstyles were variations on a curly-haired theme. They had long tendrils pulled free of a romantic knot at the nape of the neck or were mostly freed hair with a few pieces pulled back or somewhere in between. I would not be wearing the traditional bald look—the one where the bride pulls every scrap of hair off her face and piles it on top of her head, then frees a few locks of hair and subjects them to a curling iron, giving her a look somewhere between an eighteenth-century French courtier and a Hasidic Jew.

Joanne sat with the pictures in her hand, but didn't look at them as I handed them to her. Instead, she looked at my mother. My mother smiled politely back.

Joanne cocked her head, stared for a minute longer.

"Your hair is parted on the wrong side for your face," she said.

My mother took this in. She looked at herself in a nearby mirror. "You know," she said. "You're right, it is."

I looked at Joanne.

Despite her instinctual knowledge of hair-parting techniques, she seemed not to have applied any techniques at all to her own locks, which were closely cropped at the side of her head in something resembling a bowl-cut-meets-the-Marines.

Joanne glanced through the pictures quickly, nodding. "Okay," she said. "We can do any of these."

I looked at her. The sleeves of her sweatshirt were dirty.

"Do you think they'll look good?" I asked.

"Oh yeah," she said. "You've got great hair."

Great hair, which was apparently parted on the correct side of my face.

"Okay then," Joanne said, standing up. I had expected some kind of test run or general hair experimentation, but none came. Before we knew it, we were being ushered out the door.

My mother and I stood in front of the salon, blinking in the sunlight.

"Well," she said. "That was quick."

"I thought she was going to, like, show me something with my hair, you know?"

"I know," said my mother. "That's what I thought."

As we slid into the rental car I wondered if I should be worried. After all, it was just hair. And I had a lot of it. How bad could it be?

That afternoon the four of us went to the florist. Or rather, we went to a store that clearly thought it was in some way connected to the floral trade in that there was an attached greenhouse that smelled like dirt and there were baskets and vases for sale, but there were no flowers to be seen. There was a table filled with maple syrup in little maple leaf–shaped glass bottles, and chalky smelling soaps labeled MADE IN VERMONT and little packages of nicely wrapped teas, but nary a flower. The store was in one of those typical old, dark buildings you find in Vermont, the ones that look like they were built 250 years ago and not touched since. The floorboards creaked as we clomped over them, examining the store, picking up pieces of Vermontalia and setting them back down, waiting for someone to appear. After a while, a harried-looking woman with a blond ponytail popped her head in from the greenhouse and asked if we needed help.

"We're here for a meeting with Colleen," I said.

The woman smiled. "That's me. You must be Hana."

Colleen and I had spoken on several occasions, and not once had the conversation gone smoothly. The first time I called to ask if they had any pictures of the floral work they'd done. There had been much rustling on the other end of the phone, after which there was a long silence followed by a dial tone. I called back and got Colleen, who informed me she was the owner and apologized for hanging up on me.

"We've had two weddings this weekend," she told me. "So everything is just a bit crazy."

I inquired again about the pictures. I wanted to get a sense of their style, although if I didn't like it my only other option would be to haul flowers up from New York myself, as they were the only florist within at least a twenty-mile radius of the inn.

"Oh, yeah," said Colleen. "We always forget to take pictures of our stuff, so unfortunately we don't have anything to show you."

"Oh," I said.

"Sorry about that."

How I was supposed to hire a florist without seeing even one picture of an arrangement they had put together was beyond me, but in the end I hired them anyway. I figured, a flower is a flower is a flower. How bad could they be?

The next time Colleen and I spoke things didn't go much better.

"Hi," I said when she got on the phone. "I'd like to make an appointment to meet with you. I'm planning a trip up to Vermont in May and I wanted to make sure you were available."

"Okay," she said uncertainly. "Weekends are generally bad for us because we've got weddings, but I think we're pretty free in May."

"How about the last weekend in May?"

"Oh, we can't do it Mother's Day weekend."

I wrinkled my forehead. Mother's Day never had been and never would be the last weekend in May. One would think a florist would know this.

"Okay," I said. "How about the last weekend in May?"

"Memorial Day weekend is bad too," she said. "We absolutely can't do it Memorial Day weekend."

Memorial Day weekend was also not the last weekend in May.

"Okay," I said. "How about the last weekend in May?"

"Is that Memorial Day weekend?"

"No."

"Okay. Then that should be fine."

Somehow I had anticipated this meeting would go more smoothly. Maybe it's all the snow and ice up there in Vermont, I thought. They have those long cold winters, probably don't get out much, maybe aren't used to things like, say, talking to customers or making appointments. But the lack of flowers at the florist's made me reconsider my hasty rationalizations.

"So," said Colleen. "Why don't you pull up chairs?" She motioned to four rickety stools, which we set about dragging across the concrete floor towards the counter where she was standing.

"Now, let's start with the bouquet, because everything depends on that."

I breathed a sigh of relief that I'd ultimately decided to have a bouquet. I could only imagine the tizzy it would have thrown the floral selection process into if I'd strolled in and announced I would be walking down the aisle with a book.

I opened up my wedding binder and began pulling pictures from it. First I handed her the cover I'd torn off of *Martha Stewart Weddings*.

"These are the colors I was thinking of," I said.

"Lovely," said Colleen. "Now, these are all roses. Are you thinking you want roses?"

"I don't want roses," I said. "I was thinking something more interesting than roses."

"Hmm," said Colleen. "I think the only flowers you can get in this color that time of year are roses."

I looked at my mother and Marlene. They both sat silently staring at Colleen. They gave no indication as to whether they believed this information or not. Finally my mother said something.

"Can you show us some examples?" she asked.

"Ah, yeah. Well . . ." said Colleen. "As you can see, we don't really have any flowers in the store right now."

She pulled a heavy book down from a nearby shelf, blew dust off the cover, and thumbed through it. Locating the page she was looking for, she slid the book over to me.

"We would use this one, probably," she said, pointing to a tiny photo of a rose. "And this one, and maybe that one."

I stared at the tiny dots in the book, which seemed to be some kind of flower encyclopedia. From this I was supposed to pick flowers? All the wedding magazines had led me to believe that visiting the florist would approximate a religious experience. The florist would whip up one arrangement after another at my whim. There would be marigolds and impatiens and birds of paradise and all those flowers with silly names like lobelia ruby slippers and queeny purple hollyhocks and who knew what else. There would be fields of soft golden petals and the deepest blues and all would bow before me, Bride of the Flowers. Or, at the very least, there would be a flower or two.

Colleen walked over to a nearby refrigerator that looked old enough to have belonged to the inn back when George Washington was sleeping there, and took out a half-dead rose.

"We could also use this," she said. "Although of course it would look different because it would be more lively. And then, let me see." She rummaged around in the refrigerator and came out with another flower the color of a long-dead fish. "And how about this one."

"What is it?" I asked, taking it from her delicately, lest it disintegrate in my hands.

"It's a magenta calla lily." She considered the flower for a moment. "Or, at least it was. Of course it wouldn't look quite like that."

"And what about the gold flowers," Marlene asked. "The picture here has gold flowers. Could you dye roses that color?"

"What about adding a little curly willow?" my mother said. "Curly willow is always a nice rustic touch."

I stared at the assortment of dead flowers in my hand while the mothers and Colleen went on to debate the bouquet for about half an hour. Prior to walking in here I had held only two opinions. One:

no roses. Two: pink and champagne. Both of those opinions had been quashed mere moments into the bouquet discussion, at which point I was no longer interested in the conversation. I stared at Steven, who was sitting on his stool inspecting the floor.

"What do you think about that?" my mother asked me.

"Huh?" I had lost track of the conversation.

And this was how it went. I would offer an opinion, discover that whatever I wanted was not possible for whatever reason, and then I would leave it to the mothers to discuss ad nauseam. And then, every so often, I would be asked to make some kind of final decision. I snuck a side-glance at Colleen at one point, who was clearly confused at the fact that I was having trouble staying awake during what was supposed to be the most important discussion of my life to date—my wedding bouquet. I looked at the assortment of dead and dying flowers in my hand. It was hard enough for me to get excited over real flowers, let alone imaginary ones.

At some point the bouquet discussion ended. Something had been decided, although I had long since given up paying attention.

"Well," said Colleen. "That was easy. So now let's do the boutonnieres for the men."

"Okay," I said, biting the inside of my cheek to keep myself awake. I nudged Steven. "This is your part."

Steven widened his eyes and shifted on his stool. It was his effort to look attentive.

"Do you have any ideas?" Colleen asked me.

I looked at Steven, who shrugged.

"What about a single calla lily?" Marlene said.

"Okay," I agreed. As mother of the groom I figured her opinion took precedence over anyone else's on the boutonniere front.

"What color?" asked Colleen.

I sighed. "Well, the ties are going to be pink or champagne, so I guess one of those maybe. Probably not pink." I turned to Steven. "I assume you don't want to wear a pink flower."

"Well his boutonniere should probably be different than everyone else's," Colleen said.

"What color tie is he wearing?" my mother asked.

"We don't know yet," I said.

"White is nice," said my mother. "That could look very simple and sophisticated."

"Pink is nice too," said Marlene. "What about pink?"

I looked at Steven, who was now staring blankly at the wall.

"Or champagne is a good neutral color," said my mother.

"Well, which do you think he'd prefer?" said Marlene.

"Well, why don't you ask him," said Steven. "He's sitting right here."

Marlene blushed. I think she'd forgotten her son was actually present. She reached across the counter and put her hand on his arm. "I'm so sorry, sweetie," she said. "You're right. Which would you prefer?"

"Champagne," said Steven.

I raised my eyebrows at him. He glared back. I knew that he couldn't care less whether his flower was pink or champagne or white. He just didn't want to be ignored.

Once the boutonnieres were out of the way we moved on to the table arrangements and the remaining ceremony flowers. The wedding was going to have a few different locations. On Saturday night there would be a rehearsal dinner for all guests in the barn. This would require flowers. Sunday, the night of the wedding, there would be the ceremony outside, which required a few flowers, then a dinner in the inn's restaurant, which required more flowers, and then dancing and cocktails in the barn, which required even more flowers. Somewhere around here, I faded out. The mothers had begun to debate whether there should be flowers in both the men's and the women's bathrooms or only in the women's. And what kind of flowers should they be? And did they need to be in the wedding colors, or was it more important that they smell nice? At which point, I couldn't take it anymore. I didn't want to think about minutiae, I didn't want to be obsessed about flowers or flower colors. In fact, I was sorry I'd even picked out wedding colors in the first place.

At long last, after a brief interlude where my mother suggested using streamers in the barn, forcing me to remind her that this was a wedding, not a senior prom, followed by a sudden group obsession with integrating curly willow, a long, dead-looking branch-like thing that looks like the kind of flower one might use at Dracula's wedding, into every possible arrangement, we were finally done.

As we were sliding off our stools and stretching our legs, Colleen turned to me.

"Oh," she said. "I almost forgot. You should send me some ribbon to wrap the bouquet in. It can even be two kinds of ribbons, or I can sew cute little buttons or fasteners on. Lots of brides like buttons on their bouquet."

"Whatever you have here is fine," I said, eyeing a few rolls of ribbon on the counter.

"But you have such a better ribbon selection in New York," she said. "Really some absolutely lovely ribbons." I stared at her for a second.

"Okay," I said, "I will send you ribbon."

And this is why being an obsessive-compulsive bride is so insidious. You think you're home free, that you've debated every little detail conceivable, and just as you're about to slip away, some issue like the bouquet ribbon creeps up on you and grabs you by the throat. I didn't have the least interest in tromping around the garment district searching for the right ribbon (and I knew that once given the task of finding ribbon I would be compelled to find not just any old piece of ribbon but the perfect ribbon), but how could I say anything else? How could I say, no I want your crappy ribbon, pick it out, I don't care, when she had so clearly established that her ribbon was for slackers and people with no taste, and that my New York ribbon was far superior.

As we left Colleen I checked my watch. We'd been in the florist's for three hours. It felt like a lifetime.

That evening as Steven and I were getting ready for bed, I asked him about the boutonniere controversy.

"You know," he said, "it's like the whole sexist thing in reverse. I mean, you're always saying how people just assume that you're into the whole wedding and that you have opinions on all this stupid shit just because you're the bride. Well, people just assume that I don't have any opinions. And, I mean, it's my wedding too.

Just because I'm male doesn't mean I can't have an opinion on a flower."

"That's true," I said. "The world is a horrible, horrible place."

"It's just so infuriating," Steven huffed. "Oh, he's a guy, so let's ignore him completely because he can't possibly have any opinions."

"Yeah," I said. "But in all honesty, you didn't really have many opinions there. I mean, do you really care if your boutonniere is pink or yellow or white?"

"No," said Steven. "But that's not the point."

The next morning we met with Holly, the wedding coordinator at the inn. Holly looked like she'd binged on the L.L. Bean catalog back in 1984 and hadn't gone shopping since. She had long, straight brown hair pulled back into a loose, no-nonsense ponytail, and that morning she was wearing a navy blue corduroy jumper. There could have been duck embroidery involved in her outfit somewhere—I can't be sure.

Then again, having grown up in Connecticut, where people love L.L. Bean, I myself had owned the same maroon Eddie Bauer sweater worn by approximately 63 percent of my high school graduating class. (The remaining sweaterless 37 percent all owned the same bright yellow L.L. Bean duck boots.) So in some sense Holly's attire was my heritage as a New Englander. It looked familiar. It reminded me of junior high.

Holly led our little group into the barn, where the dancing would be after dinner, and we sat down on the chintz couches in front of the fireplace. The barn looked exactly as you would expect a converted barn in Vermont to look. Antique patchwork quilts covered the walls. Flowered couches, wooden tables and chairs were arranged across the room. There was a built-in bar in one corner and a piano in the other. An enormous eight-foot-long gun was mounted above the fireplace. I stared at the gun for a while, wondering if I could work up the nerve to ask Holly to take it down for the wedding on the grounds that guns were scary and therefore not decorative.

"Oh, this is lovely," my mother said. "The quilts are just gorgeous."

"You think so?" I asked.

"It's really nice," said Marlene. "It's not at all like I thought it would be. I mean, when you said barn I was thinking it was going to be, like, a barn. You know. Just a plain barn. But this is really nicely done."

I breathed a silent sigh of relief. At least the mothers liked it. Either that or they were still competing for the title of Most Supportive Mother in a Wedding Planning Setting.

Holly presented the mothers with a stack of photo albums. I smiled to myself. Unlike Colleen at the flower shop, Holly had remembered to take pictures at her events, because unlike Colleen, Holly was not the only game in town.

As the mothers were poring over the albums, I noticed a couple standing over in the corner by the piano. They were a youngish looking pair, and the woman was hugely pregnant.

"Oh look!" said Holly, spying the couple. "It's the Johnsons!"

The couple nodded hello and walked over to where we were sitting.

"The Johnsons were married here, oh, how long ago was it?"

"Last year," said Mr. Johnson.

"This is our anniversary," said Mrs. Johnson, rubbing her belly.

"So," said my mother. "Would you recommend getting married here?"

"Oh definitely," said Mr. Johnson. "All our guests said it was the best wedding they'd ever been to. Some of them are still talking about it."

"No kidding," I said.

The Johnsons smiled at us, then walked back towards the piano, where I suppose they were reliving some utterly romantic moment when Mrs. Johnson wasn't the same size as the barn.

"This is pretty," said Marlene, pointing at a picture in one of the albums that showed a huge tent set up by the swim pond down the hill from the inn. The tent was all lit up and it looked beautiful.

"That's a good idea," I said. "For the rehearsal dinner."

Holly craned her neck to look at the picture.

"Oh yes," she said. "That was lovely. That was their dinner the day before the wedding. It cost about fifteen thousand dollars."

The air went out of the room for a minute.

"For the rehearsal dinner?" I whispered.

Holly nodded.

"Well," I said. "So much for that."

Steven cleared his throat. "We were thinking about doing the rehearsal dinner at White Gates." White Gates was the largest of the outbuildings. It was set down the road from the inn and had a lovely patio area that faded into Vermont greenery and hills. There was even an apple tree.

"How many people are you expecting?" Holly asked.

"Everyone's invited to the rehearsal dinner," I said. "So, probably . . . ninety people, maybe?"

"Well," said Holly. "That's too many for White Gates. You can only have thirty people there at most."

There was silence. I may have even whimpered a little. White Gates had been one of the major appealing items about the inn. I loved the idea of having a rehearsal dinner in an old colonial house, maybe grilling outside by the patio. It would be almost like having it at my own home. Vermont was something like Connecticut, with all the trees and the beautiful silences, and although we'd never lived in a colonial, we had lived near a colonial, so I figured White Gates was about as close as I could get to having the wedding at my childhood home. When we'd booked the inn, no one had ever mentioned a limit of thirty guests.

"Why is that?" asked Marlene.

"The plumbing is very old. It can't handle more than thirty," said Holly.

"What if we rented Porta-Pottis?" my mother asked.

Holly wrinkled her nose.

"I don't want Porta-Pottis at my wedding," I grumbled. "Make people come all the way up here and then tell them they have to pee outside."

My mother glared at me. "So where would you suggest having the rehearsal dinner?" she asked Holly.

"Most people have it here in the barn," said Holly. "Or outside in the garden."

I didn't want to have the rehearsal dinner in the barn because the dancing the next night would be in the barn. And according to the wedding magazines, I would be able to get what I wanted. It was my wedding, after all. It was the most important day of my life. If I wanted to have the rehearsal dinner in White Gates and back up the plumbing and destroy the sewer system for the entire southern half of Vermont, as a bride that was my God-given right, was it not? But apparently Holly had not been reading wedding magazines. Holly didn't think I had a right to much, and she let me know. Not only couldn't we have the rehearsal dinner at White Gates, but, as it turned out, we couldn't have a hot dog vendor at the softball game.

At a Jewish event, if a moment goes by where food is not being served, everyone panics. What if, God forbid, someone at that very moment gets hungry? So we'd planned a lot of food. There would be food in the in-room baskets when people arrived on Saturday, followed by a buffet dinner. On Sunday, the day of the wedding, there would be a huge brunch, but then there was a gap of time, from one until four, when there would be no food. The inn served cookies and tea at four, and then hors d'oeuvres would be served at the cocktail hour at six, but no food for three hours in the afternoon—that was unthinkable. And so on the car ride up we had collectively hit upon the idea of having a hot dog vendor at the softball game. We would prepay for the hot dogs and the sodas, and it would be cute and silly. But Holly didn't see the point. There would be a big brunch, she said. No one would be hungry for hot dogs two hours later. She clearly didn't understand that hunger played no part in the equation. Nonetheless, hiring an unauthorized hot dog vendor was not in the contract Steven and I had signed way back in the fall.

"What if the inn made us hot dogs?" I asked.

Holly wrinkled her nose again. "The inn can't make you hot dogs. The kitchen will be busy with the wedding preparations."

"They can't make us hot dogs?" I said. "How hard is it to make a hot dog? I mean, you go to the supermarket, you buy a bunch of hot dogs, I could do it."

Holly shook her head.

I got the subtext. The inn wouldn't make us hot dogs because Holly thought hot dogs were a silly idea. Even worse, she thought they were gauche, perhaps. Or maybe too New York. Whatever the reason, she was against them, and there would be no hot dogs.

Sitting on the chintz couch in the barn, I marveled over the fact that it seemed I had chosen to become obsessed with the wrong things. I didn't want roses. I wanted hot dogs. I wanted the rehearsal dinner in a colonial building, not in a barn. But no one cared what I wanted. The mothers, on the other hand, seemed to have entered into an agreement to become obsessed with flower placement. After flipping through the photo albums and arguing about hot dogs and Porta-Pottis, we strolled around the barn.

"The basket of sunflowers should go here, don't you think?" asked my mother, pointing to an empty corner.

"Sure," I said. There were going to be sunflowers?

"What if it went over there?" asked Marlene.

"Over there would be good too," said my mother.

"Which night is this?" I asked.

"Well, let's see," said my mother. "Saturday there will be the smaller basket of sunflowers. Then Sunday night there's going to be the really big arrangement with the curly willow and all the wild-flowers in the entrance somewhere. So we really need to find two spots for them."

"Can't the florist just find somewhere to put them?" I asked.

"Well what if she puts them somewhere stupid?" my mother snapped.

"Oh my God!" I said. "It would be chaos!"

She ignored me.

"You really can't put them over in that corner," said Holly. "There's a heating vent there."

"But it will be August," said Marlene. "Will the heat be on?"

"It could be chilly," said Holly.

"Well if it's chilly where else could we put them?" said my mother. Marlene, Holly and my mother all stared into various spaces in the barn.

I looked around for Steven. He was nowhere to be seen.

"I'll be right back," I said, and slipped out the barn door. Steven was standing on the porch outside the barn.

"I can't take it," he said.

"Oh, you missed the latest. Should the sunflowers go here? Should they go there? What if it's chilly? What if it's hot? What if there's a typhoon?"

"I just don't care," said Steven. "I just want it to be over."

"At least no one asks you your opinion."

"Yeah," he said. "I was annoyed about it yesterday, but now I'm kind of happy."

I stared at the mountains in the distance.

"I guess I'd better go back in."

Steven glanced at me.

"I'm sorry about this, babe," he said. "I didn't realize this was going to be so much work for you."

"Neither did I."

"Should I be doing more?" he asked. "I mean, I don't really know what I can be doing. Should I have more opinions?"

"How can you have an opinion on something you don't have an opinion on. I mean, I'm a girl, so I can kind of force opinions on flowers and stuff if I have to." I shook my head. "It's fine. I guess it's part of being female. You have to do all this stuff that sucks. It's kind of like when I was thirteen and I got my first bra, and I was like, really? I'm going to have to wear this thing every day for the rest of my life until I die?"

Steven looked at me. "How is that like this?"

"Well, this is better, I guess, because I only have to do it once. Imagine if I had to plan a wedding every day for the rest of my life."

The fact was, Steven could have voiced more opinions, but no one was expecting him to. In fact, people were expecting him to do exactly what he was doing: having no opinion at all. So for him to actually express a thought would require not only creating an opinion on something that he didn't have, but then violating gender lines in offering an opinion on something no one expected him to care about in the first place. But for me, the opposite was true. I was expected to care. I was expected to have opinions. And in some ways, it was easier to make up an opinion than insist I didn't have one. But the funny thing about opinions is this: once you make up an opinion, you suddenly care about it. I didn't have much of an opinion on hot dogs until I was told I couldn't have them. And then I wanted them desperately.

The flower discussion had ended by the time I walked back into the barn, and had segued into a conversation about where the seating-card table would go. For this, terrifying as it was, I had a genuine opinion.

"Outside," I said.

"But if it's windy the cards will blow off," said my mother.

"No they won't," I said. "Not if you do the Martha Stewart thing."

Ah hah. Checkmate.

Both mothers stared at me quizzically while I rummaged around in my wedding binder and eventually produced yet another piece of paper torn out from *Martha Stewart Weddings*. On it was a picture of a seating-card table decorated with ribbon that had been ingeniously sewn across the tablecloth. The cards slipped underneath the ribbon, which was sheer enough to read through.

"Do you know this thing?" I asked Holly, handing her the piece of paper.

Holly smiled. The mothers stared at me as though I had descended from the heavens to bring them the word of Martha.

"Sure," said Holly. "If you buy the ribbon and send it to me I'll sew it for you."

The last stop on our whirlwind wedding tour of Vermont was the town's cheese factory, where I had planned to arrange the in-room baskets. But if Holly had seemed obstinate, it was only because I had not yet met the cheese lady. I was already pretty close to losing it by that point. I had been shown dead flowers, had been denied hot dogs, and had been consulted to death on minutiae.

The four of us walked around the cheese factory gift shop picking out items for the baskets, then assembled them by the cash register. For a moment, it was fun. We picked out two kinds of cheeses, crackers, pretzels and mustard, maple candies, little bottles of maple syrup, Vermont chocolates, wondered aloud whether the cheese in the shape of the state of Vermont was too over the top, and then finally announced our intentions to the woman behind the cash register.

"We're planning a wedding at the inn the last weekend in August," I explained. "And we want to put baskets with all this stuff into the rooms."

"Okay," said the woman.

"Plus I was thinking I wanted to put some apples in there. Do you have apples?"

"Well," she said. "We can certainly make the baskets for you, but we wouldn't be able to put any apples in them. We don't sell apples."

I stared at her. I felt hot tears gathering in my eyes.

And here, I have a confession to make. I had a theme: Apples.

I wasn't really calling it a theme; it was more like a persistent motif. There was a tiny apple on the invitations and the response cards, I'd planned to put an apple on the menu cards, there would be apple pie for dessert, and, worst of all, I'd incorporated cocktails into the theme. There would be a signature-themed drink. Apple martinis. I had seen the enemy and it was I. So when the cheese lady said she couldn't get me apples, I felt like my head was going to explode. It had been such a long weekend. And now my apple theme would be ruined. Ruined! Of course, it was absurd. Who cared if there were apples or not? I'll tell you who. Me. I cared. I wanted apples.

"You know," my mother whispered into my ear. "This stuff isn't so great. I could get us nicer baskets in Chicago."

I looked at Steven, who, seeing I was about to lose it, pulled me into a corner for a conference.

"I don't get it," I hissed. "How fucking hard is it to get an apple. I mean, it's Vermont, for God's sake. They grow them on trees here. So, like, I'm going to have to go to the supermarket and pick out a hundred apples and bring them here or something? I mean, there are like five people in this town. Between the inn and the cheese store not one of them can figure out how to get me apples? Why is everything so hard?"

"I know," said Steven.

"And my mother's like, oh, let's just get them in Chicago. But the whole point is that everything is from Vermont. I mean, people are going to schlep all the way up to Vermont so I can give them cheese from Chicago? It's ridiculous."

Steven rubbed my back. "Just take a breath," he said. "We'll figure it out."

I was whispering loudly enough for the cheese lady to hear me, but I didn't care. I wanted her to hear. I wanted her to look at me and think I was a bride on the verge of a nervous breakdown. And in the end, it worked. Perhaps realizing she was about to lose a fairly large sale, the woman suddenly said, "You know, I could probably get some apples."

"You could?" I said.

"Sure," she said. "I could go to the market and get some apples. Do you want red or green?"

And from that point, we were rolling. She brought out a basket catalog for me to look through, she said she'd assemble everything, she even suggested which color baskets she thought would look best with the wedding colors.

"And before I forget," she said as we were finishing up. "I was thinking I could tie nice little bows on the baskets, just to make them more special."

"Okay," I said.

"So," said the cheese lady. "Can you send me ribbon?"

9

The Happiest Day of My Life

Married couples tell each other
a thousand things without speech.
—*Chinese proverb*

FTER THE TRIP TO VERMONT, SOMEHOW IT BECAME
easier to ignore the obsessive-compulsive impulses. This was
partially due to the fact that most of the decisions had
been made and the only things that remained were executional.
There were ribbons to buy and guest schedules to design and invitations to mail out, but all the hardest things had been accomplished. But it was also that I had come to the realization that
wedding magazines were just a bunch of bullshit designed to drive
brides crazy. Or rather, I guess I'd known that all along, but just in
case there had been any doubts, I'd proved it to be true. The magazines had intimated that I would have control over things like which
flowers bloom when, and that if I wanted I could have tulips in
December. I had begun to believe that the rest of the world would
move mountains to make me happy, but it wasn't the case. The rest
of the world just kept on doing what it always did.

And so, when I had the misfortune to stumble upon an article
in the latest *Martha Stewart Weddings* on how to get the right stamp

cancellation on your invitations as I had just finished stamping the envelopes, I didn't beat myself up over it.

The article explained that you should preferably have your invitations stamps hand-cancelled as opposed to dumping them in the mailbox where, once they get to the post office, they will have nasty machine-printed bar codes stamped on them. Even better, suggested the article, there were towns with names like Darling, Romance, and Bliss that would "cancel your stamps for you, imprinting them with their sweet names."

After all, why make things easy on yourself and send out the envelopes from your local post office when you can make things twice as complicated by taking all your envelopes and mailing them to Kissimmee, Florida? And, although by that point I had had enough wedding mania to read the article and think, you've got to be kidding me, followed by a brief fantasy of sending my stamps to be cancelled in Hell, Michigan, I felt a tiny stab of guilt when I dumped the envelopes in the mailbox on the corner. Perhaps, said a little nagging voice in the farthest reaches of my head, you should have worried more about the stamp cancellations.

But for the most part, the summer passed in an organizational haze. Some tasks were surprisingly easy, such as getting the menus printed. I picked up the menus from the stationery store, mailed them to a printer in Staten Island, and three days later they showed up at my doorstep looking lovely. Other tasks were ridiculously complicated. Like the chocolate. One of the things I wanted and actually got was a sweet table. Instead of cake, after dinner there would be a table filled with local cheeses, fruits, crackers, breads, and chocolates. Holly had recommended a local chocolatier about twenty minutes away from the inn, and I had dutifully called them up and ordered a few pounds of chocolate. The problem was getting the chocolates to the inn. The chocolate company would not deliver them, despite the fact that they were twenty minutes away. Instead, they offered to FedEx them to the inn. When I pointed out that this meant that in order to get a box of chocolates down the street they would first have to travel to Memphis, Tennessee, the chocolate company suggested that if I wasn't happy with the situation I was welcome to come pick the chocolates up myself and drive them over to the inn the day before the wedding. Which is what I agreed to do. Because really, that's what a bride should be doing the day before her wedding, no? Chauffeuring chocolates around Vermont.

After the invitations went out the gifts began arriving. Receiving gifts, particularly when one has a wedding registry, amounts to something along the lines of a vast sociological experiment. Because you know exactly what the gift-giver's options were, and you know the exact amount of money they've spent on your gift, since you picked it out yourself. So when we received a twenty-dollar set of wine glasses from some relatives on my mother's side I called her up and asked for an estimate of their net worth.

"Don't they have two houses?" I asked.

"They sure do," she said. "And he drives a Lexus."

Other people called our parents and informed them that they didn't see anything on the registry they liked, and therefore wanted to know what else we might want. This was particularly confusing because the whole point of having a registry in the first place was so that people won't have to call you up and ask you what you want. In theory, everything you want is on the registry. And really, who cared if the gift-giver didn't like anything on the registry? It wasn't going to them. It was going to us. But I guess this is the sociology of gift giving. People want to send you something that they see as representative of their personality, even if their personality representation isn't necessarily something you want hanging around your house. You therefore must live with a butt-ugly set of ceramic dessert plates or a piece of Judaic art depicting a Jewish bride and groom in renaissance costume, as opposed to the really nice set of crystal highball glasses you spent several weeks hunting for.

The registry took a surreal turn when a couple whose wedding would be two weeks after ours sent us a roasting pan we'd registered for. We'd been involved in a rotating catch-22 with them—they were only vaguely connected to us, so no one expected that they would attend our wedding, since it was in a different state, but we couldn't rightfully decline their invitation until they'd declined ours. So when they turned us down, we heaved huge sighs of relief that we not only wouldn't have to drag ourselves out to their wedding in the New York 'burbs, but that we were now thankfully excused from buying them a gift. Then the roasting pan arrived. Which meant, of course, that we would now have to buy them a gift.

In a moment of what I thought could only be perceived as ironic brilliance, I decided that I would buy them the exact same roasting pan they'd bought us. Sadly, they hadn't registered for it, and I had to settle for a set of sheets. It was probably just as well. I didn't know them at all—they were on Steven's side of the guest list—and the humor most likely would have escaped them.

As the summer dragged on, fights and moments of panic came and went. My father and I argued almost every week. When I called to find out how to spell one of his friend's names, he told me he was too involved in the details of the wedding and wanted to be left alone. When I vetoed his suggested that the softball game be fast-pitch he yelled that he wasn't involved enough.

My mother had her own meltdown over the bridal shower situation. The situation was this: there wasn't going to be a bridal shower. This, she'd decided, was not right, despite the fact that she'd never been one for etiquette. In fact, she could usually be categorized as being the anti–Emily Post. If there was a rule of etiquette (for example, that at dinner parties one shouldn't meet guests under the table for whispered conferences, or that when engaged in conversation with one's child one generally shouldn't suddenly decide to execute favorite yoga positions) she violated it. Nonetheless, she'd somehow latched on to the idea that I should have a shower, and that she should throw it. Her idea was that I should fly to Chicago where she would invite a host of friends whom I not only had never met, but who also were not invited to the wedding. She cajoled, she bribed, she appealed to my inner materialist (these people want to buy you presents, she'd snapped when I told her I was having none of it). But I put my foot down. There would be no shower.

And she wasn't the only one panicking over the fact that I was shower-less.

"My mom is really upset that you're not having a shower," Steven said one evening as we were hand-writing seating cards.

"Really, honestly upset?" I said.

"Apparently so. She wants to throw you one."

"Well," I said, "she'll have to duke it out with my mother first."

A few weeks later a set of cute, yet sensible, lingerie arrived in the mail from Marlene, along with a note thanking me for including her in the wedding planning. It was a very sweet, if somewhat odd, gesture. I guess she figured that if I didn't have a shower I would have nothing to wear on my wedding night for my first night of married sex. And so, as mother of the person who would be on the receiving end of my lingerie-clad body, she took it upon herself to provide me with some.

About a week before the wedding everyone around me became suddenly fixated on the weather. My father forwarded me daily forecasts from the Weather Channel website, most of which said it would rain the entire weekend. It could have just been me, but I thought I detected a smidgen of glee in his e-mails. Marlene and I took to speaking several times a week about the details of the wedding. In one of these conversations I asked her if she'd checked the weather forecast.

"I can't," she said. "I'm too nervous."

"I've checked it," I told her. "Do you want to know what it says?"

She hesitated. "Okay."

"Well, some days they say it's going to rain. Some days they just say it's going to be cloudy."

Part of me was trying not to obsess about the weather, which was, more than any other part of the wedding, completely out of my control. I told myself this, but I also knew that if it rained it would be my fault. Kimberly called to suggest I bring up some board games in case it rained. The whole thing was stupid anyway, I decided, as the wedding was going to be in the mountains and, as everyone knows, the weather in the mountains is utterly unpredictable so there was absolutely no point in paying attention to the forecast. Still, I checked several times a day, sometimes hourly, to see if the Weather Channel had replaced the little gray cloud icon with a happy smiling sun.

As the wedding approached, I felt like I had entered a kind of automated state where I went through the motions of life. People sent me e-mails with small problems (Kimberly's shoes had been dyed the wrong color and wouldn't match her dress) and big problems (a group of friends who were driving up from Manhattan had yet to rent a car for the biggest car-rental weekend of the year). There were last minute cancellations and last minute acceptances. Both my father and Steven's father sent me a news clipping about a bride who had been arrested on her wedding day for destroying the catering hall after they ran out of alcohol. And my grandmother, who had been behaving as though she wasn't sure she was going to live until the wedding, suddenly decided she was going to make it after all, and began calling me daily with questions (Will there be a safe in the room for her jewelry? Was it okay if she wore gold shoes instead of cream, since gold was in the color scheme, right? And you know what? She couldn't wait to see me! Really! How exciting—I was getting married!).

And then, finally, the wedding weekend was upon us. It was as though the summer were made of a rubber band, pulled taut in the early months as time dragged by endlessly, then snapped quickly shut, and before we knew it we were arguing with the rental car agency over a lost reservation a few days prior to the wedding. The rental car agency said they had deleted our reservation when we didn't show up at the appointed time to pick up the car. The fact that there was an appointed time was news to us, but it didn't matter. The SUV we'd booked was gone. After tears and arguments about company policy and threatening cell phone calls to other rental agencies, all of whom were teeming with overworked New Yorkers rushing to get in cars that would take them far away from the city's depressing and insufferably steamy Labor Day weekend, someone found us a blue minivan.

As we pulled out of the rental car garage into the clogged streets of midtown Manhattan I looked at Steven, who was in the driver's seat. I usually drove, especially in the city, an experience I viewed as a competitive sport and Steven viewed as terrifying, but minivans scared me. I'd never driven one, not that Steven had either, but he'd decided to step up to the challenge.

"Well," I said, once we'd heaved out of the parking garage and onto the street.

"Here we are," said Steven. "We're getting married."

"We're getting married," I echoed. "And we're in a minivan. The symbolism is, like, too much to bear."

"Don't think about it," said Steven.

He edged the van forward two inches, then sighed as the light turned red.

I peeked into the cavernous back of the van, then stared ahead at the traffic.

"I feel like I should be yelling at some imaginary kids back there or something," I said.

Steven turned his head to the back of the van. "Stop hitting your brother!" he yelled.

I laughed. "Who wants to watch the *Finding Nemo* DVD again?" I asked the backseat.

"I don't care who started it," Steven yelled again. "Do you want me to stop this car? Because I will!"

The traffic crawled forward another half an inch.

An hour later we reached Kleinfeld. As I got out of the van and pulled open the door to the bridal salon it was as though I'd entered a dream state. I saw myself, hair piled on top of my head and hastily pinned back with a big plastic clip, stained shorts, sticky in a tank top in the August heat. I saw myself open the door to the building as if from on high, looking down at the dirty Brooklyn streets, looking at the blond girl with the minivan on her way to her wedding. It was me, but it wasn't. The freezing air-conditioned air sucked me into Kleinfeld through the glass doors and then suddenly I was downstairs (I was an old pro now, walked right by the nervous newly engaged girls perched on the stiff couches in the waiting area, didn't even bother to check in with the front desk, knew exactly where I was headed) and then Rosa was bringing out my dress.

The dress had been stuffed with paper and tissue so that it looked like there was actually a body inside of it on a hanger. Rosa unzipped several layers of sheeting, then flung them to the side of the hanger and revealed the dress as though it were a work of art.

"OK," I said, thinking, *yup, that's the dress all right.*

"It's beautiful," Rosa prompted.

I then realized that I had missed my cue. That it was beautiful, or ugly, or any other adjective, was not news to me. I'd seen the dress a thousand times at this point, and had already bought it, so it wasn't as though I was going to say, no, take it back. But apparently I was supposed to be admiring it.

"Oh yes," I said, slowly picking up on the concept. "It's beautiful."

Two men in tight black T-shirts with "Kleinfeld" spelled out in white letters appeared next to the dress. I looked at them, nodded, and then we were out on the street and they were loading the dress into the minivan. We folded down the backseats and they stretched the dress out carefully on the floor of the van. It was all wrapped in white cloth and lay there on the floor like a shroud. I stared at it as they snapped the van doors shut. There was something terrifying about it.

The dress continued to freak me out once we got it home. I watched Steven carry it up the stairs to our apartment, and it swayed over his shoulder, ghostlike, longer and heavier than any garment I owned, including my scuba wet suit. Somehow I had liked it better when the dress was in Kleinfeld. In my apartment, suspended from the French doors separating the bedroom from the living room, it seemed to take on anthropomorphic qualities, especially all stuffed with paper breasts, and I began to feel like I had brought home a living, breathing entity. And then I began to worry about it.

My relationship with my dress had been tenuous at first. I'd loathed it in the beginning, then grown slowly to accept it. But now, in my apartment, it became abundantly clear that I now owned this ridiculously overpriced object. Here it was in front of me. I could do whatever I wanted with it. I could put it on right then and cook up a plate of spaghetti marinara if I wanted. In Kleinfeld there had been so many rules involved in the dress. So many ritualistic, almost worshipful acts you had to follow before you could even get near the thing. You had to take off your shoes. You had to speak softly. You had to layer on uncomfortable undergarments. But here, in my apartment, it was no longer a ritualistic object. It was just a weird piece of clothing and it was staring at me.

The next day we spent the morning loading up the minivan with wedding paraphernalia. We hung my dress up in the back and then filled the rest of the space with boxes of softball T-shirts (in the end my brother had acquiesced and gone with light blue and dark blue shirts that read, simply, BRIDE and GROOM, respectively), bats, bases, Steven's suit, two suitcases full of assorted wedding weekend attire for a range of temperatures, tennis racquets in case anyone wanted to borrow one, three boxes full of printed menus and seating cards and schedules for the guests, a large plastic bag filled with champagne-colored yarmulkes and a pink wicker basket filled with the implements of marriage: the *ketubah* and a silver wine goblet that had graced my family's table on every holiday.

It was hot and overcast, and we rode up to Vermont in silence.

I took out the digital camera and snapped some pictures of Steven driving, then experimented for a while with taking artsy pictures of my toes. I wanted the drive up to be fun. I had imagined us laughing and having a grand old time in the minivan that was supposed to be an SUV, but there was nothing left to say.

"So," I said. "Here we are. We're going to get married."

"Yup," said Steven.

We stopped on the way to the inn to pick up the chocolates, then arrived at the inn in the early afternoon on Friday. I found Holly, and the three of us sat in the lobby in front of an empty fireplace going through the boxes of wedding stuff. In a move that showed my neuroses were rubbing off, Steven insisted on double-checking all the seating cards against the seating chart one final time.

"It looks like the weather will be nice," said Holly as Steven thumbed through the cards mumbling to himself.

"It does?" I asked, turning to look out the window.

"I think we'll be fine," she said.

For some reason, this made me feel that the weather really, truly would be fine. Holly must know, I thought. After all, she lives here.

After Steven had exhausted his obsessive-compulsive tendencies by going through the seating cards a second time, we walked across the street to get the marriage license. The wedding industry barely mentions the license, despite the fact that out of all of the elements of a wedding, it is actually the only one you truly can't get married without. Usually it's a sidebar in the magazines that says, "Don't forget to get the marriage license!" Maybe this is because there's nothing exciting about the license from the wedding industry's perspective. There's no way to make it look nicer, there's no fancier version of the license, no way to have it dipped in gold or surrounded by flowers, no way to incorporate it into your wedding theme unless you're going with a Governmental Documents motif.

The marriage license bureau was also the post office—a tiny one-story wooden building painted barn-red with white trim. There was a little covered wooden porch that had a bulletin board outside where people had hung signs for local music events and yoga classes. The whole building was unbelievably cute; it was the kind of structure Disney might design for Ye Olde Pony Express Office. As we brushed past the bulletin board I noticed a flyer for a Howard Dean rally happening that weekend. It was funny to think that the rest of the world would be going on about its usual business of playing music and exercising and going to political events while I was getting married. It's like when someone you know dies and you're amazed to discover that outside the funeral home or outside the hospital, just across the street even, people are going on with their lives, as though it's a normal day. And you want to scream from the rooftops, how can you people all act so normal! Don't you know??? It was a lot like that.

We walked into a dusty office overflowing with papers. There was a huge wooden desk to one side, the kind where you sit on a stool and do things with an abacus and ledgers, although this desk was inexplicably covered with felt finger puppets. A small woman in jeans sat behind a metal desk in the middle of the room. She looked up at us as we walked in.

"Marriage license?" she asked.

We nodded.

"It was either that or dog license," she said. "But you don't usually have couples coming in for dog licenses."

She was nothing like I'd imagined the Town Clerk would be. Steven had called a few weeks earlier to make an appointment to get the license, and had been greeted with extreme puzzlement. "Just come in and talk to the Town Clerk," he'd been told. And so for weeks now I'd been picturing said clerk as an old gnarled man with reading glasses perched over an enormous wooden desk. The desk was there, in the corner, but in the man's place was this small, unassuming woman.

We filled out some paperwork, which involved both of our parents' names and our full names, and then had to spell and respell all the names for the clerk as she typed them onto an official-looking piece of paper.

"Too many *s*'s and *c*'s and *k*'s," explained the clerk.

I discovered, to my amazement, that there was no place to write what would be my new, married name. I had been going back and forth for months on whether I would change my name, and in the end had decided that whichever way the mood struck me when we got the marriage license, that would be the way I would go. But with no space for my married name, I would now have to make an extraordinary effort to take Steven's name if I chose to do so. That is, I would actually have to think about it.

"Now," said the clerk, looking over the paperwork. "This rabbi who's marrying you, is he certified in the State of Vermont?"

I shrugged and looked at Steven.

"Probably not," he said.

"Uh oh," said the clerk.

"Uh oh?" said Steven.

"Well, it's not a big deal, but if he's not certified then you have to get a waiver that says he can marry you."

"Okay," said Steven.

"But you can't get it today," she said.

At which point, I suppose I should have passed out. After all, I had just spent a year planning a wedding for a marriage that was not going to actually be legal. And yet, somehow it didn't faze me. Perhaps it was because I was numb from head to toe in anticipation of the weekend, perhaps it was because it seemed like such a silly, trivial thing. Perhaps it was that after all the time and energy I had invested in thinking about colors and guest lists and getting my parents to show up in the same state at the same time, the legal side of it seemed somewhat superfluous. I had a sudden fantasy of us rushing off to City Hall when we got back to New York and never telling anyone. It would be our little secret. We would have two anniversaries. Somehow it almost felt more romantic that way, and then I was utterly enamored of the idea. We would have the big public wedding, and then we'd have our own little private wedding to make it all legal. What a terrific idea!

"Well, it's not a big deal," said the clerk. "I'll just find out on Monday if you need the certification or not. You'll probably just need the rabbi to sign something."

"Okay," Steven said.

"Now," said the clerk. "Who's going to pay?"

I blinked.

"Pay what?" Steven asked.

"The processing fee. It's forty dollars."

"Oh," I said. "I think I have forty dollars."

"You're going to let her pay for the license?" the clerk said to Steven.

We looked at each other.

"No," said Steven, as though who paid for the license mattered one iota to either one of us. "I think I can cover it."

Steven opened up his wallet and rummaged around.

"Uh oh," he whispered.

"What?" I said under my breath.

"I only have twenty dollars," he whispered.

The clerk looked up.

"Well why don't you both pay twenty dollars," she said, making no pretense of having not overheard our whisperings. "That's nice and even."

We all laughed, as though this were the silliest thing anyone could have said. Money would not be an issue in our marriage. How absurd.

"Okay," I said. "We'll both pay twenty dollars."

"We split everything fifty-fifty," Steven said to the clerk, smiling. "Right down the middle."

A few moments later we walked out of the post office, receipt in hand.

"It's so weird, isn't it?" I said to Steven.

"Which part of that exactly are you referring to?"

I snickered. "I meant the whole license thing. I mean, here we are getting married, and it's like, we could just as easily be getting a dog."

"Maybe we should have gone for the dog instead," Steven said.

I rolled my eyes. "Ha ha. Funny."

"See," said Steven. "That is what we call irony. Because we were talking about licenses, and you said . . ."

"All right!" I said. "I get it."

Steven chuckled to himself. He liked to explain his jokes. The dumber the joke, the more he liked to explain it. He thought it was funny.

"I guess we should go unpack, huh?" I said.

"Okay."

We started walking in the direction of our room. We were staying in the honeymoon suite, which was the upstairs of a little white house across from the main inn.

"Hey Steven," I said.

"Hm?"

"We're getting married."

"So you've said."

"Are you nervous?"

"Not really. It feels too surreal to be nervous."

I sighed.

"Are you nervous?" he asked.

"I don't know," I said. "I'm numb."

"Me too," said Steven. "But I'm really glad to be marrying you."

I smiled. "Aw. I'm glad to be marrying you too."

Steven's parents were the first to arrive. They drove up to the town line as we were walking down the road, hand in hand, coming back from dropping off the last in-room basket at a bed and breakfast down the hill from the inn. They honked at us as they approached, then slowed to a stop and rolled down their windows. I loved the fact that we could hold a conversation in the middle of the road with no fear of being run over or yelled at by passersby.

My father, his wife, and my grandmother pulled up to the inn next. My father's wife arrived in tears, hysterical about something, perhaps the idea of being near my mother, and insisting that she needed to use the phone that second. My father demanded to know why there was no cell phone service in the area, how could I have been so stupid as to plan a wedding in a town that had no cell phone service and then compound my stupidity by not informing anyone that they would not be able to use their cell phones. Steven went to entertain his parents while I helped my father and his wife find their rooms.

"How's the room?" my father called out to his wife, who had walked in first.

She shrugged. "Okay I guess."

She spied the basket of cheese, apples, and assorted goodies that had been placed in everyone's room, just like the cheese lady had said they would.

"That's the in-room basket," I said.

"You should put something on the baskets so people know they're from you," she said.

"There are guest agendas that they're putting in all the rooms tomorrow," I said through gritted teeth.

Deciding I needed to be elsewhere, I walked across to the main inn to check on my grandmother. She was staying in a suite on the second floor, and as I peeked my head in the door I could tell she was unhappy. She was standing a little unsteadily by the closet, staring into it, the back of her little blond puff of hair turned towards me.

"How's your room, Gammy?" I asked.

"There aren't enough hangers," she said.

"I'll get you hangers."

"Just have someone send up some hangers."

"Okay," I said. "How's everything else?"

She looked around the room, her lips scrunched and her eyes sad. Ever since my parents' divorce she'd had sad eyes, which had only gotten sadder with my grandfather's death a few years later.

"This is some crazy place to have a wedding," she said.

I knew what she was thinking: it wasn't fancy enough. She didn't see the rustic charm or the appeal of sleeping in a place that had been standing in the same spot for over two hundred years. She wasn't going to be imagining herself sitting in the lobby having conversations with Ralph Waldo Emerson or Rudyard Kipling or any of the famous people the inn listed as having stayed there. She just saw creaky floors and dusty corners and faulty plumbing.

"Okay Gammy," I said. "I'll go see about your hangers."

My mother and brother were the last to arrive, pulling in that evening just as we were beginning to wonder about them.

"There's no cell phone service," my mother said breathlessly through the rolled down car window as she slowed down in front of the inn.

"No," I said. "There isn't."

My heart was pounding as I watched her pull into the parking lot. Just knowing that she and my father were in the same town was making me want to go run and bury my head in a pillow. The dream-like state I'd entered into that morning was now overcome by a burst of panic as I realized what it was going to be like to suffer through an entire weekend with both my parents. I just tried to shove it down and not think about it.

The rest of the guests began arriving the next day. Although it was overcast, the rain had held off and for Vermont it was fairly warm. I had made a silent deal with the weather gods that it was fine if it rained on Saturday as long as it didn't rain on Sunday. So far they seemed to have signed on.

Steven and I sat in rocking chairs on the front porch of the inn, rocking back and forth quietly. Every now and then a car would pull up to the inn, and the people inside would roll down their windows and yell out to one of us. There would then be hellos, introductions, a discussion of the drive, and comments about how beautiful the location was. Then they would roll up their windows and park behind the inn; and we would go back to our rocking chairs and await the next car. As we sat there rocking silently I marveled to myself at how astonishing it was that people were actually coming. I mean, it's hard enough to get people to commit to going out to dinner. But here we'd picked a date, told people we were getting married, and like magic they just showed up. I would continue to find this astonishing throughout the weekend with every aspect of the wedding. The band, whose members we'd never met and had communicated with primarily through e-mail, materialized at exactly the time they'd said they would. The florist, the wind trio, the photographer, they all came, just as they'd said they would, and suddenly it was real. They weren't just random voices I'd been speaking to on the phone or ghost-fingers typing e-mails, but actual people.

I'd slept very little the night before, and the day passed just as the previous one had. I lived in my little bubble and watched myself talk to people and be the happy bride. I smiled at my relatives and suddenly knew little tidbits of information about Steven's guests. I found that I was easily able to remember people's names by virtue of having written them on envelopes, seating cards, seating charts, and countless spreadsheets.

And again, amazingly, people did the things we'd told them to. They arrived with tennis racquets and headed for the courts. Others rented bikes and rode around. People with children went off to look at the sheep at a nearby farm; the younger crowd folded up trail maps into their back pockets and went hiking; the older crowd marched off dutifully to the cheese factory to watch cheese being made. As hosts, Steven and I did none of this. We ran around making sure everyone was happy. By the late afternoon someone mentioned getting something to eat and I realized that I had not only entirely forgotten about both breakfast and lunch, but that even so I wasn't remotely hungry.

That evening I went back to the honeymoon suite and put on the little white lace dress I'd bought for the rehearsal dinner. It looked to me like something one would wear to a wedding in the Valley of the Dolls, and I thought it was funny. And still, none of it was real. I watched myself step out of the shower, get dressed, put on my makeup. I watched as I went to the barn for the rehearsal dinner; and I thought to myself, I just want to go to sleep.

The ribs were pork and they were delicious. Not one person said anything to me about the fact that we were serving pig. I savored those minutes sitting there eating my ribs. The bulk of my friends had arrived late in the day—their carful of people from Manhattan had been delayed, they explained, when they all decided they didn't have the right clothes and had to stop at a mall in Massachusetts to go shopping—and it was lovely to sit with them, to just sit, and listen to them talk and laugh. They sounded like they were having a good time, and for a few moments it took my mind off of my parents, both of whom had gone into hiding. My mother had been holed up in her room for most of the day; my father had been glued to a football game in the living room of his house.

Steven sat next to me as we munched away on the ribs. We'd been able to see some of each other during the day, but it seemed as though one of us was always being hustled off into some activity by one guest or another. Someone wanted to meet one of us, say hello to the other, show us something, explain something else. I can't recall a word that was said that evening. I look back at it and all I hear is white noise.

That night, my last night as a single woman, I slept fitfully. I'd taken a big fat sleeping pill before I got into bed, but I was so wound up it had almost no effect. Well, I suppose the lack of effect could have had something to do with the fact that I'd been taking the sleeping pills almost every night that week and I was building up a tolerance. The first time I'd taken a pill I almost passed out while walking from the couch, where I'd swallowed the pill moments earlier, to the bed. But now I lay awake all night. I was exhausted, but sleep would not come. At around four in the morning I took another sleeping pill, knowing full well that they were supposed to last for eight hours. It put me out for three hours; at seven . . . ping. . . . I was up again. I lay in bed for another hour, repeating to myself: this is my wedding day. Here it is. My wedding day. This is it. Now get up already.

I crept out of bed while Steven was still sleeping and pulled back the window curtain. No rain. In fact, it looked like there might even be a little sun. I got back into bed and curled up next to Steven. He opened his eyes and looked at me.

"Happy wedding day," he whispered.

I closed my eyes and smiled. "Happy wedding day."

We lay like that for a while, then finally one of us suggested we get out of bed and greet the day. We dressed in silence, almost as though we were conserving our thoughts and words for the deluge of conversation that we knew awaited us throughout the rest of the day. We walked over to the inn for breakfast, and as soon as Steven pushed open the door we were swept away into the madding crowd of guests.

"Here they are!" someone cried. Then Steven was at the opposite end of the room talking to someone, greeting someone else, and I was being pushed and pulled along an endlessly running river of good mornings and so-nice-to-see-yous. At one point I looked up to survey the room and discovered my parents sharing a breakfast table with a smattering of what used to be their collective friends. Steeling myself, I decided I'd better check on the situation, and sat down at the table. To my amazement, the conversation was, if not amicable, at least polite. Which isn't to say that it wasn't incredibly tense and didn't make me wish I could order a round of Bloody Marys for the table. But at least they were trying. I managed to nibble a few bites of bagel before someone pulled me away into some other table's conversation, and then before I knew it, breakfast was over and it was time for the softball game.

I'd seen my brother and Steven's brother walking around handing out T-shirts, to the delight of the breakfast crowd. Someone had handed me a BRIDE T-shirt, and then Joshua was telling me he couldn't hand out the shirts fast enough. People thought they were great. Even the people who weren't playing wanted one. I breathed a sigh of relief that we'd decided to order extra. My two hipper-than-thou friends, Jami and Liz, met in the lobby and discovered that they had both chopped up their T-shirts in exactly the same way, sawing off the sleeves and hacking the neckline to pieces.

"I'm totally wearing this around Brooklyn," Liz was saying to Jami, who replied that she was sure she'd be the only one in Williamsburg with a BRIDE T-shirt.

"I'm never wearing this shirt again," my father was saying to someone within my hearing range. "Now, if it said Schank-Shaklan wedding I might wear it again. But BRIDE? I'm going to walk around with a T-shirt that says BRIDE?"

I tried to tune him out and find someone who was having a good time.

"Where's everyone else?" I asked someone standing next to me.

"They're already out on the softball field. They can't wait to get going," said the person. Maybe it was my mother.

I walked over to the field behind the inn and discovered most of the guests engaged in batting practice. It was one of the funniest things I'd ever seen. There on the field were almost all the people I'd known since I was a baby, all wearing light blue BRIDE T-shirts, swinging bats and running around bases just as I'd asked them to. With everyone in uniform it almost looked like a real softball game. More people arrived, and then someone was suggesting we take team photographs, so we all got into groups and posed with our teammates. Some people kneeled in front with their softball gloves like it was a real team photo, and then Steven's team was posing and he was lying down in front like the team mascot. Then Steven and I were standing together talking and people were coming over and asking us to pose for pictures.

"Because he's the groom and he's wearing a shirt that says GROOM," they all explained. "And you're the bride and you're wearing a shirt that says BRIDE."

"Yes," one of us would reply. "We see the humor."

And then we were drawing up a batting order and the game had started. I had decided I would only bat since I'd never been much of a fielder; and I figured that if I were daring enough to try fielding, this would be the one game where I would get my nose broken by a high fly ball. So Jami agreed to field for me. Just as the game was getting under way the sun broke through the clouds and it was the most gorgeous day I'd ever lived through. The sun made the mountains turn a bright emerald shade of green, so bright they seemed to sparkle. I was suddenly aware of all the possible shades of green one could find in a mountain scene—the dark pine-green of the mountain top, the lighter emerald farther down, fading into a yellowish green by the base, the immeasurable blue of the sky, the white puffs of cloud. All the colors, combined with the remnants of the sleeping pill and the surrealness of the fact that this was my wedding day, made me feel like I'd taken a heavy dose of hallucinogenic drugs.

The sounds of the softball game getting under way came to me like soft musical notes, with the low crack of the bat and high-pitched yelps of glee punctuating the air every now and then. I sat with a group of my friends who weren't playing—Kimberly with her swollen belly and flowy shirt, Amanda pushing her new baby in a stroller, Liz, who had decided, despite raving about how much she loved her T-shirt, that she wasn't much of a ball player. We sat and marveled at the beauty of the day and the fact that in a few hours I would be married. It just happened that we were all watching the game when the first drama of the day began to unfold. Someone hit a fly ball out to center field, and the crack was so loud that my friends and I all turned to watch the ball soar into the sky. I followed it as it flew high into the air and the center fielder, too far away for me to determine who it was, ran in and got under the ball. And then, suddenly, the ball was rolling away on the ground and the center fielder was lying face down in the dirt.

"What happened?" I said to no one in particular. I saw Steven run across the field to the downed player and said a silent prayer of thanks that he wasn't the one on the ground. I spied my mother sitting on the bench closer to the field and walked over to her. The center fielder was still lying on the ground.

"Who is that?" I asked her.

"Steven's brother," she said, her voice thin with rising panic.

"Oh, shit," I said.

Other players were now kneeling by the lump on the ground that was Steven's brother, Danny. I saw Steven's father rush over to his son, and then Danny was up and wobbling slowly off the field. Time must have passed, but it seemed like only minutes later someone was telling me that Steven's uncle, a doctor, thought Danny had a concussion, and he was off to the emergency room. This being Vermont, the nearest hospital was an hour away in Brattleboro.

After Danny left a somewhat subdued form of play continued. I walked back over to my friends and we picked up our conversation.

"Well," I remember saying to someone. "You've got to figure that something is going to go wrong. Hopefully that's it and it's out of the way."

No sooner were the words out of my mouth than I heard a kind of commotion on the field. I heard angry voices and yelling. What happened next I'm still not quite clear on. All I know is that I turned to the field and saw my father, Steven's father, Steven, and assorted other guests screaming at each other. I ran over to Steven and grabbed his arm.

"What's going on?" I panicked. "What happened?"

"Nothing," he snapped, walking away from me. "Nothing, let's just play."

"But what happened?"

"It's stupid," he yelled back. "It's not important. Can we just play please?" This last part was directed toward the cluster of men in BRIDE and GROOM T-shirts yelling at each other near the pitcher's mound.

I ran over to the bench where my mother was sitting. "What happened?" I asked her.

"I don't know," she said. Again, there was panic in her voice. "Someone said someone else was cheating, and now they're all yelling at each other."

A few minutes later a hostile form of play resumed. I felt sick inside. People were angry and I didn't know why. Steven's brother was in the hospital. And I suddenly remembered that the rabbi had yet to arrive. Checking my watch, I realized it was past one—time for me to start getting ready.

"All right ladies," I called to a cluster of my friends, trying to pre-

tend that everything was fabulous. "I'm going to get ready. The
salon people are coming at one, so come by then if you want your
hair or nails done."

I found Steven standing in a tight circle of guests, talking in the
short, clipped tones of someone who is beyond furious. Seeing me,
he nodded in my direction and walked over.

"Okay," I said. "I'm off to make myself beautiful."

"All right," he said. "Go do your girl things."

I put my arms around his waist.

"Can you please just tell me what happened?"

"It's not important," he said.

"It's obviously important," I replied. "I want to know why you're
so upset."

"I don't want to upset you."

"I'm already upset."

"Let's talk about it later."

I looked at him. He'd never been so evasive, but I knew he gen-
uinely didn't want me to get upset about whatever it was that was
making him so angry, and for that I loved him. It was completely
unlike me, but I just decided to let it go. The fact was, I really didn't
want to know what it was. Whatever the issue, I just wanted it to
go away. I wanted to return to the moment of bliss right before
Danny got hit in the head.

"Okay," I sighed, resting my head on his shoulder.

Steven hugged me hard. "I love you," he whispered.

"Oh babe," I whispered back. "I love you too."

We stayed like that for a moment. I didn't want to leave him. I
felt like he was my only ally in a town filled with suddenly hostile
guests.

I pulled away on inch or so and looked at him. "The next time
you see me I'll be in a wedding dress," I said.

"I know," he said. "I can't wait."

So much of the weekend is a blur, but the shower in White Gates is
a vivid memory. It is dark and cool in White Gates, and it feels won-

derful to stand there under the water. I'm in Kimberly's shower and she has all kinds of interesting products lined up on the floor. Ordinarily I wouldn't pry into someone else's beauty products, but I am the bride, and I figure that if there is any day to pry, this would be it. I open up various bottles and sniff the contents. She has an interesting-looking shaving foam that I try out on my legs, even though they have been waxed smooth and don't need to be shaved. I put conditioner in my hair and slowly pull it through the wet strands with a plastic comb, just as I always do, just as I have done in every shower I've taken for the last fifteen or so years. Only now, this is my last shower as a single woman. Everything I do that afternoon I think, *this is the last time I will do this as a single woman. The next time I brush my teeth, the next time I smooth on deodorant, the next time I pluck my eyebrows, I will be an old married lady.*

My friends arrive half an hour later, along with two women from the local beauty salon. I am getting my nails painted in a shade picked out three months ago by Ellen, while Kimberly is getting her hair done and my mother is showering and Ellen is finding us sandwiches because she's discovered that I haven't eaten much more than a bagel in the past three days. Jeannette, one of my friends from college, is sitting on the couch and talking to me as though it is just any other day and we're just two friends hanging out. The hairdresser is blowing Kimberly's hair out with fat round brushes and I'm thinking it looks a little poofy, but maybe that's what Kimberly wants, now that she's pregnant and lives in Connecticut. Maybe this is how pregnant women in Connecticut wear their hair. My nails are looking atrocious, the polish is running down into my cuticles, which have been clipped ragged, but I really don't care that much and somehow I'm imagining that when they dry they'll look fine. The only other time I've had my nails manicured was for my bat mitzvah, and while I hated having them polished, I was fascinated by the fact that when you get a manicure the polish chips off in big, satisfying chunks, which makes you want to do nothing all day but sit around and chip polish off your nails, much as you sometimes feel compelled to peel the skin off your back in whole flakes a few days after a bad sunburn. It is bad for you and it looks terrible, but you can't stop picking at it. I'd hated the feeling of having polish on my nails, and I believe even way back then, when I was thirteen and supposedly a woman but really only on the cusp of teenagedom, I knew that the next time I wore nail polish would be the day that I got married.

The hairdresser and the manicurist are blabbing away while they do Kimberly's hair and my nails, and Kimberly seems to be panicking that they're taking too long. They have three hours to do all our hair and nails, and they've already spent almost forty-five minutes on her hair. They've spent just as long polishing my nails, but that's because I can't sit still and every time they finish with one hand, I flail it around to dry the polish and bunk it into something and then they have to redo the nails again. The hairdresser and the manicurist are telling stories of past clients they've had, and I think there is some questionable racial content thrown in for good measure, so we try to ignore them and we don't tell them we're having a Jewish wedding. I always feel compelled to laugh with hairdressers to make them feel like they have a good audience, which, my theory goes, will make them like me and make them do my hair better. So I'm trying to laugh, but I'm also thinking about how long it's taking the hairdresser to do everything because she can't seem to talk and style at the same time, and she won't shut up. And I'm thinking about Danny and asking someone to find out if he's back from the hospital yet (he isn't) and if the rabbi has arrived yet (he hasn't) and then it's Panic City, but all I can do is sit and act pleased to be a bride on her wedding day.

And then my nails are done and my mother comes downstairs all freshly showered in a T-shirt and shorts and is ready to have her nails done. Ellen arrives with sandwiches. She forces me to take a bite of turkey sandwich, specially prepared for me without mayonnaise, which I hate, and as I chomp into it I also chomp down on my lip and I draw blood. I hurry Ellen into the kitchen and away from my mother because I know if she finds out I bit my lip, she may freak out, and I can't have anyone else but me freaking out right now. Ellen and I sit in the kitchen and she hands me a chunk of ice, which I put on my lip. I accidentally bite my lips all the time—a combination of having a naturally puffy lower lip and being a zealous, if somewhat distracted, eater. I can feel that I might cry because I don't want to walk down the aisle with a swollen lip, but Ellen looks at it and says, just keep the ice on for another few minutes and it will be fine. So we sit there, cold water dripping from the corner of my mouth onto my chin, and it is my wedding day.

The ice is almost gone when someone comes in and says the flowers have arrived, do I want to take a look. So we go out to the driveway and there is Colleen with her van. She says hello and slides the door open so we can peek inside. It looks like a bunch of flowers to me, but I say they're beautiful. And then she hands me my bouquet, which is comprised exclusively of pink, champagne, and burgundy–colored roses. I look at it and I think, I don't want to get upset that it's all roses, at least the colors are mostly right, I will focus on the colors. Then she produces a flower for my hair, which is a rose twisted up with a bunch of baby's breath, the little white floral sprays you usually see on the wrist of a prom queen. They are so precious and dainty and absolutely the opposite of what I had in mind for my wedding day, and my friends all agree that they look stupid, but we all say, well, whatever. Then we go back to the living room and Ellen is having her hair twisted up into a French twist at the back of her head, which looks fine, and then, horror of horrors, the hairdresser produces a curling iron. I had specifically said no curling iron when we'd met with her back in May, and when Ellen sees the curling iron out of the corner of her eye she practically jumps out of the chair.

"No curling irons, please," she snaps.

The hairdresser recoils from Ellen as though she's been bitten, and explains that there's nothing wrong with curling irons, but Ellen will have none of it. She thinks they're cheesy, and most of New York City agrees with her.

And then, finally, it is my turn in the chair, and I'm a bit apprehensive after watching what she's done to Kimberly and Ellen, but I figure I have a lot of hair, and we've discussed the style I want, so it will all be fine. After much pulling and twisting, she hands me a mirror. She's taken a large mirror off the wall from the hallway of the house, as apparently she has not come with her own, and it is huge and requires two hands and lots of bicep action for me to keep it aloft. It is also an antique decorative mirror, which means that it is warped in the center like a funhouse mirror, so that my nose stretches out like Pinocchio's and my forehead looks the size of a small lemon. I can't see much, but what I can see looks awful.

"Is there another mirror?" I ask. I can hear the desperation creeping into my voice. Someone finds a small pocket mirror and hands it to me, and I stare at my reflection.

My hair is slicked back from my face and tied in a loose knot at the back of my head. The curls look simultaneously plastic and frizzy. I have never seen my hair look worse, not even when I've just woken up from a long night of barhopping.

"I look like I just came back from a run," I whisper. And then I start to cry. At first it is just small tears appearing on my cheeks, and then it is, to my mortification, a huge sob that wells up from somewhere deep in my diaphragm and forces itself violently out. I hand someone the mirror and bury my head in my hands, and I cry and cry. I cry for my parents, who cannot speak to each other and have to hide in their rooms, I cry for Steven's family who now has a son in the hospital with a concussion, I cry for my guests who hate each other because of some stupid softball game, I cry for the year of my life that has passed while I planned and planned and has now culminated in my sitting in a chair in Vermont sobbing, and most of all, I cry for my hair. My poor hair, which has so much potential and only wants to be loved and beautiful, and could be, if only I had a competent hairdresser.

"I'm sorry," I say to the hairdresser. "It's not because of my hair." Then I excuse myself and run to the bathroom and lock the door and have a good long cry and it feels fabulous. It's the best thing that I've done all weekend. When I'm finished I come out of the bathroom and find Ellen sitting outside.

"Who else is out there?" I ask.

"Just Jeannette," she says. My mother and Kimberly had both gone upstairs to get dressed before the tears began to fall.

"Don't tell my mother," I say. "Or Kimberly."

"I won't," she says.

I go back into the bathroom and splash water on my face and then walk back into the living room and sit back down in the chair in front of the hairdresser.

"Let's try it again," I say. I explain what I want her to do, and, now silent, she redoes my hair. When she is done, she hands me the small mirror. It's a looser version of the hair I had a few minutes earlier, and the curls look a little happier. I won't say that it was the best hairstyle in the world, but it was passable.

"Thank you," I say. And then I look at my watch and discover I have only half an hour to get into my dress and put on my makeup before the photographer arrives.

Ellen and Jeannette and I run upstairs to join Kimberly and my mother in the big suite where everyone is getting dressed. My mother is already in her dress, which turns out to be not brown at all, but a shimmery amber color that is stunning and goes perfectly with the wedding colors.

"You look beautiful, Mama," I tell her.

She smiles sadly at me. I guess she doesn't have anyone around to tell her that anymore. Or maybe she doesn't think she looks beautiful, or maybe she's just sad because I'm getting married and there is something sad about a wedding.

Then Ellen is doing my makeup and Jeannette is helping me into my gown and my mother is fastening my grandmother's diamond bracelet onto my wrist and I am sliding my great-grandmother's art deco diamond earrings into my earlobes. Everyone is marveling over how beautiful the dress is, and the instant Jeannette zips it up, I feel thrilled to be in it. I look at myself in the mirror and look at my dress and now, suddenly, I am crazy in love with the dress. It is the most beautiful garment I've ever owned, and I want to sleep in it and eat breakfast in it and wear it always.

There is mad chaos as Ellen is finishing Kimberly's makeup and my mother is fluffing out the dress and Jeannette is smoothing out the train and then suddenly there is pounding at the door and we're all yelling who the fuck is that and it is my father's wife demanding deodorant and someone is hurrying her out the door.

Someone announces that the photographer is here, and someone else says that the rabbi has arrived, and I feel much better about things, but I'm still worried that Steven's brother isn't back yet. And I finally decide it's time, and I pull open the door to the suite and ask someone to tell the photographer that I'm about to walk down the stairs and that I want her to take a picture of Steven's reaction when he sees me, because Steven is supposed to be at the bottom of the stairs waiting for me. We'd decided in a moment of completely clear thinking several months earlier that we wanted to see each other before walking down the aisle. And right now there is nothing I want to do more than see Steven and have him wrap his arms around me. I desperately want his presence. I don't care about the wedding or the guests or anything right then. I just want to be with him.

"Wait!" yells Kimberly as I pull the door open. I turn back towards her and she snaps a picture of me. "The last picture of you as a single woman," she says, and I smile and yell down the stairs that I'm coming down. Someone yells back that they're ready for me and I carefully lift up my train and walk down the rickety two-hundred-year-old stairs. As I turn the corner halfway down the staircase I see Steven's parents and my parents and my brother and my grandmother all waiting at the bottom, smiling up at me, and then I see Steven and I lose all composure once again and burst into tears. I start to run towards him, but my nose is now running so I make a beeline past him towards a box of tissues. And then, tissue in hand, I turn to Steven and bury my face in his shoulder and sob, and again, it is my happiest moment of the day.

Then we are taking pictures and somehow the mad rush to get me out the door seems silly now, as we've all the time in the world to loll in the sun in our wedding finery. To everyone's relief Steven's brother materializes, looking a little dazed but generally okay. Then there are endless combinations of photographs, but the photographer has carefully orchestrated it so that my mother and father are never in a picture together. And then I'm standing out by myself on the front porch of White Gates, looking down the hill at the ceremony site. Phantom people have arranged white chairs in a semicircle down there by the swim pond, and there is a very simple, pretty chuppah and I'm looking at it thinking, *huh, someone is getting married today. How nice. What a beautiful day for it.*

My father joins me on the porch, and we smile at each other uncomfortably.

"Well," says my father. "You do look more beautiful than I've ever seen you look." He says it begrudgingly, in a way that makes it sound like he usually thinks I look like crap. Even so, I appreciate it, because my father never tells me I look beautiful, not ever. And anyway, I am in my bubble, and I feel beautiful no matter what. I feel, dare I say it, like a princess. I am dressed in the finest silks and satins and I have flowers in my hair (albeit baby's breath) and I suddenly can do nothing but smile.

"Thank you," I say.

My father puts his hands in his suit pockets. He has chosen a dark gray suit over the pink-and-gray-striped Versace, and is wearing the tie I sent him. A single calla lily is pinned to his lapel. Someone must have distributed the boutonnieres. That was nice of them, whoever it was. I watch my father surveying the ceremony site, and I'm proud of how handsome he looks in his wedding attire.

"So," says my father. "You sure you want to do this?"

I smile because it is just the sort of thing I expected him to say. "Yes."

As the word comes out of my mouth, I know that it's true. I have never been more sure of anything than I am at that moment. There is nothing in the world I would want more right then than to walk down the aisle and marry Steven.

I hear a flurry of activity out on the patio, and my father and I walk through the house to see what the commotion is about. It is the rabbi, who has finally arrived. My father stares at the rabbi and turns to me.

"He's not wearing a yarmulke," he says.

"I told you," I say. "I told you he might not."

"No you didn't. You never said anything about the rabbi not wearing a yarmulke."

"Yes I did. I told you. Maybe you forgot, but I told you."

"No," says my father. "I would have remembered something like that."

"Well," I say. "Ellen is going to go talk to him about it. We have it taken care of. Ellen is going to ask him nicely to wear a yarmulke."

"I'll talk to him," says my father.

"Ellen will do it."

"I'll do it. I can be very charming."

I look at my father, at his gruff beard and smooth pate and perpetually angry eyes. He doesn't look it, but I know that it's true, he can in fact be charming. He can be friendly and witty and lovely. He just doesn't usually choose to be.

I sigh.

"Okay. Talk to him."

Then I am off taking more pictures. Steven is around somewhere, but I don't see him and we don't talk. I am managing things. I am sending someone down to the swim pond with a basket of yarmulkes for the guests. I am asking someone to check if the ceremony musicians have arrived. I am making sure all the right permutations of pictures have been snapped. The thought flashes through my brain that what I am doing is akin to putting on a full-scale Broadway production. There are sets and costumes and musicians and choreography and there is even an audience. And then I am walking by my father, who is sitting in a white wooden chair on the patio, and he is fuming. I try to walk by him quickly, because I don't want to know what he's fuming about, but he grabs my arm as I pass.

"The rabbi refused to wear a yarmulke," he hisses into my ear.

I look at him. This sounds unlike the rabbi.

"What do you mean he refused?"

"He refused," my father snaps. "Just flat out refused."

"I doubt that," I say.

"Ask my mother," he says. "She was there. She heard it."

I look at Gammy, who is slumped in a nearby wooden chair.

"It's true," says Gammy. "He was not nice."

"Well," I say. "I guess the wedding is off."

But my father does not laugh. He does not see the humor, and I don't have time to explain how ridiculous it is that he's decided that we must adhere to this one tradition despite the fact that we all ate pork ribs last night. I don't have time to sit down and tell him that Steven and I have talked about it, and that this wedding is about a marriage between me and Steven, not me and my father, not me and the rabbi. And that we have decided that while I would prefer it if the rabbi wore a yarmulke, we are not going to make a big deal out of it. I don't have time to tell him that marriage means that Steven and I are going to be a family, and that as a family we have a right to create our own rules and make our own decisions as to what aspects of the Jewish faith we choose to practice, and that those choices may not be identical to the choices my father has made about his own religious practices. And I don't explain that while the rabbi isn't wearing a yarmulke, my father should get down on his knees and kiss my feet for the fact that Steven is wearing a yarmulke, for the fact that there are yarmulkes at all. I don't have time to say any of these things because I am getting ready to walk down the aisle any minute now, and also because I see that not only is my father fuming, but out of the corner of my eye I see the rabbi fuming, and the last thing I want is a rabbi who fumes his way through the marriage vows. And so I put it out of my mind. I file it away in the back of my head and I decide I will not let my father rain anger on my wedding day.

But just as I have decided this, the rabbi comes over and asks if he can speak privately with Steven and me. Steven is then at my side, and the three of us are walking back inside and sitting down in the dining room. It is dim and slightly musty in the dining room, and it's nice to just sit down for a minute.

"Do you remember," says the rabbi, "when you came and met with me in the synagogue and we talked about sovereignty?"

Steven and I nod. The rabbi had given us a lengthy talk on our second visit about how getting married meant that we would be sovereign unto ourselves. This meant that while we should still respect our parents, we would now be honorbound to also respect each other. We shouldn't, in other words, let our parents shape and dictate our marriage. It was from this very talk, in fact, that Steven and

I had come to the conclusion about the yarmulkes. It is from this talk that I now draw strength to stand up to my father.

"Your father has suggested that he would like me to wear a yarmulke," the rabbi says to me.

I nod slowly, as though this is the first time I am hearing this information.

"Which I'm happy to do, but only if that's what you want. If it's someone else imposing their values on you, then I won't do it."

"Oh no," I say. "I'd like it if you would."

"Okay," he says. "I just wanted to make sure that it was what you wanted."

I smile to myself as the rabbi stands up and excuses himself. I like the idea that the rabbi thought my father was forcing his arcane and old-world value judgments on me, as though my father were a nineteenth-century immigrant just off the boat from Poland, demanding that his Americanized daughter keep a kosher home and submit to an arranged marriage. How very *Fiddler on the Roof.*

As I sit in my chair the rabbi is gathering everyone into the dining room for the *ketubah* signing. I notice that he is now wearing a champagne-colored yarmulke. Steven is sitting next to me and the rabbi is reading from the *ketubah* and I feel the rest of the wedding party—our collective friends and families—shifting heavily in the background. I can hear that they're not sure where to put their hands or exactly how to stand. Then we are signing the *ketubah* and we must have signed the marriage license, although I have no memory of it. But I do remember thinking, well, that's it, we're married, and the ceremony hasn't even begun yet, and it's all so very strange.

And then we're all standing out on the patio watching the guests arrive down the hill. They can't see us, but we can see them, and it's like observing a wedding from heaven. I can hear strains of familiar music floating up the hill, and it dawns on me that it is being produced by the wind trio. They are playing Bach, just as we asked and argued and bickered over. It sounds lovely, but it also sounds like it comes from very far away, and again it is hard to believe that *this is it.* Then we're all making our way down the hill to the apple tree, where Holly meets us. Steven is gone; he must have walked down the aisle already. Kimberly and Scott, the best man, are gone down the aisle as well. I am standing with my parents and my brother and my grandmothers now. Focusing for a minute, I notice that both of my grandmothers are holding their pocketbooks and looking somewhat confused.

"Mama," I say to my mother. "They're both holding pocketbooks."

"Ma," she says to her mother. "What, you think you're going to buy something as you go down the aisle?"

I turn to Holly, who has materialized at my elbow, and ask her to do something with the pocketbooks. The grandmothers both seem worried about surrendering their bags, and only do so after multiple assurances that they will be reunited with them at the end of the ceremony. They also look dazed, and I think for a second about how sad old age can be. I think about my grandfathers who aren't here, especially my father's father, who would have loved to watch me, his only granddaughter, walk down the aisle. I think about Gammy, who is here but isn't really. Only parts of her personality are left, as though the rest has simply evaporated as she aged, leaving her stuck trying to walk down the aisle with a pocketbook, an act that her former self never would have allowed. And as I watch my brother loop arms with my grandmothers and walk down the aisle, I think about my parents, who are also here but they aren't.

It is just the three of us now, standing under the apple tree. My father on my left and my mother on my right, and here we are, the three of us, my family, on my wedding day. Even though my brother was born when I was just on the edge of turning three, I always think of him as a newcomer, an interloper who ruined the wondrous age of the Family Of Three, where I was the sole focal point, the little child in plaid pants with the helmet of white-gold hair who received nothing but unadulterated love and affection from her parents. The child whose parents loved each other too, so much that they took pictures of each other doing the most mundane things, like mowing the lawn with a hand-powered metal lawn mower or sitting in flowered clothing in their backyard.

I look at my parents, and I notice that we are all smiling now. We are still all slightly on edge—after all, we're about to walk down the aisle—but then my father says something sarcastic and silly and we're all laughing, even my mother, and for just a moment, we are a family again. And right then I realize that this was the moment I planned the entire wedding for. If weddings are about fantasies, then this was mine: I wanted my family back together again, even if it was for a few fleeting seconds. And right then, as I bask in the warmth of my family, it is all worth it. The months of tears and obsession and ribbon and Martha Stewart. It is all worth it.

I hear the music stop, the sounds of the oboe and the flute and the bassoon are replaced by the soft sound of water bubbling from a nearby stream, and then I know that everyone else is in the ready position. The guests are in their seats, the wedding party is under the chuppah, the grandmothers are seated, and Steven is waiting for me. The music starts up again; this time it is one of the Jewish selections I picked out, not the one Steven hated but a different one, and again I can't help but think, wow, I picked out that music back in March and here it is, in August, being played exactly as I asked. Holly nods at me and I link arms with my parents and we begin our walk down the aisle. One minute I am standing at the foot of the aisle listening to the beautiful music and watching all the guests turn around to look at me, the star, the next I am kissing my parents good-bye as I leave them and step up to the chuppah.

"I'll see you later," I say to them. Even as I say it, I think it's a funny thing to say, and they look sad, like they don't want me to go.

The ceremony begins, there are Hebrew words to repeat and there is wine to sip, rings are exchanged, and all I can think about is how happy I am to finally be standing next to Steven, how it feels like an eternity since we've seen each other, how all I want is for the ceremony to be over so I can kiss him. We stand next to each other, and I feel like an invisible wall of Plexiglas separates us. I can't touch him and he can't touch me and for those ten or fifteen minutes, it is excruciating. Finally I hear a delicious crunch as he breaks the wine glass under his foot, and I practically leap into his arms. I kiss him and kiss him, I throw my arms around him and try not to sob, I am so happy to be close to him. Then he looks at me, and the happy klezmer music starts up somewhere and the guests are clapping and shouting *mazel tov*, and we both start to laugh because the whole thing is so silly and ridiculous. We've planned a big, fancy wedding and we've pulled it off.

Afterword

It is only a slight exaggeration to say that as Steven was sliding an engagement ring on my finger I was thinking about how I wanted to write a book on planning my wedding. As we stood in our living room on a sweaty August evening, my hair rumpled, my shirt sticking to my back, pretending that I hadn't been needlessly crabby all afternoon and that my life was now fabulous thanks to the diamond that had suddenly taken up residence on my ring finger, I felt one thing: ridiculous. This was not how it was supposed to be. In every movie, book, play—in every anything I had ever encountered over the course of my life that portrayed this very moment in a woman's existence—the woman was never crabby and sweaty and feeling silly. She always knew exactly how to react. Sometimes she stormed off or threw the ring at the guy, but usually she became instantly happy. Which isn't to say I wasn't happy. I was. I loved Steven. I wanted to marry him. But the rest of it felt . . . odd. What was wrong with me? Why wasn't I giddy with excitement?

Well, nothing was wrong with me said the rational part of my brain. I just wasn't that kind of girl. The giddy kind. The one who cheered her teammates on effortlessly in JV volleyball. The one for whom wedding planning and baby showers and nail polish came naturally. There were allegedly women in the world, and this became even more apparent as I began immersing myself in Wedding Land, who loved weddings. They loved pink. They loved ribbons and flower arrangements and wanted to grow up to be princesses. And those women, it seemed, were running the bridal industry. Worse than that, they were intimidating every other woman out there with their uber-femaleness. They were publishing magazine after magazine reinforcing the princess bride persona, they were staffing the reception areas of bridal stores, they were writing lists on The Knot of 187 tasks to do for your wedding.

But what I've discovered since the publication of *A More Perfect Union* is this: nobody thinks they are *that girl,* the super-girly-female. In fact, that girl may not even exist, or if she does there are maybe only ten of them in the world, each wielding the power of a thousand mascara applicators. I have spoken with women who work at bridal magazines, I have received e-mails from women who maintain pictorial lists of their favorite cakes in their online Knot profiles, I have talked with readers who have planned extravagant weddings. None of them thinks they are girly-girls, or at the very least, they know someone who is girlier than they are, who makes them feel a tad insecure. I can point to friends on either end of the girly spectrum—I know people who are way girlier than I am, and I have friends for whom I am probably the epitome of girliness.

Much of *A More Perfect Union* deals with the way the wedding industry makes women feel insecure by essentially out-girl-ing everyone. There is, I am quite confident, no girlier entity on the entire planet than the wedding world. And the result is that women who have previously led normal, nonwedding-related lives, suddenly find themselves competing on a field they didn't even know existed. Women who had previously been perfectly content with their level of girliness, whatever it was, watch terrified as they move a few notches over on the spectrum in an attempt to prove that they, too, can create a perfect floral centerpiece.

One's level on the girliness spectrum is information that most women walk around knowing without articulating, like your jeans size or the fact that you hate peas. For example: one might be a size six and girly enough to get weekly manicures but not girly enough to love baby showers. Or girly enough to love baby showers but not girly enough to wear a floral dress to one. And so on. But while on the surface the girliness spectrum seems to be about making nail polish or clothing decisions, on a deeper level it is about the way we choose to live our lives: about how we choose to marry, whether we decide to have children, whether we opt to have careers or be stay-at-home moms. Where we fall on the spectrum, at the heart of the issue, is the struggle between traditional and so-called feminist sex roles. And weddings are emblematic of this struggle. Which is why the decision about how one marries is so fraught with drama for many women, who find themselves sliding over toward traditional weddings and taking on traditional female roles and tasks when they had previously lived out most of their lives thinking they were fully empowered, self-aware feminists.

For people who have not been through this struggle, women who either embraced the girliness or were content to get married in cargo pants and order takeout Chinese to celebrate, a book about weddings is easy to dismiss, and A More Perfect Union has received some criticism on both ends of the continuum. On the one hand, there were people who responded to the book by saying, "Well, of course women have princess fantasies. Duh." This criticism is one more variation on the belief that if something is an issue primarily of import to women then it is silly and dull.

A book about the effect soccer has on world politics—great, bring it on, make it a bestseller. A book about the effect yoga has on world politics—um . . . probably not going to happen. Intellectual discussions about body image, weddings, or pregnancy? Absurd. Or, if we really have to talk about those types of things, let's just group them together under "women's issues" and dismiss them.

The vast amount of writing on motherhood provides a perfect example of the world's inability to address these "women's issues" seriously. It seems like practically every day someone else is publishing a book on how to be a better mommy, how to balance motherhood with work, how not to balance motherhood with work, the value of staying at home, the new official correct way to be a mother, and so on. One of these writers recently made the point that in no other body of intellectual discussion is it acceptable to completely disregard anyone who has come before you. Women who write about being mothers frequently don't take the time to go back and read historical theories on motherhood the way you might if you were writing about, say, Abraham Lincoln. And this is in part due to the fact that women themselves don't feel that writing about a women's issue is as serious as writing about Lincoln. They don't treat it as an intellectual subject. The same goes for weddings.

So I suppose I shouldn't have been surprised when my book was dismissed as one more dopey women's book by some people who seem not to have gotten past the copyright page. Because who cracks open a wedding book with plans to take it seriously?

And then, on the other end of the continuum, there were the people who wondered what kind of neo-feminist-career-track-high-powered-professional woman writes a book about weddings anyway? Because we are so beyond that now, and on to more important issues. Women are thinking about physics and the stock market and neuroscience, goes the hyper-feminist argument. Women should not be thinking about weddings.

This is the more dangerous, more insidious argument. Because people who are simply dismissive about weddings as a "women's issue," or people who assume that of course a woman's wedding is the happiest day or her life, can be proven wrong by the scores of women who live their lives against the grain, by women whose happiest days include things like winning promotions, closing big deals, or any other type of professional or personal success. But the critics who argue that women should be better than all of this wedding silliness, who respond to the very real, scary situation that many women find themselves in when planning their weddings of suddenly behaving like someone else by saying, essentially, "we should be beyond this," do women a greater disservice than any wedding magazine could. Because ignoring a problem does not make it go away. If anything, it only makes the problem worse.

Whereas the traditionalist critics wondered why I'd bothered to write a book about weddings in the first place, the arch-progressive critics seemed to want me to apologize to Betty Friedan for failing to burn my bridal magazines, for having the kind of wedding that, in all likelihood, Betty Friedan herself probably had. These critics insist on asking: if you thought wedding planning was so stupid, so girly, so not you, *why did you do it*? To these critics all I can say is, I tried not to! That's the whole point.

Who knew weddings were such a hot button issue? marveled the collective forces associated with the publication of the book, my friends, my parents, and anyone else who knows me and my writing. But I should have anticipated that offering any opinion that can be considered feminist or neo-feminist or post-feminist or any kind of—ist with fem- at the beginning, is dangerous territory. It opens you up to attacks. It makes it easy for people to tell you you're not being the right kind of girl. In what must be the ultimate irony, the women who think they are defenders of the feminist title are essentially doing the same thing that twelve-year-old girls are doing in the schoolyard, or that bridal magazines are doing to would-be brides: they are telling you how to be female. So when we look at the size and girth of the bridal industry, at the fact that even the women who compile lists of "my favorite china patterns" on The Knot think they're *not that kind of girl,* at the fact that women who dare to speak up can eagerly anticipate venom from both ends of the feminist continuum, it becomes glaringly apparent that the blame for Wedding Land must fall to women ourselves.

Since the publication of *A More Perfect Union* things have gotten worse for brides. *Bridezillas* has since hit the airwaves, televising the humiliation of women who have succumbed to the image the bridal industry salivates at—that of the bride so consumed with perfection that she will stop at nothing, spend any amount, berate anyone, to have things her way. I have yet to understand who agrees to be on this show, but that aside, I find it to be completely unwatchable. It's like witnessing half an hour of pain—a car wreck in slow motion, family relationships torn apart, the groom's inevitable descent into irrelevance, a bride who can't even stop herself long enough to enjoy the day she has spent so much time and energy creating. And worst of all, these poor women's nervous breakdowns are served up to the public as comedy. Instead of asking what societal forces have created such an abundance of insane brides that a network is able to fill a weekly TV series, viewers are encouraged to cackle at otherwise high-functioning women who are brought to their knees by the wedding industry. Women think they've come so far, is the underlying message of *Bridezillas*, but look what happens when you take a career woman and stick her in a wedding gown: she reverts to the marriage-crazed banshee we knew was in there all along.

And the media is no longer stopping at brides. *My Super Sweet 16*, on MTV, portrays one spoiled teenager after another complaining that she wants her "big day" to be "perfect." Gee, where would she get an idea like that? Even worse, there are now numerous prom-related magazines on the stand, usually published by the same people who put out bridal magazines, in an effort that nicely parallels the cigarette industry's philosophy of "get 'em young." Hook those young girls into obsession as early as possible. Get them obsessing about their prom dresses, their big day to be a princess/celebutante/movie star. That way they'll already know how to act come wedding planning time, which will save everyone a lot of effort. Ready-made Bridezillas! Genius!

I've been asked a few times what advice I might offer to brides who find themselves becoming obsessed with wedding planning. My advice used to be, remember that it's not about the wedding: it's about a marriage, about starting a life together, about love and family. When you're getting divorced no one is going to say, "I really thought it would last because they had such lovely place cards at their wedding." But now I'm not sure that that's good advice. Because the truth is that when you can't help but become obsessed, having someone tell you to just stop obsessing isn't really all that useful. It's like saying to an alcoholic, "Know what? Maybe you should drink less."

So now my advice is this: know that there is no such thing as the girliest girly-girl. Know that even the women who can give you a forty-two-page typewritten treatise on what kind of wedding cake they want think they might be faking it. Know that no matter what you do there will be people who think your wedding was too traditional or too wacky or just not their kind of thing. And know that, if all goes well, you will never plan another wedding. At the very least, if you're hugely obsessed, you will probably never plan another wedding like the one you're planning now. So savor it. Revel in your dip into uber-femininity. Make everything pink. Learn about all the flowers that are indigenous to your region and force all your bridesmaids to go out into a meadow and pick their own bouquets because you want a "hand-plucked" look. Get as girly as you want to be. Because after your wedding, you will tuck your dress away in a corner and you probably won't look back. You will go back to being the woman you used to be before this whole silly wedding thing happened. So breathe deeply. And enjoy.

References

The following is a list of books that I found useful in researching the wedding world, wedding history, marriage, and divorce. Some of these have a lot of great facts and figures, others are just a terrific read, particularly if you are in the midst of planning a wedding.

Coontz, Stephanie. *The Way We Never Were: American Families and the Nostalgia Trap*. New York: Basic Books, 1992.

Geller, Jaclyn. *Here Comes the Bride: Women, Weddings, and the Marriage Mystique*. New York: Four Walls Eight Windows, 2001.

Heyn, Dalma. *Marriage Shock: The Transformation of Women into Wives*. New York: Villard, 1997.

Ingraham, Chrys. *White Weddings: Romancing Heterosexuality in Popular Culture*. New York: Routledge, 1999.

Pleck, Elizabeth H., and Cele C. Otnes. *Cinderella Dreams: The Allure of the Lavish Wedding*. Los Angeles: University of California Press, 2003.

Maushart, Susan. *Wifework: What Marriage Really Means for Women*. New York: Bloomsbury, 2002.

Monsarrat, Ann. *And the Bride Wore . . . The Story of the White Wedding*. London: Gentry Books, 1973.

Nissinen, Sheryl. *The Conscious Bride: Women Unveil Their True Feelings About Getting Hitched*. New York: New Harbinger, 2000.

Roiphe, Anne. *Married: A Fine Predicament*. New York: Basic Books, 2002.

Seligson, Marcia. *The Eternal Bliss Machine*. New York: Morrow, 1973.

Tanenbaum, Leora. *Catfight: Women and Competition*. New York: Seven Stories Press, 2002.

Wallerstein, Judith, Julia Lewis, and Sandra Blakeslee. *The Unexpected Legacy of Divorce*. New York: Hyperion, 2000.

Acknowledgments

Eternal thanks to Stephen O'Connor for suggesting I expand an essay about getting engaged into a book. Also to Lis Harris, Patty O'Toole, and Michael Scammell for their wise advice, and Ellen Cohen, Melissa Heltzel, and Carol Paik for reading more than their fair share of the manuscript.

This book would not have come into existence without the support of my family: my father, Roger Schank, who said he thought it was about time I wrote a book; my mother, Diane Schank, who bought me my first dictionary when I was seven because she thought I had a way with words; my brother, Joshua Schank, who says that my writing simultaneously makes him want to laugh and jump out a window.

Thanks to Kate Lee, who has been way more attentive than I ever thought an agent would be, and to my editor, Greer Hendricks, for seeing the potential in the manuscript despite being only one day post–maternity leave.

I'm indebted to my in-laws, Marlene and Allen Shaklan, for putting up with my writing about them even though they're not my blood relatives. Sorry about that.

Most of all, thanks to Steven Shaklan, who not only lived through this experience with me but then relived it through countless drafts, obsessive conversations, and late-night panic attacks.

Printed in the United States
By Bookmasters